BARBARIANS

RICHARD FREDERICK RUDGLEY
1931-2002

When we compare the present life of man on earth with that time of which we have no knowledge, it seems to me like the swift flight of a single sparrow through the banqueting-hall where you are sitting at dinner on a winter's day with your thegns and counsellors. In the midst there is a comforting fire to warm the hall; outside, the storms of winter rain or snow are raging. This sparrow flies swiftly in through one door of the hall, and out through another. While he is inside, he is safe from the winter storms; but after a few moments of comfort, he vanishes from sight into the wintry world from which he came. Even so, man appears on earth for a little while; but of what went before this life or of what follows, we know nothing.

Bede

A son is better
though late begotten
of an old and ailing father.
Only your kin
will proudly carve
a memorial at the main gate.

Hávamál
(The Sayings of the High One)

BARBARIANS
Secrets of the Dark Ages

RICHARD RUDGLEY

First published in 2002 by Channel 4 Books, an imprint of Pan Macmillan Ltd,
20 New Wharf Road, London N1 9RR, Basingstoke and Oxford.

Associated companies throughout the world.

www.panmacmillan.com

ISBN 0 7522 6198 3

9 8 7 6 5 4 3 2 1

A CIP catalogue record for this book is available from the British Library.

Designed by seagulls
Printed by Mackays of Chatham plc

Front cover photograph © Werner Forman Archive;
back cover photograph © David Wason/Granada Media.

Photo credits: p1 (top) G. Tortoli/Ancient Art & Architecture Collection Ltd,
(below) David Wason/Granada Media; p2 (top) Mary Evans Picture Library, (below)
David Wason/Granada Media; p3 Kunsthistorisches Museum, Wien; p4 (top) Mary
Evans Picture Library, (below) Naturhistorisches Museum, Wien; p5 (top) David
Wason/Granada Media, (below) Richard Rudgley/Granada Media; p6 (top) Mary Evans
Picture Library, (below) Peter Rooley; p7 St Edmundsbury Borough Council/West Stow
Anglo-Saxon Village Trust; p8 (top) The British Museum, (below) R. Sheridan/Ancient
Art & Architecture Collection Ltd; p9 (top left) The British Museum, (centre right, top
right) R. Sheridan/Ancient Art & Architecture Collection Ltd, (below) The British
Museum; p10 Mary Evans Picture Library; p11 (top) Mary Evans Picture Library,
(middle and below) Werner Forman Archive/Viking Ship Museum, Bygdoy; p12 (top)
Mary Evans Picture Library, (below) Werner Forman Archive/Viking Ship Museum,
Bygdoy; p13 Werner Forman Archive; p14 (top) Paul Lord/Granada Media, (below)
Werner Forman Archive/Statens Historika Museet, Stockholm; p15 Werner Forman
Archive/Statens Historika Museet, Stockholm; p16 Mary Evans Picture Library.

GRANADA

This book accompanies the television series *Secrets of the Dark Ages*,
made by Granada Media for Channel 4.

Executive Producer: Liz McLeod
Series Producer: David Wason
Directed by: Mark Elliott and Chris Malone

CONTENTS

Acknowledgements

I would like to thank all the people whom I met on my journey through Britain and elsewhere in Europe in search of more tangible links with the past than books alone could provide, particularly: Lindsay Allason-Jones on Hadrian's Wall; members of Angelcynn, especially Colin and Ben Levick; Richard Bailey on Lindisfarne; Alan Baxter, manager of West Stow Anglo-Saxon Village; Dan Carlsson for a fascinating tour of Gotland; Joanna Caruth of the Suffolk Archaeological Unit at Lakenheath; Martin Carver, excavator of Sutton Hoo; the swordsmith Hector Cole; Richard Darrah on Anglo-Saxon woodworking skills; Angela Evans, curator at the British Museum; Manuela Farneti at the beautiful church of Sant' Apollinare Nuovo, Ravenna; Michael Gebühr on the Nydam boat in Schleswig; Sauro Gelichi at the mausoleum of Theoderic; Edwin and Joyce Gifford for having me on board the *Sæ Wylfing*; Catherine Hills on the Anglo-Saxons; Olaf Höckmann in Mainz; horse archer Kassai Lajos in Kaposmero, Hungary; Lola Luque for help in Cordoba; Sergeant McHale for escorting me round RAF Lakenheath; Soren Nielsen at Roskilde Viking Ship Museum, Denmark; Knut Paasche, curator of the Viking Ship Museum, Oslo; Ricardo Perezsbrino, surgeon in Cordoba; Dominic Powlesland at West Heslerton; Julio Samso on Islamic science in Spain; Jorn Schuster, curator at the Burg Bederkesa Museum; Laura Sole at Bede's World, Jarrow; Jonas Ström for showing me the *Krampmacken* in Gotland; Janos Tari, for interpreting for Peter Tomka in Hungary, and Tomka himself; Maria Teschler-Nicola and Karin Wiltschke-Schrotta of the Naturhistorisches Museum, Vienna; Brunetta Zavatti (see photo), for her mosaic making; Karoline Zhuber-Okrog and Elisabeth Reicher of the Kunsthistorisches Museum, Vienna.

I would also like to thank all those people who worked with me on the Granada Media television series *Secrets of the Dark Ages* made for Channel 4: Mark Atkinson, Mark Elliot, Alex Horsfall, Birgitte Johnson, Bill Jones, Faith Lawrence, Paul Lord, Roger Lucas, Chris Malone, Liz McLeod, Alison Neslany, Tim Pollard, Karen Stockton, Graham Veevers and David Wason. At Channel 4 Books: Charlie Carman and my long-suffering editor Gillian Christie – the support and understanding of both has been greatly appreciated; Christine King, my text editor; and my agent, Andrew Lownie.

Thanks to Benedict for help with references concerning Gotland; to my mother-in-law Dorothy for her invaluable support during the last stages of the writing of this book; to Bernadete for her much appreciated help; and to my dear wife Robin for her fortitude in difficult circumstances.

The dedication is to the memory of my father, who died during the writing of this book.

BARBARIAN
TIMES

The very word 'barbarian' conjures up images of violence, savagery and contempt for learning and the world of books – so to try to put across the barbarian viewpoint in a book is rather ironic. Yet the word also evokes heroism and drama, however tainted by blood and destruction. So what were the barbarians really like? Were they truly as bad as their reputation suggests, or did they have genuine cultures and subtle beliefs of their own? Was their era simply a black mark in the history of humanity, or did they actually contribute a legacy of lasting significance? In fact, just who were the barbarians? Where did they come from? What was the driving force behind their restless migrations, their conflicts with each other and with Rome? Who were their warriors, their diplomats and their leaders?

These are among the questions that are raised in this book. History should never be written in black and white, but always in shades of grey. We must guard against the temptation to portray the 'civilised' Romans as pure as driven snow and the barbarians as the harbingers of darkness and ignorance. There are two sides to every story, yet the barbarian version of events is barely known. This book is an attempt to turn the tables and catch a glimpse of what those times might have meant to the barbarians themselves.

The era of history that *Barbarians* deals with is sometimes called by the neutral name of the Early Medieval Period (the Early Middle Ages), from AD 300 to 1000 – beginning with the decline and fall of the western Roman empire and ending with the coming of a new millennium. In England, part of this period (or sometimes even the whole period) has often been called the Dark Ages, an era little known and little understood, whose very name embodies this obscurity.

The term 'Dark Ages' is a loaded one that can be read in two ways. Firstly, it is seen as dark in the sense that there are few written records to illuminate the period, compared with those before and after it – and writing is understood to be a marker of civilisation. Secondly, the Dark Ages have been portrayed by conventional history as a time of moral, cultural and social decay, precipitated by the collapse of Rome and, therefore, civilisation itself. We are led to believe that the torch of civilisation flickered only in the monasteries that dotted the landscape of a Europe engulfed in the darkness of barbarism. While this period of our history may well have been dark in the first sense, it is wrong to accept the second interpretation without greatly qualifying it. The period should not simply be stereotyped as one of cultural backsliding and ignorance, a yawning chasm between the fall of Rome and the domination of Europe by Christianity.

Many historians prefer not to talk about the Dark Ages at all, and use different terms to describe this period. In Germany it is known as the Age of Migration, or time of *Volkerwanderung* (wandering peoples), in recognition of the fact that this was a period of great upheaval and change in the make-up of the ethnic map of the continent.

The Barbarian Peoples

In this mysterious and complex period of our past, there were a great many barbarian tribes competing for power and land on the European stage. Some of them were destined to disappear or dissolve into the ethnic mix that characterised the continent at the time. The names of others, such as the Franks, the Angles, the Lombards and the Saxons, survive to this day on the maps of Europe: in France, England, Lombardy and Saxony. Most of the names of these past peoples (or ethnonyms as they are sometimes called) appear only here and there in the ancient records: the Alamanni, the Alans, the Avars, the Gutones, the Tervingi, the Heruli, the Antes, the Rugians, the Suevi, the Scirians and the Gepids were among those who were either swallowed up by other ethnic groups or simply played too minor a role in the great political machinations of the time to merit further attention from the chroniclers.

It would be a mistake to clump all the barbarian tribes together as one homogeneous entity; they each had their individual identity. For the purposes of this book, they can be broadly divided into Celtic peoples, Germanic peoples, a number of Iranian tribes and the Huns.

The Celts emerged during the second millennium BC, long before our story begins. They were once a major power in continental Europe but Roman conquest of their territories (and Germanic expansion) had drastically reduced their influence by the first century BC. Pushed out of central Europe, they tried to hold on to the region of Gaul, the old name given to most of France, Belgium, the Netherlands and neighbouring regions, and after which the Celtic inhabitants of this area were called. Under the leadership of their commander Vercingetorix, the Gauls fought hard against the forces of Julius Caesar but could not maintain their independence. Gaul became a Roman province, and Celtic autonomy on the mainland was now a thing of the past. The Britons with whom the Romans came into contact were Celtic peoples who had already established themselves in Britain from as early as the fifth century BC. Before the Roman domination of western Europe, the Britons had established many trading links and cultural exchanges with the continental Celts. In Ireland, too, Celts kept their cultural traditions alive and, to a large extent, independent of Roman influence. The Celtic people spoke (and still speak) languages that belong to a distinct group. The Celtic languages that have survived into modern times are Welsh, Cornish, Breton, Manx, Scots Gaelic and Irish.

The barbarian peoples speaking Germanic languages can be conveniently divided into three broad groups: eastern, western and northern. It must be said that this is a division of their languages rather than strictly a reflection of their geographical location. The eastern peoples included the Goths (who split into two groups, the Visigoths and the Ostrogoths), the Vandals, the Gepids and the Burgundians. Although their origins were in the eastern part of the continent, it must be remembered that the Dark Ages were a time of great migrations, and many tribes ended up settling in western and southern Europe. All these peoples subsequently merged with other ethnic groups, and no longer exist as separate entities. Similarly, none of their languages survive as living tongues. Some historians prefer to describe the East Germanic peoples as simply Gothic peoples; I refer to each people by their name rather than by either of these group terms – although these bigger entities can be useful in attempting to understand the bigger picture.

The West Germanic peoples consisted of numerous tribal groupings, among them the Franks, Angles, Saxons, Alamanni and

Frisians. The modern languages that belong to the West Germanic branch include English, German and Dutch. The North Germanic group were the Scandinavians: the Vikings or Norsemen. The Scandinavian languages of today – Danish, Swedish, Norwegian, Icelandic and Faroese (but not Finnish) – belong to this branch.

All the Celtic, Germanic and Italic tongues, including Latin, are branches of the great Indo-European language family; another branch is that of the Iranian-speaking peoples, who lived over a much larger region in antiquity than the present borders of Iran. A few of these tribes (such as the Alans and the Sarmatians) ventured westwards into Europe, where they came into contact with the Romans, the Germanic peoples and the Huns. The Huns were a nomadic people who inhabited the vast steppe lands that stretch from Mongolia in the east to the Black Sea in the west. During the Dark Ages, they also moved westwards into Europe and became a major force in the political landscape of the time. Both their language and their culture were very different to those of the European barbarians.

Historical Sources and Propaganda

The dual influences of classical education and Christian beliefs have moulded much of the world view of the European peoples. It follows that our view of our own history is formed by these two pillars of western society. Almost all the historical information we have about the Dark Ages comes from the written records of classical and Christian authors. The barbarians did not, as a rule, read or write and so speak only through the filter of Rome or Christendom. The glories of Roman civilisation speak for themselves through the architectural splendours that adorn the European continent – and if they did not speak volumes enough, then the writings of a thousand Roman authors remain to recount their story in their own words. But what of the story of the barbarians?

It is misleading to accept classical and, later, Christian sources at face value. Any attempt to equate these 'civilised' views with the plain truth would be an error. The barbarians and pagans had their own side to the story and it is this that needs telling alongside the traditional account. The archetypal image of the barbarian as savage, violent and ignorant is only a one-dimensional caricature: good political propaganda but very poor history. Even the most infamous barbarian of them all, Attila the Hun, will be shown to be a far more sophisticated and rational being than his role as the 'Scourge of God' suggests.

The Romans inherited the snobbish attitudes of the Greeks towards their ruder neighbours, trading partners and enemies – the word 'barbarian' derives from the Greek and was thought to best describe the *bar bar* sounds of 'savage' languages. This superior attitude to lesser beings is tellingly echoed in more recent times, as the great European powers of the nineteenth century carved out their colonial empires. The beginnings of modern anthropology are intimately intertwined with colonialism: the subject peoples and 'untamed' tribes needed to be studied in order to control them better, and their languages learnt where possible to communicate with them. This is not to say that the only interest was merely to exploit this knowledge, but it was certainly useful to the colonial powers.

Returning to the times of Greeks and Romans, it is clear that they laid the foundations for this anthropological science. Their writers did not just record history; they also sought, in their own way, to give an anthropological account of the other peoples that they came into contact with. They too needed to have some understanding of the other cultures that surrounded them; they too saw themselves as superior, with a mission to rule and civilise. The prejudices concerning the 'natives' of the British and other colonial dominions clearly echo those of the Greeks and Romans.

These prejudices took many forms, but there were always a few underlying themes. The basic fact that the barbarians were not ruled over by a stable system of kingship but by a shifting series of chiefs and temporary tribal alliances made them primitive and unpredictable in Roman eyes. Their lack of writing – and therefore the fact they did not abide by a written body of law – was also seen as a sign of their cultural backwardness.

Yet neither their forms of government nor their lack of written laws meant that barbarian societies were anarchic. Societies that rely on oral tradition are perfectly capable of administering themselves and are just as likely to maintain law and order as any more 'advanced' society. The succession to power of chiefs was likewise no more unpredictable than the rise and fall of kings and emperors. Even a cursory look at Roman history makes it clear that the empire suffered as many power struggles and unexpected changes in leadership as the barbarians experienced in their own societies. To give but one example, only two emperors in the whole of the third century were fortunate enough to die from natural causes!

Another recurrent theme of Roman anthropology is that barbarians could not control their appetites – their insatiable desire for food, drink, sex and gold. (Though the Romans, with their notoriously extravagant banquets and rapacious use of the wealth and manpower of their subject peoples, were hardly in a position to preach.) Not surprisingly, the Romans were also contemptuous of barbarian religion. It was hardly considered religious at all, but simply a confused mass of superstitious practices that the barbarians themselves barely understood. This kind of attitude is later echoed by many European accounts of the native peoples of Africa. Implicit in both accounts is the underlying belief that the Imperial powers are superior, and that the subject peoples or unconquered 'savage' tribes live an inferior material and spiritual life. It is, of course, now understood that the traditional African societies have their own religious life and are not simply ruled by mindless super-stition. The same was true of the European barbarian tribes; it was simply that the arrogance of the Romans blinded them to this fact.

The other main prejudice voiced by the Romans about the barbarians was that they were unable to make rational decisions and were prone to act in inexplicable ways. All these accusations – lack of law, stable government, self-control, religious belief and rationality – were down to the fact that the Romans simply did not understand the inner workings of the barbarian cultures they came into contact with. True, they often knew enough to control them, trade with them and negotiate with them, but beyond that their own sense of cultural superiority meant that they over-looked the subtlety and complexity of barbarian life. Although the word 'barbarian' still conjures up many of these prejudices even today, I shall use the term without resorting to inverted commas every time. It will soon become apparent that I do not use it in a disparaging way.

The barbarians were seen as the outsiders, the savages and the enemies of Greece and Rome, peoples to be suppressed, domi-nated and civilised. But this Mediterranean stranglehold on the enemies within (barbarian Europeans) and without (Asiatic hordes) could not sustain itself for ever, and Rome fell to the inex-orable rise of new powers on the world stage. The barbarians were not just bit-part actors in the great dramas of Imperial Rome and the conversion of Europe to Christianity. They were major players in their own right. They acted out their own plots and their own destiny. The vibrant, colourful and often violent lives of the key personalities of the Dark Ages need to be told. The roles they played in the history of our continent were not just those of villains in the theatre of war but of statesmen, artists, visionaries and heroes. This is their epic story.

This book is divided into three parts. The first part is largely concerned with the story of the Romans, the Celts, the East Germanic (Gothic) peoples and the Huns. We start with the fall of Rome: the conflicts of rival emperors and barbarians, the decay and eventual abandoning of the British outpost, the attack of the Vandals across the river Rhine, the lust for golden treasure among the barbarians on the Danube and those who have sought to profit from it in more recent times. The Goths, the first of the Germanic peoples to adopt writing, were independent yet appreciative of the Roman way of life, which they partly adopted and turned to their advantage. The mysterious Huns, whose name is a by-word for all things barbaric, are shown to be a significant culture in their own right – powerful, organised and fiercely independent.

The second part of the story traces the history of the Anglo-Saxon world: the West Germanic people's migration from their continental roots to Britain, and their interaction there with the Celts. The fecund mixture of indigenous British culture and the recently arrived immigrants resulted in a society with its own artistic and technological innovations, and the development of distinctive national characteristics. Unearthed by archaeologists, the people's villages, swords, ships and sometimes extravagant burials are enduring reminders of a world of ideas that would otherwise remain unknown.

The last part follows the Anglo-Saxons on to their conversion to Christianity, and the new wave of learning that was transmitted from remote monasteries. From being a cultural backwater, England began to exert an unexpected and powerful influence on the development of European civilisation. The history of the North Germanic peoples (the Vikings) is recounted too, their epic sea voyages opening up a whole new phase of the European story. From their homeland in the far north, the Scandinavians created a civilisation that shows their legacy was much more than sensational stories of their piracy and raiding expeditions would have us believe. The story ends with the entry into Spain of the first wave of Islamic peoples – a reminder that the Europe we know today owes a cultural and scientific debt to Islamic civilisation that is all too often forgotten.

Part One

ROMAN TWILIGHT

Chapter One

ALL ROADS
LEAD TO ROME?

In the second century of the Christian Era, the empire
of Rome comprehended the fairest part of the earth, and the
most civilised portion of mankind. The frontiers of that
extensive monarchy were guarded by ancient
renown and disciplined valour.

Edward Gibbon (1737–94), *History of the Decline and Fall of the Roman Empire*

The Romans, like every imperial power since, had a vested interest in propagating their own version of history. There are few written barbarian accounts to contradict the Roman view that their civilisation was the cultural and political centre of the known world. Yet if we read between the lines and look at the significance of discoveries made by archaeologists, many cultural voices can be heard and many barbarian achievements emerge out of the darkness.

Each and every barbarian society had their own view of the world in which they lived. While they no doubt understood the importance and political power of the empire, they nevertheless still saw their own culture as the centre. There was never a universal consensus that Rome ruled supreme; the barbarians always strove to assert their own rights and interests, whatever the balance of power may have been. Long portrayed as simple-minded barbarians, these ancestral Europeans were much more than that – in many ways their art, their society and their cultural legacy have shaped and moulded the destiny of Europe more than the Roman empire that once held them in its vice-like grip.

If all roads led to Rome then there at its heart lies one of the most enduring symbols of the ancient world – the Coliseum. It is an enormous monument to the civil engineering skills of the Romans, but it is also an emblem of the barbarity at the heart of the imperial machine. Here, at the place where the roots of empire lay, was a reminder that savagery was hardly the sole prerogative of the European tribesman. In AD 80 the Coliseum opened and 2,000 gladiators are said to have died during the first hundred days for the gratification of the spectators.

With Roman writers being our main and sometimes only source of information concerning many of the barbarian peoples of the so-called Dark Ages, it is hardly surprising that our vision of this period of history is seen through the distorting lens of Roman bias, custom and propaganda. The Roman empire had a massive impact on the development of European civilisation and its technological and administrative transformation. The Roman roads embody this sense of the continent linking up – the arteries of communication pumping goods, soldiers and ideas from the heartland to the periphery of the empire. Yet Roman rule was not so straightforward and unified, for the empire itself split into two – the western and eastern empires – each with its own agendas, allies and enemies; each with its own destiny. We cannot hope to understand the barbarians unless we have a basic grasp of the history of the Roman empire to which many of them were subject.

The Growth of Empire

Rome grew from being simply a city state to become the super-power of the western world over a period of 200 years – the third and second centuries BC. This powerful republic was democratic to an extent but, in reality, it was an oligarchy, a state run by a small cluster of aristocrats who ruled by means of the Senate. The rapid expansion of Roman territorial interests and military requirements necessarily involved administrative problems on an unprecedented scale. The growth of the Roman enterprise required fundamental changes to be made in the way that the whole organisational machinery operated.

Among these changes was the development of a professional army in the first century BC. The Senate decided, unknowingly to the detriment of their own interests, to make the career soldier reliant on his general for his security in retirement. The State, by not providing a pension or other provision to the army, gave away too much power to the generals, who thought nothing of exercising it in times of crisis. Almost incessant civil wars led to the demise of the republic and the rise of the emperors, the first of whom, Augustus, reigned from 27 BC.

Although there were constant interactions between the Romans and barbarians throughout the following centuries, the imperial forces managed to keep the upper hand. The time when the barbarians could really shake the foundations of the Roman world was still some way off. It was not really until the third century AD that serious difficulties began for the Romans. At that time, the other superpower of the time, the Persian empire, was going through a major period of change as the Sasanians, a new dynasty of kings, sought to flex their muscles and strove to regain the much larger empire that was under the sway of the Persians long ago before the time of Alexander the Great.

There were a host of other problems that would need to be dealt with by whoever took the reins of power: the barbarian threat, disease, an ailing economy – an empire with a thousand and one problems. The old guard, that is to say the aristocratic senators of the city of Rome, had long since ceased to get all the top positions in the running of the empire. For this elite, it was bad enough when the senatorial posts and even the imperial seat could be filled by the provincial gentry of Spain or North Africa. One can only imagine their horror when a commoner named Maximin I became emperor by the popular consent of the Roman army. Even worse, from their point of view, was the fact that he was from the outlying regions of the empire. According to a Greek historian of the time, Herodian, he belonged to a semi-barbarous tribe in Thrace (modern-day Bulgaria and Macedonia). A later historian saw him as having even 'lower' credentials – of mixed barbarian stock, one of his parents being a Goth and the other belonging to the Alan people. This source also tells us that he was born *outside* the empire – a true barbarian.

How many of these details we can rely on is difficult to say, but we can be sure he was at least partly barbarian in origin. This gives a clear indication that it was a rapidly changing world and the old order was having to come to terms with some very uncomfortable developments. Yet the Senate was still in a position of strength and backed the murder of Maximin in 238 by some of his own soldiers while he was in the north of Italy.

Certainly, the line between the Romans and the barbarians was gradually becoming more blurred. It would be wrong to think that the Romans were able to simply dominate the barbarians they encountered. Similarly, the barbarians were not all hell-bent on the destruction of the empire and the looting of its coffers. Many barbarians wanted part of the action themselves, preferring to work inside the imperial system rather than threaten it from without. They had much to gain by doing everything they could to ensure the health of the empire. The Romans were often reliant on barbarian forces as auxiliaries and mercenaries. There were conflicts in many provinces and on many frontiers and, as the decades wore on, the defending of Roman interests was undertaken more and more by both commanders and soldiers on the ground who were of barbarian stock.

By the 240s the Romans were beginning to feel intense pressure from the Germanic tribes on the Danube frontier. In 246, the then emperor Philip led a successful campaign to beat them back. Only two years later a confederation of Goths, Vandals, Carpi and other motley tribes overran the eastern Balkans. In the resulting upheaval, a new pretender to the throne appeared in the form of Decius, the general who successfully extinguished the barbarian uprising. In 249 he took on Philip and his army in battle and won. His time on the throne was short and he himself was killed in a battle against the Goths in 251.

Things were generally taking a turn for the worse, and the next twenty years or so saw even greater upheaval. The key to the successful function of the empire was the army, and the key to the army was their wages. Problems with paying them obviously set in motion a host of other problems and the possibility of uprisings, civil wars and power struggles. During this time the coins, meant to be silver, had been debased to being little more than silver-plated bronze. This artificial and transparent attempt to keep the economy buoyant failed and, as the historian Roger Collins has pointed out, no one seems to have been taken in by this – as shown by the sheer size and number of hoards of coins from these troubled times. The size of these hoards shows that their lower intrinsic value was well understood. The number of separate hoards shows that, in these economically unstable times, many people thought the safest place to put your money was in the ground.

During this time the continent of Europe was racked not just by an economic depression and a partial slide into anarchy, but by outbreaks of plague and starvation. Yet there were outlying regions of the empire, such as Britain, Spain and North Africa, which continued to live in peace and prosperity – the problems of the rest of the empire seemed to leave them comparatively unscathed. Despite these areas of relative calm, a succession of emperors found that they needed to be in two or more places at once. Keeping the empire going in the midst of all these problems was a juggling act in which dropping one of the balls could have disastrous consequences.

It was against such a backdrop that the institution of having one man at the top supposedly running the empire began to falter. It was a huge task and, although some of the emperors of earlier times had not really been up to the job, the fundamental stability of the empire meant there was no real danger of the whole system collapsing. Things were different now with the difficulties that faced the empire in the late third century, and solutions simply had to be found. Out of dire necessity, the organisation of the Roman empire underwent a major overhaul in the reign of Diocletian, who was in power from 284 to 305. Many of the reforms that took place under his leadership grew out of the ideas and policies of his predecessors, but he was the one to boldly put it all into practice.

Almost immediately after coming to power, Diocletian decided that two heads were better than one and in 286 chose a general named Maximian to share power with him, initially as a junior partner with the title Caesar and then promoting him the following year to an equal with the title of Augustus. Diocletian was to be in charge of the eastern part of the empire and Maximian the west. It could be said that Diocletian was taking something of a gamble by sharing power in this way – not that his predecessors who had sought to rule single-handedly had been exactly secure. But he seems to have been a good judge of Maximian's character and no attempt to break the partnership was made by his fellow Augustus. Maximian had enough to do without plotting against Diocletian. Keeping his part of the empire in order required him to deal with a host of troublesome barbarians from Saxon pirates in the English Channel to Berber tribesmen in North Africa.

Diocletian continued to pursue his radical solution when, in the year 293, with the full agreement of Maximian, he split power even further. Each of the Augusti were to be supported by a Caesar – Constantius for the western part of the empire and Galerius in the east. This was kept in the family by marrying off daughters of the respective Augusti to the Caesar of the same half of the empire. Everything seemed to be ticking over and the four rulers were able to contain and pre-empt the rise of rebellious would-be emperors.

That this new system was anything but a personality cult has been made clear by Roger Collins, one of the few historians who provides a scholarly overview of the whole era. The coins minted at this time do not portray individuals. The same imperial head was used on all the coins and only the inscriptions gave away which of the rulers was being depicted. The message was that the four were, in a sense, part of a greater unified whole.

Diocletian did not limit his radical reorganisation to the upper echelons alone. He also sought (as did his first major successor, Constantine) to change the structure of the army to suit the needs of the time. Two distinct units were created: the Limitanei and the Comitatenses. The first type, as its name suggests, were frontier units at the limits of the empire whose role was to hold at bay the barbarians outside. The Comitatenses were mobile units of the army who went anywhere there was a need for them. The boundaries of the empire became more clearly delineated on the land-scape – massive fortifications were constructed to strengthen the hand of the frontier garrisons. Like any system, it had its strengths and its weaknesses.

On the plus side, if a frontier was pierced and the Limitanei were unable to stop the enemy, the Comitatenses provided a second line of defence, a second army to be defeated. Even better, if the intelligence they received from their scouts was good enough the mobile units could be standing side by side with the Limitanei before the enemy was even at the gate. On the down side, if the mobile units were far away or otherwise engaged then the fate of a province could be left to the Limitanei. Once the barbarians broke through this barrier, they could run amok at will.

The turn of the fourth century saw an empire that was increasingly rule-bound, as the emperors sought to keep a firm grip on the reins of power. Christianity had suffered intermittent persecution under the empire but this rose to an unprecedented level under Diocletian's campaign against it that began in 303. The Roman empire had no problem with the diversity of religious groups among its subjects, provided there was no political threat from allegiance to this or that cult or sect. Christianity was different. Unlike many of the other religious groups of the time, the Christians were not *laissez-faire*. For them, it was all or nothing: if you were not a Christian, the gods you worshipped were not really gods at all but demons – which they believed to be the case with the pagan gods of the empire.

The refusal of Christians to participate in the state-run ceremonies in which such Roman gods were venerated more as a civil act than a strictly religious one created a major problem. Refusing to be involved in such rituals was an act of sedition; this seems to have been behind Diocletian's decision to persecute them. The Christians were not to be wiped out; indeed, after Diocletian's reign, the emperor Constantine converted to Christianity – thus guaranteeing the Church a very rosy future indeed.

Constantine and Christianity at the Crossroads

In 305 the joint reign of Diocletian and Maximian came to an end when they voluntarily stepped down for 'the greater good'. The four-fold division of power was still in place, but within a few short years it was history. After a complex and protracted power struggle for control it all came to a head in a showdown in 312 just outside the city of Rome. The battle of the Milvian Bridge, between the massed forces of Constantine and Maximian's son Maxentius, resulted in the victory of the former and the drowning of the latter in the river Tiber. This defeat of a major enemy meant that Constantine was able to add the territories of Africa and Italy itself to the combined provinces of Spain, Gaul and Britain which he already had under his authority.

According to the account given by Bishop Eusebius of Caesarea in Palestine (who is known as the father of church history), writing just a few years after the event, Constantine is said to have converted to Christianity because of a vision he had on the eve of the battle of the Milvian Bridge. His success the next day convinced him that God was shining down on him.

He stayed in Rome after defeating his rival and decided to waste no time in implementing a new building programme on a grand scale. It was he who oversaw the building of the great basilica of St Peter's, along with numerous other architectural innovations. Naturally the Church itself experienced a rapid change of fortune. The previously modest economic standing of the clergy was soon to be a thing of the past. A number of buildings were handed over to the bishops and their riches soon rivalled those held by the conservative forces in the Senate where paganism still reigned. The official Christianity of the emperor was, as the historian John Wallace-Hadrill so aptly put it, Christianity 'with the detonator removed'. Constantine had removed a major threat by incorporating it; however sincere his conversion may have been, it was also a clear instance of his political acumen.

Constantine had his eyes on the eastern part of the empire and forged temporary alliances and fought civil wars against his rivals until, finally, in 324, he reigned supreme after successfully taking the port of Byzantium. The following year he decided that this was to be his new capital and had it consecrated under the name Constantinople in 330. It was to remain the seat of the eastern emperors until it was taken over by the Ottoman Turks in 1453. It is now the site of the modern city of Istanbul.

Constantine the Great, as he was subsequently known, certainly earned his name. His domination of the empire, his role as the first Christian emperor, his building of St Peter's basilica and his setting up of a new capital mark him out as a truly exceptional emperor. Yet his lust for power and worldly gain made him little different from his pagan counterparts. Despite his acceptance of Christianity, he hardly strikes us as compassionate, ruthlessly ordering the killing of his wife, eldest son and father-in-law on separate occasions both before and after his conversion.

All roads did not lead to the city of Rome in the time of Constantine – he changed the seat of power, moving it far away from its ancient site. This was not the first time that Rome was overlooked in favour of other cities: Ravenna, Milan, Thessalonica and Trier had been centres of administration for the empire and official residences for the emperors. Rome as an idea and as a civilisation could certainly be said to have had all roads leading to it, but the city itself was far from being the sole centre of power and influence.

At the time of Constantine's death in 337, we can still make out a fairly straightforward division between two worlds – the stable and settled world of the Romans and the volatile and restless world of the myriad barbarian tribes. But times were changing. The barbarians grew in strength as the Romans relied more and more on their military aid in defending the empire against other tribal groups. Increasingly, the destinies of the two were merging. The historian Norman Davies cites the early fifth century writings of a priest from Marseilles named Silvian, who tells us how some Romans sought refuge with two barbarian peoples, the Goths and the Franks: 'seeking a Roman humanity among the barbarians, because they could no longer support Barbarian inhumanity among the Romans'.

This blurring of the line between Roman and barbarian cultures was having a profound effect on the destiny of the continent. Roman civilisation offered opportunities for the ambitious barbarian – power, wealth, and prestige opened up new worlds of experience. While the *nouveaux riches* among the barbarians sought to emulate Roman values, it would be wrong to think of the cultural interaction as just one-way traffic. In clothing, for example, the Romans succumbed to a new fashion already established among the Germans – the wearing of trousers. Despite being outlawed by the emperor Honorius in 397 they became an integral part of the civilised wardrobe, a place they still hold today. This is just one of the many instances of barbarian cultural influences that make up our modern European culture.

The barbarian Germanic tribes were becoming an increasing threat and inflation was rampant. The economy was falling further into a steady and irreversible decline as the fourth century wore on. It was withering at the very roots with agricultural production dropping across the length and breadth of the empire. A plethora of barbarian tribes were growing like vigorous weeds in the orderly fields of the Roman world. The integrity of the language was also under threat as the major provinces of Italy, Spain and Gaul were growing into separate linguistic branches. As the historian Wallace-Hadrill put it: 'Men were thinking and feeling as Europeans; but they still called themselves by the old name – Romans.'

The individual histories of the barbarian peoples are inevitably intertwined not just with Rome but with the ever-changing skein of alliances, disputes and migrations that typify this dramatic, restless and energetic cluster of cultures. Rome itself faced two problems – the enemy within, that is to say the barbarians inside the empire, and the enemy from without, most notoriously the Huns from the east. The comparatively stable map of modern Europe was very different to that which delineated this period of great migration and displaced peoples. Yet the outcome of all this movement was the eventual settlement of peoples and the roots of the modern states of Europe. Before plunging back into the churning core of the struggle for the mainland, we must pick up one of the other strands of the story – the Roman intervention in a place once thought to be beyond the pale of the civilised world: the island of Britain, which was to become another building block in the edifice of Roman civilisation.

Chapter Two

THE EDGE
OF EMPIRE

To separate the Romans from the barbarians.

Aurelius Victor, fourth-century biographer of Hadrian,
on the reason for the building of Hadrian's Wall

Britain was a Roman province with a difference. The separation of
the island from the European mainland made it difficult to incor-
porate into the empire in the first place, and this continued to be
a key factor in the following four centuries of Roman rule. The
Roman interest in and eventual occupation of Britain made a
major impact on the indigenous people, and heralds the beginning
of detailed historical information about the island. Before this
time, most of what is known about Britain and its inhabitants
comes from archaeological rather than written evidence.

History and writing go hand in hand. Under Roman rule,
there were more people who could read and write than there
would be for a few hundred years after the end of the occupation.
One of the main reasons for this was the fact that literacy was a
prerequisite of army life. The Celtic inhabitants of Britain found

themselves taking part in a very different social world in the towns that began to grow under the influence of the colonial power of Rome. It seems that the population grew rapidly.

Roman Invasion

Celtic Britain was, despite the Channel that divided it from mainland Europe, a very active trader with the rest of the continent even before its incorporation into the empire. Particularly close links existed between the south of the country and the northern part of Gaul (present-day northern France, Belgium and the Netherlands). Julius Caesar's campaign in Gaul brought him into conflict not just with the Gauls themselves but also with the British barbarians who fought alongside them against the Roman invaders. His conquest of Gaul was followed swiftly by a concerted campaign against Britain. Whether the two expeditions he mounted to Britain in 55 and 54 BC were simply punitive campaigns to teach the Britons a lesson for interfering in the Roman invasion of Gaul, or whether he had something more ambitious in mind, remains a moot point.

The first invasion was not a success. The legions fought their way into Kent but within a matter of weeks had returned to Gaul, perhaps to deal with more pressing problems. But Caesar did not want such an ineffectual campaign to be repeated. The second time around he brought a force of 32,000 men over the Channel in a fleet of 800 ships. The military might of the Romans made itself felt and allies and enemies were made in the patchwork of small kingdoms that made up the south of the country. Caesar left with an agreement from a number of defeated kings that they should pay an annual tribute to Rome. Britain was no longer quite at the edge of beyond – it was now within the Roman sphere of influence and would not last much longer outside the empire.

When Claudius succeeded the murdered Caligula as emperor, he was not considered highly in many quarters. He was a rather eccentric character who had somehow found himself centre stage, much to the surprise of even his own family. He soon proved himself to be much more intelligent and determined than his detractors thought him to be. He needed a feather in his cap in order to consolidate his position and to assert his authority; adding Britain to the provinces of the empire would certainly do the trick. A formidable army was dispatched to do just that in AD 43.

Four Roman legions (each consisting of about 5,000 troops) were augmented by an equally large force of auxiliaries, making the invading army 40,000 strong. Auxiliary troops were not only important from a military point of view; they also did much for the process of barbarian integration. Auxiliaries were guaranteed Roman citizenship on their retirement and their sons were able to sign up in the legions. As the expert on Roman Britain, Peter Salway, put it, such auxiliary units 'provided a continuous process of turning unlettered barbarians into literate Roman citizens and were a major element in the assimilation of new peoples into the empire'.

Such was the force that confronted the Britons. A full-scale professional army like that of the Romans was simply beyond the economic means of the natives to equal. The chariot-driving warrior class among the tribes of Britons was effectual but small. Most of their compatriots were farmers called up for army duty. They had neither the training nor the equipment that the invading army took for granted. Furthermore, they could not continue fighting all year round without their own communities starving as a result of neglecting their crops and livestock.

Despite the Romans' advantages, it was not easy going and they suffered heavy casualties. Nevertheless, it soon became clear that the campaign was going to succeed. Once victory was assured, Claudius himself arrived on British soil, with a troop of elephants, in time to lead the army in its triumphal entrance into Colchester. Eleven British kings formally surrendered to the new order. Power was consolidated over the next few years, at least in southern and central England. The west and the north posed more difficult problems.

Druid Destruction and Iceni Uprising

In AD 59 and 60 the appointed governor of Britain, Suetonius Paulinus, decided to launch an all-out assault on Wales. The Druids, the ancient priesthood of the Celts, had seen their religion and authority collapse before the onslaught of the legions. It was on the island known to the Romans as Mona and to us as Anglesey that they made their last stand. If we are to believe the Roman accounts, the Druids practised human sacrifice in a number of forms. They are reported to have built colossal figures out of wood and straw and put live animals and people inside them before setting the whole thing alight. (This ancient story was the basis for the sacrifice of a policeman in the 1970s film *The Wicker Man*.) But this time the blood of the slaughtered was to be on Roman hands.

Paulinus knew that the Druids were not only priests but also the leaders of the opposition to Roman rule. The combined force of his cavalry and infantry stormed the island, and the mass slaughter of the Druids and the desecration of their sacred groves was the result. Wales looked to be on the verge of being successfully assimilated into the Roman province when an uprising among the Iceni tribe of Britons (inhabiting parts of what is now Norfolk, Suffolk and Cambridgeshire) forced Roman attention back to the east.

The fairly peaceful co-existence of the Romans and those Britons with whom they had reached terms seems to have turned sour due to overbearing arrogance and downright corruption on the part of the colonisers. In AD 60 Prasutagus, the king of the Iceni, died, leaving the emperor Nero as one of his heirs. Prasutagus thought by doing so that the alliance he had nurtured with Rome would remain in place after his death. The Romans, however, simply saw this as capitulation on his part and took away the hereditary estates of the Iceni upper class.

The account of what happened next comes from the Roman historian Tacitus, who no doubt heard it from his father-in-law, Julius Agricola, who was in Britain at the time. The Iceni king's widow Boudicca protested at the injustice of the Roman decision to remove all power from her people. As a result, she was flogged and her daughters dragged off and raped. The Romans, through their own barbaric behaviour, brought upon themselves a ferocious wave of barbarian revenge. Boudicca roused the Iceni and began a campaign of total destruction against Roman interests in the region. Colchester was burnt to the ground and its Roman citizens and sympathisers slaughtered in the environs of the half-built temple of Claudius. London was the next destination on the bloody trail of revenge.

The governor Paulinus, hearing news of the rebellion, rushed back to London but although he arrived before Boudicca he and his cavalry could not stop the town burning. The governor retreated to the Midlands, where he could combine his force with that of two other legions and their auxiliaries. This was the force that Boudicca's army met in the Midlands in the battle for Britain. It was a resounding victory for the Romans: the rebellion was crushed with perhaps as many as 80,000 Britons killed. The devastated Boudicca is believed to have poisoned herself in the aftermath.

The peripheral regions of Roman Britain – Wales, northern England, Scotland and the tin-rich Cornish peninsula – all continued to pose problems for the colonial administration. But within the heartland of the province, urban development flourished during the first and second centuries. Urban expansion with all its trappings created a network of towns and cities organised by centralised authorities. It was a Britain very different to the one that greeted the first Roman visitors: amphitheatres, law-courts, public baths – all clear signs that Mediterranean civilisation had made its indelible mark on the physical and social landscape of Britain.

A Wondrous Wall

Hadrian (who reigned from 117 to 138) was an emperor with a difference. He flew in the face of the established policy of constantly seeking to expand the limits of empire. Maintaining and strengthening the existing empire seemed a much more sensible course of action to him and, however unpopular it made him, he was determined to put his beliefs into practice. He spent much of his time visiting the various provinces and playing an active role in their reorganisation. Among the provinces for which he had big plans was Britain. He initiated a bold scheme for reclaiming the fens of East Anglia and turning them into useful agricultural land. London too went through a major facelift under his guidance. But he is best known for the great wall that bears his name and still dominates the landscape of northern England.

Winding across country for 73 miles from Newcastle upon Tyne to Bowness-on-Stow, it is the single most impressive legacy of the Roman occupation of Britain: the most dramatic realisation of Hadrian's goals for his empire. It was designed to draw a line between the civilised world and those outside its borders – as the quote at the start of this chapter makes clear. Inscriptions tell us that the building of the wall was undertaken by a number of different legions, and also give us the name of the governor who was in Britain at this time. Other sources tell us that he held this office between 122 and 125. From this, we know that the wall was started in one of these years.

In Britain, Hadrian's Wall is the obvious place to start in trying to understand the mosaic of cultures that made up the Roman empire. Even the Roman emperor Hadrian was not actually Italian but belonged to a prominent Spanish family. The three legions that built the wall – the II, VI and XX – were all composed of Roman citizens, but this did not mean that they had to be Italians. Very few were, and there were troops from Romanised barbarian tribes throughout Europe, including Germanic people and Gauls, in these legions. Later, the auxiliary units that were actually posted to man the wall were, if anything, even more ethnically mixed – their ranks being drawn from as far afield as Africa and Syria. The Roman military machine played a key role in moving diverse peoples from Europe and beyond all over the empire. Multi-cultural Britain existed long before the modern era and these movements of people, which were echoed throughout the empire, must have had a marked influence in the spread of ideas across the continent.

Living on the other side of the wall were a number of barbarian tribes who were probably less dangerous than the Romans thought they were. Most of the time they were too preoccupied with their own feuds and protecting their own territories to pose a serious threat to Roman interests. According to Lindsay Allason-Jones, a specialist in Roman Britain, the Romans found it hard to put themselves in the position of these barbarians who, unlike themselves, had no desire to forge themselves an empire. Perhaps because they did not understand the mind-set of the northern barbarians, they judged them falsely by their own Roman standards. There is no evidence that the wall was ever seriously damaged by barbarian attacks.

It has been suggested that the building of Hadrian's Wall was not so much a reaction to any real threat but more of a training exercise to keep the otherwise unoccupied troops busy. A constant anxiety of the Romans was the potential problem that foreign soldiers within the army might rebel. Typically, such troops were posted a long way both from Rome itself and their own homelands to minimise such risks. Keeping them busy building roads and, in this case, a mighty wall kept them out of trouble.

The wall was also a powerful statement in itself: a monument to Roman might. Not only was it a considerable feat of engineering; it also demanded impressive organisational skills. To simply feed the legions while they were constructing it was a major achievement in itself. The wall stands as a testimony to the Romans largely because it was built of stone, whereas most other frontiers of the empire were fortified by earthworks and ditches that have not survived so completely as Hadrian's monumental labours.

Archaeologists have found a great deal of Roman weaponry in sites scattered along the length of the wall. Such artefacts show quite clearly that, contrary to what one might think, they were not always at the cutting edge of military technology themselves but relied heavily on foreign weapon systems. A special kind of curved sword invented by barbarians in Bulgaria was used at the wall. Parts of Syrian bows have been found, showing that this kind of weapon had also been appropriated by the Roman military. The bow is of a special type known as a composite bow, so named because it was made up of various materials – different kinds of wood and bone. Each part was specially selected for its particular properties: strength, flexibility and so on.

It was this very weapon, the composite bow, which was having such a devastating effect on Roman fortunes far to the east around the time that Hadrian's Wall was finally abandoned. The horse archers of the Huns were the supreme masters of the composite bow and their repeated assaults on the eastern front are described later in Part One. In the light of the evidence of these weapons, it is clear that the cultural exchange between Romans and barbarians was not simply flowing one way. The barbarian cultures were not simply sponges soaking up the knowledge and trappings of their imperial 'superiors'. The colonising power found itself drawing inspiration and innovation from its barbarian subjects.

There are many other archaeological finds that give us a picture of the ethnic diversity that existed among the occupying forces in this windswept northern outpost of the empire. Numerous memorial stones provide potted and incomplete thumbnail sketches of individual soldiers who were stationed at the wall. One such stone commemorates an auxiliary named Dagvalda who was from Pannonia, a Roman province in what is now Hungary. The stone was raised by his wife Priscina, yet the reason for his death remains untold. Other stones tell similar stories of men from all over the known world who served and died far from home on Hadrian's Wall. That their families came with them we know, but their life stories remain unrecorded and therefore unknown.

It is impossible to put a date on the abandonment of the wall as it was not a sudden event but a slow decline. Although 410 is the year when dramatic events elsewhere in the empire forced the Romans to finally leave Britain, many had already left long before then. The wall had already begun to crumble and its maintenance and upkeep had long since ceased to be a priority. In fact, while thousands of visitors make the trip to see the wall today, it did not seem to have made much of a stir at the time in the wider Roman world. Even Hadrian's biographer gives it only a line. In the greater scheme of things, it was simply a wall built far from the centres of power in an obscure part of the empire.

Britain after the Romans was certainly a different place. The towns that had provided the backbone of the Roman administration fell into decline as many people abandoned them in search of a more secure life in the countryside. The lack of a central Roman authority marked a return to more traditional Celtic systems of social organisation. In southern Britain the pressure coming from a host of foreign aggressors from various directions was felt keenly soon after the Roman departure. From the north the Picts (the barbarian tribes of Scotland) started to move southwards, while Irish and continental pirates sought to take full advantage of the fact that the legions were no longer around to repel them. There was, from the point of view of Roman civilisation, a gradual return to barbarism.

As the Romans were abandoning Britain, their empire was plagued by major threats from other barbarians far from British shores. Vandals and other tribes were pressing on the Rhine frontier, a situation that would culminate in a catastrophe for the Romans on New Year's Eve 406. And events in the Balkans, where the Goths and Huns were challenging the might of the empire, were to change the direction of history.

It is now time to leave the outpost of Britain (to which we shall return with the Anglo-Saxons later in the book) and focus once again on the bigger picture: central and eastern Europe. I wanted to get a real idea of what was happening at the time, and decided to go in search of archaeological clues that could bring back something of barbarian life that I could not get from the history books alone. I would go to Mainz on the banks of the Rhine, where sixteen hundred years ago there had been an extraordinary act of vandalism.

Chapter Three

WANDERLUST AND GOLDLUST

*I shall now say a few words of our present miseries...
Savage tribes in countless numbers have overrun all
parts... The once noble city of Mainz has been captured
and destroyed. In its church many thousands have been
massacred... And those which the sword spares without,
famine ravages within. I cannot speak without tears...*

St Jerome, in one of his letters written in 409 (epistle 125)

The main markers of the eastern edge of Roman dominion were two mighty rivers, the Rhine and the Danube. The Rhine was one of the most important natural avenues in the Roman world, both for trade and for its strategic significance: it was a key supply route for the commercial and military requirements of the empire. Around 12 BC the Romans set up a fortified camp as a base for two of their legions. This was to be the foundation of the city of Mogontiacum (later to be known as Mainz). Its original purpose was to be a settlement from which the legions could start campaigns to expand to the east, and by AD 70–80 Roman expansion had made the Rhineland an integral part of the empire. In Roman times the river at Mainz was about a hundred metres wider than it is today, making it an even more difficult barrier to pass. Naturally, defence of the Rhine was paramount for the security of the empire and it was regularly patrolled by river boats. In the 1980s the discovery in the centre of Mainz (in the environs of the Hilton hotel) of the wrecks of five such boats gave archaeologists and historians the opportunity to gain a rare glimpse into the way such Roman vessels were made. Numerous kinds of boats were built in the Roman shipyards, and these particular models were specially designed for use on the large rivers of the continent; as such, they would have been totally unsuitable for use along the coast or the open sea.

The archaeologist Dr Olaf Höckmann was instrumental in the discovery of these ancient river craft, and he kindly agreed to give me a guided tour of the stretch of the Rhine around Mainz. As we stood chatting on the open deck of a small boat, the sky was grey and overcast, a persistent light rain and a damp wind gradually chilling the flesh and seeping into the bones – a misery endured by the Romans too so long ago.

Dr Höckmann told me that it has been possible to pinpoint the date of the boats, thanks to the technique of dendrochronology, a very accurate form of dating by tree ring. It was worked out that one of them was built in 376, and careful inspection of two sections of the boat that were replaced in Roman times shows that these repairs took place on two separate occasions, the first in 386 and the second in 394. All five vessels were built from oak and hammered together with iron nails. Typically, they would have had between twenty-four and twenty-eight oarsmen, and therefore the full crew would probably have numbered over thirty men.

The boats could reach speeds of up to 11 knots, and patrolled the river like clockwork. They would travel between river stations

set 20 miles apart, going downstream in the morning and returning upstream in the afternoon. The regularity of these patrols was
designed to deter barbarian assaults by boat: surprise attacks were
hardly possible under the constant and watchful eye of these
ancient river police. There were also early-warning systems in
place, forts across the Rhine on the eastern side and roving scouts
– part of the strategy designed to thwart enemy incursions. But the
real border remained the Rhine itself and the crucial defensive aim
was to hold the river.

The Romans built a bridge at Mainz in AD 27 during the reign
of the emperor Tiberius. It was about 8 metres wide and the only
way into the city from the other bank. Later the city walls were
built and further defended by a fort about a mile away from the
bridge. The bridge, with its heavily armed guard, seemed to be
impregnable to any barbarian force, which simply would not have
been able to get sufficient numbers across so narrow an inroad.
The Romans felt that the measures they had taken to defend both
the bridge and the river itself were sufficient, but they had not
allowed for a fateful night when freak weather conditions and the
guile of their enemies conspired against them...

Barbarian Invasion

By the beginning of the fifth century barbarian peoples were mass-
ing threateningly in the lands east of the Rhine. Among them were
the Germanic Vandals and Suevi, and the Alans who had wandered
far to the west from their Iranian origins. These diverse tribes came
together in a temporary alliance to mount an audacious attack on
New Year's Eve 406/7. Legend has it that this was one of the
worst winters the inhabitants of Mainz had had to endure as the
Rhine itself became a single sheet of ice.

At the time, New Year's Eve was a Christian festival. Many
barbarian tribes still held to their pagan beliefs and so had no

respect for Christian observances. This was neither the first nor the last time they would seize their chance by attacking on a religious holiday. Many Christian troops refused to fight on holy days, but whether the Roman garrison this time was caught napping due to their piety or to their over-indulgence in drink we will never know.

Countless horsemen and barbarian wagons poured across the Rhine, gate-crashing the New Year's Eve celebrations in the most spectacular and bloody manner. The size of the attacking force has been estimated to be as much as 60,000 (a figure that includes whole families so perhaps a fighting force of 20,000 would be a more realistic estimate). Whatever the number involved, the resulting carnage was horrendous.

The barbarians who sacked the city seem to have had little comprehension of the possible advantages of urban life on the scale that confronted them in Mainz. As will become clear later, while many barbarian peoples were opposed to Roman rule, they nevertheless sought to overtake the infrastructure and exploit it for their own ends. Yet for the marauding hordes of 406/7, the seizing of slaves and booty seems to have been the only goal they had in mind – and to this end they not only remained in the city but moved deeper into Roman territory. The booty would not just have been the gold and jewellery of the rich townspeople but also fine clothes, household goods and iron – in great demand for the making of weapons and tools. We can imagine too that the wine cellars of the city would have been drunk dry by the rampaging mob.

This was not the first successful barbarian attack on Mainz; there had been a number of earlier catastrophes in the second half of the fourth century. In 368 Prince Rando, leader of the Alamanni tribe (their name means 'all men'), who had long since lived in the region east of the Rhine, had, also on a Christian holiday, forced his way across the river and plundered the city's coffers. But, unlike the attackers of 406/7, he had no desire to either stay in the city or go further into Roman lands. Rando and his army were happy to simply load their wagons with booty and return from whence they came.

The Rise and Fall of the Vandals

Of the tribes that made up the deadly and effective confederacy of 406/7 it was the Vandals whose subsequent history was to have a dramatic effect on the fortunes of Rome for a long time to come. Their extraordinary migrations and exploits show them to be a far more organised and sophisticated culture than might be thought from their popular reputation as the epitome of wanton and mindless violence. Their legacy was far more than simply the word vandalism.

They first appear in the annals of history as a rather small and insignificant tribe in western Poland. How they came to be such a powerful military force is something of a mystery. They migrated and fought their way across the heartland of Europe to the southern tip of Spain and into North Africa and, from there, mounted a massive sea-borne assault on Rome itself. The sheer speed and magnitude of their movements epitomises the Age of Migration, as this time is known among German historians and archaeologists.

Even before they sacked the city of Mainz in 406/7 the Vandals had begun to work inside the Roman machine, and one of the most powerful of their chieftains, Stilicho, rose swiftly to the highest echelons of the Roman military establishment in the 390s. He consolidated his position by taking the niece of Emperor Theodosius I as his bride. On his death Theodosius left the empire to his two sons – the younger, Honorius, under the guardianship of Stilicho. Although Stilicho held the Gothic enemies of the empire at bay for a decade and even saved Rome itself twice he was never fully accepted by the Roman establishment. Whatever compromises he had had to make in his military manoeuvres (which undoubtedly raised the hackles of many of his detractors), the real reason for disdaining him seemed to be his religious persuasion. He belonged to the sect of Christianity known as Arianism. This doctrine, which takes its name from its founder Arius, held that the Son did not share in the divinity of the Father. Not only had the Vandals become Arians but so had the Goths (later chapters on whom deal with their Arianism). That these two powerful Germanic peoples were Arians was of great concern to the Catholic Church. These barbarians who had once been pagans were now something even more odious to the Catholics – they were heretics.

The spiritual heartland of the Catholic Church was in Roman North Africa, the home of its mastermind St Augustine. With the very real threat of a Vandal invasion, he feared for the future of his Church. Augustine was the most powerful and influential Christian thinker of the world of late antiquity and, as bishop of the city of Hippo, he was inevitably enmeshed in the political fabric of North African politics.

At this time, North Africa was the granary of Europe and was therefore of paramount economic and strategic importance. Its significance was not lost on the barbarians, and the Romans did everything they could to prevent them overrunning the sea routes across the Mediterranean. In 419 a number of Romans were sentenced to death for revealing shipbuilding secrets to the Vandals. Once the cat was out of the bag, the Vandals wasted no time and invaded North Africa from their Spanish stronghold. St Augustine himself died inside the walls of Hippo as the Vandals lay siege to the city, leaving his magnum opus, *The City of God*, for posterity.

Once the Vandals were in control of the whole region, they were able to stop grain and oil from reaching Europe. Under the able leadership of Geiseric they shook Rome from afar. The eastern emperors also felt the shock waves of the Vandal activity emanating from lands far to the west. So in 440 a major naval force set sail from Constantinople with the aim of taking back Carthage, the capital of Roman Africa. This was a risky business as, in the east, the Huns were already on the warpath and posing a serious threat to the empire. The stakes were high and the decision to counter-attack the Vandals was clearly not taken lightly.

Nevertheless, the imperial fleet failed to achieve their goal and it was only much later, under the rule of the emperor Justinian I, that the Vandal rule in North Africa was finally brought to an end. In the summer of 533 an army of 15,000 troops sent by Justinian arrived in North Africa, landing without resistance in the Bay of Tunis. In the ensuing battle a few miles outside the city of Carthage, the Vandals were soundly defeated. A large Vandal force that had been sent to deal with an uprising in Sardinia returned to North Africa on hearing the news of their fellows' defeat. They, together with the survivors of the first battle, fought another battle near Carthage and were defeated once more.

Geilamir, the king of the Vandals, fled to an inland stronghold but this only delayed the inevitable and he was forced to surrender as the Romans starved him into submission. He, along with what remained of his force, was sent to Constantinople. Geilamir got off quite lightly, being given an estate on which he spent his twilight years in peace. The rest of the Vandals were put into the melting pot of Germanic soldiers serving the empire and, for all intents and purposes, they ceased to exist as a separate ethnic group. The era of Vandal fame and infamy was dead and buried.

A Barbarian Treasure Hunt

In the uncertain world of barbarian Europe it was not possible to deposit one's wealth in a bank. Depositing riches and hoards in the ground was as safe a way as any to keep valuables secure. Even today some people who are suspicious of banks still hoard cash under their mattresses or in biscuit tins. But the barbarian attitude towards material wealth went far beyond a naive distrust of the banking system.

For the nomadic herdsmen among the barbarians, wealth had to be, of necessity, portable since they were often on the move. They relied on their herds just as much as the barbarian farmers relied on their own livestock. But naturally their leaders – the noble clans and military elite – wanted something more ostentatious to embody their high social standing. Gold, whether in the form of bullion, coins or jewellery and other decorative objects, was hugely important to the barbarians both economically and culturally.

This goldlust (shared, it should be said, by the 'civilised' Romans as well) needed to be slaked and a steady supply maintained. Where was all this disposable wealth to come from? Much of it was to come from the coffers of the empire. For example, the Romans paid off the barbarians in the Danube region by supplying agreed amounts of grain to feed their people and gold to satisfy their nobility. If they paid up then the barbarians would not invade. It would be wrong to think of this financial arrangement between the empire and the barbarians as nothing more than a vast protection racket. It was not simple extortion, as the Romans themselves were extracting all they could from the economies of the barbarian peoples whom they were able to dominate. The methods of the empire and of aggressive barbarians such as the Huns are best looked at as simply two sides of the same coin.

Annual payments to the barbarians varied, but were usually in the region of the high hundreds or low thousands of the Roman gold coins known as solidi. Some seventy-two solidi could be minted from a pound of gold, so considerable amounts of precious metal were changing hands. At the height of barbarian power in this relationship – under the reign of Attila the Hun – nearly half a million solidi per year were being paid out. Many of these coins were melted down and fashioned into all kinds of objects desirable to barbarian taste.

It would be quite wrong to think that these people were simply vulgar and unsophisticated *nouveaux riches* with no class or style. They and their craftsmen drew upon many influences from the Romans, Persians and other 'civilised' peoples but had their own cultural traditions that also inspired their artistic labours. In fact, one of the most powerful reminders of the richness of the barbarian cultures is their supreme skill as craftsmen. Although their woodworking and textile making were undoubtedly highly accomplished, it is their metalwork that has survived for us to admire today. The items they produced are all the more amazing as they often lacked the permanent workshops (and elaborate equipment and tools) of their Roman counterparts, creating their masterpieces in the back of a wagon or other makeshift setting.

The little-known but extraordinary barbarian treasures of the Danube have come down the ages to us in two basic and very different forms: as the contents of rich burials and as hoards of treasure temporarily hidden in the earth to be recovered later by their owners. For reasons unknown, in many cases the owners failed to return to claim their deposits, leaving them to be found by the treasure hunters and archaeologists of future generations. One such hoard is the fabulous barbarian treasure of Pietroasa. Most of this dates from the fifth century, but at least one of the silver platters seems to have been made in the fourth century beyond the borders of the empire in territory dominated by the Goths.

Pietroasa is a village in the Wallachia region of Romania, to the north of the capital Bucharest. This particular tale begins in 1837 with two local peasants named Ion Lemnaru and Stan Avram, one being the father-in-law of the other. Together they were quarrying limestone when, to their great surprise, their digging revealed a number of objects embedded in the mud. Cleaning them off, they saw an array of golden treasures appear before their eyes: rings, a bowl, a tray, a jug...

Secretly, they bagged up the treasure and told no one what they had found, unsure of what to do with this most unexpected gift – or curse – from the earth. A year later, their house had to be demolished, so they got one of their relatives to hold on to the hot property for them. The next chapter in the story has the two peasants starting work on constructing a bridge for a builder named Verusi. Believing that their new boss was both trustworthy and more worldly-wise than themselves, they let him in on their big secret. He offered (but clearly not out of the goodness of his heart) to take a piece from the hoard to a Bucharest jeweller in order to obtain a valuation.

On his return from the capital two things were clear in his mind. He now knew – or thought he knew – something of the true value of the pieces, and he was sure that the peasants had no idea of the magnitude of what they had found. For a paltry sum of money and a few clothes he persuaded them into handing over the treasure. As the hoard weighed 88 pounds (about 40 kilos), he got himself a real bargain and they were well and truly duped.

Then the plot thickens as the tenant farmer for whom the two peasants usually worked got involved, putting together the rumours he had heard. He wanted part of the action and a substantial part at that. Verusi's greed prevented him being generous and, in exchange for the farmer's silence, he offered a single golden trinket and a small one-off cash payment. Insulted, the farmer blew the whistle on the unfortunate peasants by letting the local bishop (who was the actual owner of the land on which the treasure was dug up) in on the secret.

Verusi was not about to give up without a fight, and split up the trove and buried it near the recently built bridge. As the official investigation got under way, a letter of Verusi's was discovered, hinting at the whereabouts of the treasure. Nearly half the original 20 carat treasure (weighing just under 44 pounds) was uncovered, making it one of the single biggest treasures ever unearthed from the soils of Europe. The other half remains undiscovered to this day.

The case came to trial two years later in 1839. But the hapless peasants languishing in jail did not live until the end of it. As if to prove justice is blind, the swindling and conniving Verusi was acquitted of the charges against him. The hoard became a national treasure – and that should have been where the story ends. But the restless golden hoard seemed to have a wanderlust all of its own...

By 1867 the magnificent treasure was fully restored and after an international tour took pride of place in the National Museum in Bucharest. It was open to the public gaze in a display case, but what one particularly observant (and criminally minded) visitor to the museum noticed was that the display case was sometimes left unlocked at the end of the day by the rather desultory security guards. On a dark and stormy winter's night (it really was!) the eagle-eyed cat burglar broke through the ceiling of the room containing the treasure, the sound of this forcible entry being covered by the noise of the storm raging outside. He lowered himself down on a rope until he was in reach of the treasure. Having misjudged the size of swag bag required for the job, he was obliged to manhandle the objects, distorting and partially crushing them in the process.

He made his getaway undetected and unsuspected. As the horrified museum staff wandered around in a daze the next day, one of the curators noticed something gleaming in the snow outside. The thief had dropped it in his haste to leave the scene of the crime. The police wasted no time in tracking down the guilty parties. The thief's fence was caught in the nick of time as he was preparing to melt down a golden neck ring. The arrests were made, the punishments meted out and the treasure returned to the museum. There it remained until the middle of World War I when it was moved to Russia for 'safe-keeping'. The Communist authorities held on to it until 1956 when they deigned to return it to their satellite state.

No doubt to the great relief of the Romanian government, the story stops there. But what of the other half of the story – the other 44 pounds of golden treasure hidden by Verusi? Did he return after the dust had settled and dig up the hoard in the dead of night and have it melted down so that he could sell it undetected? Did he leave it where he had buried it for fear of being caught again? And, if so, did he take his dark secret to the grave or pass the precious information on to an accomplice? Or did he simply forget where he had buried it, or had someone built on top of it so that he could not dig it up without their collusion? All these questions remain unanswered. Yet it seems possible, even likely, that buried in Mother Earth somewhere near the quiet village of Pietroasa lies a hoard as spectacular and substantial as that treasure that lies in the bosom of the Romanian nation in the National Museum in Bucharest.

Chapter Four

THE GOTHS: A ROMAN HORROR STORY

*Now from this island of Scandza, as from a hive
of races or a womb of nations, the Goths are
said to have come forth long ago...*

Jordanes, sixth-century Gothic writer

In the year 376 one of the greatest mass migrations in an age of movement was already under way. A mighty force of Huns was on the move from east to west, pushing other barbarian tribes aside. A vast number of Gothic refugees found themselves on the banks of the river Danube, the frontier of the Roman empire. They were a desperate people seeking sanctuary in the comparative safety of the troubled bosom of the Roman empire. The emperor Valens agreed to let them in on one condition – that they would fight on behalf of the Roman cause; for this, they would receive land on which they could be secure and perhaps even settle. The Goths were not about to get a better offer from elsewhere and agreed to the emperor's terms.

Once they were inside the empire, the trouble began. But before we continue with this story in which the emperor's decision to let them in was to haunt him, we must turn back to earlier times to find out how and why the Goths found themselves in such a predicament in the first place. We must go back to the dark and mythical roots of this Germanic people that lie entangled in the prehistoric past of north-eastern Europe.

The major written source for the early chapters of the Gothic story is the work of a sixth-century Gothic author named Jordanes, who lived in Constantinople. His book *Getica*, or *The Origins and Acts of the Goths* as it is sometimes known, was written in Latin around 550. He drew on a number of sources, including the oral traditions of the Gothic nation themselves and on another work (which has not survived to our day), the *Gothic History* written by Cassiodorus in the 520s. Cassiodorus was at the court of the most famous of the Gothic leaders – Theoderic, king of the Ostrogoths, whose extraordinary life is the subject of the next chapter. There are other scattered references to the Goths in the writings of Greek and Roman authors from AD 200 onwards. Yet none of these offers either the detail or the overview supplied by Jordanes. According to Peter Heather, who has written the definitive history of this barbarian people, the three central themes of Jordanes' account have shaped our understanding of the Goths ever since.

Firstly, the ancient Goth places the homeland of his people in Scandinavia. He tells us that from there they crossed the Baltic Sea and made their way across Poland until they reached the Black Sea. Jordanes also says that from the third century at the latest the Goths were divided into two groups, the Visigoths and the Ostrogoths. The third point he makes is that these two groups were ruled by ancient royal lineages, the Balthi and the Amal respectively.

Investigating the Gothic Underground

Although none of these assertions of Jordanes can be taken simply at face value, they are a very useful way to investigate the obscure history of the Goths. His own account of the early migrations of the Goths was based largely on the oral traditions of his people. Nowadays, in the light of archaeological investigations in eastern Europe, we can try to link this shadowy history with tangible evidence from under the ground. Are there enough archaeological clues to either prove or disprove his idea that the Goths should trace their roots back over the Baltic to a Scandinavian homeland? The short answer to this question is no. The archaeological trail runs cold. There are not enough links between the sites either side of the Baltic to prove it. The ultimate roots of the Goths remain in the realm of mystery and there seems little chance that this will change. We can get no further back in the Gothic story with the aid of either history or archaeology.

We simply cannot work out whether they actually came from Scandinavia, but there is some archaeological evidence that is convincingly linked to the Goths as they moved south from Poland down to the shores of the Black Sea. There are two archaeological cultures that fit the bill and can be associated with the Goths. One is the Wielbark culture of northern Poland, and the other is the Cernjačhov culture of the region to the north of the Black Sea. The scanty written sources place the Goths in Poland in the first century AD, which fits well with the earliest phase of the Wielbark culture identified by the archaeologists. In the following two centuries the typical finds associated with the Wielbark culture spread out in a southerly direction exactly as the Goths were supposed to have done according to the fragmentary ancient writings available.

A number of types of artefacts (including pottery, brooches and items associated with women's fashions and clothing) can be found not only in the numerous sites of the Wielbark culture but also in those belonging to the Cernjachov culture. Likewise, there are strong connections to other cultural practices that are very similar in the archaeology of both Poland and the Black Sea, such as the way they built their houses. In the cemeteries belonging to the Wielbark culture there is clear evidence that people were both cremated and buried. And, unlike their neighbours, the graves of their men did not have any weapons buried with them.

Neither of these two traits of the Wielbark is particularly remarkable in itself, but both were unusual in that part of the world and distinguished them not just from the practices of their neighbours but also from the people who had lived in the very same area before them. Cremation (but not burial) had been practised by the other cultures around them and these others also placed weapons in the male graves. The people of the Wielbark culture were different and their archaeology gives us some idea of how they can be linked to the Cernjachov culture. The two cultures differ in a number of ways but the burial of men without weapons seems to have a cultural practice that was transmitted from the Wielbark to the Cernjachov culture. We cannot help but think that one moving population is behind this transmission: the Goths.

The literary sources tie in neatly with the archaeology. The spread of Wielbark culture in Poland in the first and second centuries AD echoes the literary accounts of the presence and migration of the Goths southwards. There is a gradual thinning out of Wielbark sites in the third and fourth centuries. This, along with the arrival of the burial without weapons and distinctive clusters of Wielbark objects in the Cernjachov cultural zone, marks a Gothic migration to the south. It is the material evidence that shows their movement from one area to the other.

The timing too is right, for the appearance of Wielbark traits in Cernjachov culture in the third and fourth centuries coincides with the time when the written sources tell us that the Goths were present in the region. The Roman historian Ammianus Marcellinus tells us that by the fourth century the Goths ruled the land between the river Danube and the river Don. This dovetails with the area in which archaeological sites belonging to the Cernjachov culture have been found.

So the archaeology of the Goths has been traced from northern Poland all the way to the Black Sea, and this part of Jordanes' story seems to be corroborated by material evidence that has been dug up from under the ground. It seems that these archaeological finds are the remains of Gothic material culture, but we must be careful not to over-simplify things. The Goths were not a rigid ethnic unit that remained unchanged throughout their early history and long-range migrations. The actual make-up of their societies was much more complicated. They must have merged and split with many other groups over the centuries, so a certain looseness and flexibility must be borne in mind when thinking about their culture.

A Shifting Mosaic of People

The fluid nature of Gothic society becomes easier to understand when we consider how they organised themselves during this early phase of their history. Jordanes is not writing history in the way we do today. In his account, the epic journey of the whole of the Gothic people from Poland to the Black Sea takes place under the leadership of a single man whom he calls Filimer. This was not the way it would really have happened. It is possible that before they left northern Poland they may have all been part of a single kingdom, but this is by no means certain. What made the Goths what they were was not so much their ethnic unity or even their language. It was their name, a banner under which a multi-ethnic group could gather, and the fact that it was an organisation under the leadership of a royal Gothic clan.

There was no unified Gothic state as such and the various branches of the Goths would have migrated gradually under the rule of different chiefs. What is reflected in the archaeological remains are some of the distinctive but very general cultural traits that were part of Gothic life. In the widest sense they were one people and probably spoke dialects of the same language, but they were not unified politically under a single leader. They would not have moved in one great mass across Poland to the Black Sea. Smaller groups, temporary alliances and vying chieftains would have characterised their life at this time.

To see how this fluid arrangement of Gothic groups eventually coagulated into more permanent kingdoms of later times, we must now turn our attention to their role in the Roman world. The Goths enter history as a problem for the Romans. By the 230s they are attacking Roman interests across the Danube. Towards the end of the decade in 238 they sack the city of Histria on the river. Their withdrawal is agreed on the understanding that the Romans pay them off annually. To pay or not to pay was always something of a dilemma. By caving in too easily, the Romans were simply encouraging other Gothic chieftains to try their luck but, on the other hand, it was sometimes simply the best (and sometimes, in the greater scheme of things, cheaper) option to pay out.

The size and frequency of their raids increase in later years. In 249 another city, Marcianople, falls into the hands of two Gothic chieftains named Argaith and Guntheric. The following year Cniva, another of the numerous Gothic chieftains, takes Philippopolis. Things take a more dramatic turn when Cniva defeats a Roman army and kills the emperor Decius in the process. Soon the Goths and other barbarian peoples with whom they team up find another means to force their way into the empire.

The Goths and their allies prove themselves more than competent pirates, organising large-scale raids across the waters of the

Black Sea. By the 260s such barbarian alliances were reaping rewards far and wide as they burst into the Aegean – plundering Greece, Cyprus, and Asia Minor, where, as if to prove their barbarian credentials, they vandalised the temple of Diana at Ephesus (in modern-day Turkey). In the third century this was as good as it got for the Goths. The Romans managed to get the raiding down to a more manageable level by a mixture of punitive expeditions into Gothic territory and more effective defensive measures.

To return to the version of the Gothic story written by Jordanes, and his assertion that the Goths were split into two groups – the Visigoths and the Ostrogoths: Ammianus wrote of two groups of Goths that existed in the fourth century called the Greuthungi and the Tervingi. They have been readily identified with the Ostrogoths and the Visigoths respectively. This is, unfortunately, too simple an equation. The Ostrogoths and Visigoths really only came into being as distinct groups in the fifth century. Both were composite entities and the Visigoths comprised parts of both the Greuthungi and Tervingi as well as other kinds of Goths who belonged to neither of these two groups. The internal divisions of the Goths were still in a constant state of flux.

The arrival of the Goths on the Danube frontier of the empire in 376 was simply another stage on an epic journey that had led them from northern Poland and would not finally end for some of them until they reached southern Spain. This was truly an age of migration on a continent-wide scale. But the significance of this particular stage in the journey was that they were just on the verge of their fateful entry inside the empire. The Huns were undoubtedly the reason for the Goths' presence on the Danube. It was a famous example of the so-called 'domino effect' where one group moves into the territory of another, and so on. This kind of explanation for the movements of peoples was also one put forward by writers at the time. Ambrose of Milan, writing around 380, wrote:

'The Huns threw themselves upon the Alans, the Alans upon the Goths, the Goths upon the Taifali and Sarmatae.'

Usually historians portray the Huns as the intruders who pushed aside other groups, including Goths, out of their own territories with the inevitable knock-on effects, eventually threatening the security of the empire. But there is another way of looking at the role of the Goths and Huns to the east of the empire. The expansion of the Goths from their settlements in northern Poland was probably due to a population explosion that resulted from more intensive and productive farming. The rising tide of Goths moved, as we have seen, into the area between the Don and the Danube. This was the region where they were to feel the brunt of invading Huns.

But it was not the Huns who were strangers in this land but the Goths. Long before the Goths lived in this region it was traditionally under the dominion of nomads from the steppe, people who had far more in common culturally with the Huns than with the Goths. Such nomads continued to control the region long after the Goths had left as well. In other words, the northern Goths who were farming people by inclination had, through population growth, expanded into an area traditionally run by nomads whose lifestyle and culture were very different. When the nomadic Huns from the steppe pushed the Goths out again they were simply reasserting the ancient grazing rights of the nomadic peoples. It was the Goths and not the Huns who were the odd ones out in the bigger sweep of history.

When the emperor decided to let the Goths into the empire, a chain of events was set in motion which was nothing less than a horror story for the Romans. The Goths, after the initial relief of being let in, soon became disgruntled at the treatment they were receiving from the Roman officials in the region. The emperor Valens had promised them free supplies but local corruption meant that the Goths were being charged for them. The Goths were becoming a problem and were shunted from place to place. Two groups under the leadership of chiefs named Fritigern and Alavivus were moved south to the city of Marcianople (which, as mentioned above, had been sacked by their forefathers).

While a banquet between the local Roman military high command and the Gothic chiefs was taking place, hungry Goths decided to take things into their own hands and tried to break into the city to seize supplies of food. Lupicinus, the Roman general in charge, reacted quickly. Ordering his guests' bodyguards to be killed, he planned to hold the chiefs hostage. Somehow Fritigern escaped and when Lupicinus and his army came out in pursuit they were chased back into the city by the Gothic forces now under the command of their escaped chieftain. Such confrontations continued over the next two years and a major battle was inevitable. The Romans had to try to solve the problem of the Goths once and for all.

The emperor led an army of 40,000 men against a Gothic confederacy of Greuthungi and Tervingi forces in a battle that took place just north of the city of Hadrianople (modern Edirne in European Turkey) on 9 August 378. The barbarian forces were formidable. The Goths defeated and killed the emperor Valens, ruler of the eastern part of the Roman empire, along with two-thirds of his army. The account of Themistius, a philosopher and leading senator in Constantinople, records the devastation: writing in horror, he describes how 'our armies... vanished like shadows'. It was in the aftermath of this crushing and unexpected defeat of the Roman forces that the two new groups of Goths – Visigoths and Ostrogoths – gradually emerged. Roman interests recovered as they had done so often before, but the Goths had proved themselves a serious force to be reckoned with.

Under the leadership of Alaric (said to be in the bloodline of the royal Balthi clan mentioned by Jordanes), the Visigoths became a political reality. They were the most powerful group in the Balkans, and the Romans were ready to do business with them. The Visigoths could use the rivalry between the western and eastern empire to their own advantage but not owning any territory that they could call their own made them reliant on one or the other for ensuring they had sufficient supplies of food. The early fifth century was a frustrating time for the Visigoths. Alaric, despite his threats and raids on the interests of both parts of the empire, failed to secure a promising future for his people.

He had an 'agreement' with the Romans, which obliged the Senate to pay him 4,000 pounds' weight of gold. When the Senate changed its mind and refused to pay, Alaric decided to exact his revenge by sacking Rome in 410. Rather than being an expression of his power, this was more a consequence of his impotence. He could not get at the western emperor who had moved his court from Milan to the almost impregnable city of Ravenna. Nor could he put into action his plan to take the Visigoths to the richer lands of Roman North Africa. After the sacking of Rome he led his people south, again trying to forge a new Gothic kingdom. The sudden death of Alaric meant the end of the dream of reaching Africa. He was succeeded by his wife's brother Athaulf, who was clearly more pragmatic. He immediately decided to give up Alaric's ineffectual strategies. He gave up not just on Africa but realised that there was no place for the Visigoths in Italy either. In 412 he led them away over the Alps.

We shall meet the Visigoths again, on the battlefield where they faced the Huns in Gaul, but their subsequent history and their final settlement in Spain takes us away from the main arena in which the other branch of this great barbarian people, the Ostrogoths, made much more of a success in their quest for power in Italy. The Amal dynasty (the second of the two Gothic royal lines mentioned by Jordanes) produced a king who, with the possible exception of Attila the Hun, was to be the most significant of barbarian leaders: Theoderic the Great.

Chapter Five

SHADOW EMPEROR

The poor Roman imitates the Goth,
the well-to-do Goth the Roman.

Aphorism of Theoderic, king of the Ostrogoths

Theoderic was born in Pannonia in 454. He was the son of
Thiudimer Amalo, king of the Ostrogoths (the eastern branch of
the Goths, the western branch being the Visigoths), who reigned
alongside his brothers Vidimer and Valamer. Theoderic's childhood was abruptly interrupted when he was given as a hostage to
the eastern emperor at the age of eight, as a living guarantor that
his father's and uncles' treaty with the emperor would be adhered
to. Bizarre as this may seem today, such were the practices of
ancient diplomacy and negotiation. The Romans hoped that by
taking royal hostages in this way, they would turn the offspring of
barbarian kings into lovers of the Roman way of life. Thus the
young Theoderic spent the next decade at the Byzantine court. In
his case at least the Roman scheming would backfire.

Until comparatively recently, many historians have simply repeated the ancient and partisan accounts that have portrayed Theoderic as illiterate. Yet the fact that he spent ten formative years in the court makes this impossible to take seriously. It can now be dismissed simply as propaganda. He spent the greater part of his formative years in the epicentre of the empire and must have received a first-class education. Furthermore, there are sources that tell us that his daughter was a very cultured individual versed in Latin and Greek who wanted to give her own son the benefits that came from such learning. Theoderic is said to have been a retiring and clumsy youth who nevertheless had a deep interest in a large number of fields including art, philosophy, politics and military matters. How much of what he was later to achieve was planned in silence during these years we can only guess at.

When Thiudimer requested the return of his son, he must have wondered how the boy had turned out, a Gothic prince who had lived in the sheltered and learned world of Byzantine splendour. Perhaps he wondered if he had become effete and unfit for the world that awaited him outside. The emperor had no objections to releasing his teenage 'guest', believing him too ineffectual and timid to pose any problems. Neither his father nor his imperial captor was prepared for the boundless vigour and vision the young Theoderic unleashed on his release. Immediately on returning to the Ostrogoths and without waiting for his father to return from his campaign against the Suevi people, he launched a successful assault on the city of Singidunum (modern-day Belgrade). Not only did he conquer it – he also refused to hand it over to the emperor, thereby flouting the agreements that, until that time, had existed between the Ostrogoths and the Byzantine court.

His father died two years later in 474 and Theoderic was crowned king of the Ostrogoths. His reputation and power grew during the 480s when he twice saved the emperor Zeno from attempts to overthrow the throne. By way of reward, Theoderic was first given territories and then (whether with the consent of Zeno or without it) took over the rule of Italy on the understanding that he would remove the barbarian leader Odovacar, who had taken it for his own. Odovacar's ethnic origin is uncertain, but his force was drawn from many barbarian peoples. In the back of his mind Zeno may have been hoping that both barbarian leaders would destroy each other, but he had agreed to hand over the reins of power in Italy to Theoderic (even though it was Odovacar and not he that held them).

Theoderic willingly accepted the challenge and in 487 began preparations for the huge undertaking, a long march, which would involve the entire nation of Ostrogoths (some 300,000 souls – men, women and children, young and old) travelling through 2,000 kilometres of hostile foreign lands only to meet their arch-enemy Odovacar at the other end. With the harvest reaped and loaded on to carts, the mighty wagon train swung into movement in the autumn of 488. The beginning of winter found them in the land of another Germanic tribe, the Gepids, who were less than pleased to see them. Despite meeting fierce resistance, the Gothic forces triumphed and lived off the land of their defeated 'hosts' while waiting for the coming of spring. Having now persuaded some of the Gepids to join him, Theoderic led his people, like a barbarian Moses, over the Alps towards the promised land of Italy that lay beyond.

Odovacar was both forewarned and forearmed. After much strategic manoeuvring, the battle finally began near Verona on 30 September 489. The bloody conflict looked set to result in a victory for Odovacar, until Theoderic roused his commanders in the midst of the battlefield and inspired them to turn the tide to their favour. They inflicted great losses on the enemy and Odovacar was lucky to escape with his life. Theoderic's army was itself too weakened to pursue the foe and this allowed Odovacar to live to fight another day. Both leaders sought to forge alliances before their next conflict.

Odovacar moved his base of operations to the city of Ravenna, the capital of the western empire. It was to remain the capital for 350 years. It was eventually abandoned and sank into a long period of decline lasting until the twentieth century when the draining of the swamps that surrounded it revitalised the ancient city once more.

Between the Adriatic sea and great stretches of marshland Odovacar thought he would be beyond the reach of his arch enemy. But Theoderic had not come this far just to give in, and began what was to be a protracted siege of the city. After nearly a year and a half, both sides were suffering. Inside the city they were nearing starvation, while many of the besiegers had contracted malaria as a result of spending too long in the unhealthy mosquito-ridden marshes. Finally, after another six months, Odovacar capitulated and surrendered the city.

On 5 March 493 the victorious Theoderic entered Ravenna peacefully. No instant retribution was made. The army of Odovacar was not even disarmed. The citizens of the city soon warmed to their new ruler. Less than a fortnight into the new regime, Theoderic invited Odovacar to a small banquet where he stabbed him to death. Even this does not seem to have lessened him in the eyes of the people of Ravenna, who accepted his version of events – that Odovacar had been planning to overthrow his conqueror. Theoderic disposed of the entire family of Odovacar along with some generals who were his co-conspirators, and the security of his regime was firmly established.

Theoderic set to work immediately on a series of social and economic reforms. As his Italian biographers Stefania Salti and Renata Venturini put it, he 'never had complete faith in the "Italic race" which he considered to be naturally predisposed to corruption'. He wanted the Italic people to rebuild their economy under the military protection of the Ostrogoths. He envisaged a society which allowed both peoples to live side by side, respecting each other's cultures. It was not just cultural differences that made them distinct; they also belonged to different branches of Christianity: Catholicism and Arianism.

For a while things went well for the new regime. The economy picked up and the two cultures seemed to be able to work together. Things turned sour when, in 523, a law passed by the eastern emperor Justin made it impossible for Jews and heretics to take up public office. This edict was specifically designed to exclude Arians from positions of power. Until the eastern empire instigated this persecution of the Arian community, Theoderic had succeeded in creating a peaceful and harmonious co-existence of Arians and Catholics. Perhaps as an outsider and a barbarian himself, he understood the need to respect different faiths and ethnic groups for the sake of all involved. After the Arians were persecuted, Theoderic reacted in kind by a royal decree ordering that all Catholic churches be handed over to the Arians.

The Barbarian Mosaics of Ravenna

The conflict between Theoderic and his Arian Ostrogoths on the one hand and the eastern empire and the Catholics on the other is embodied in the exquisite mosaics of an ancient church in Ravenna. The mosaic art has, for hundreds of years, been presented as a lowly and minor one. It has even been called 'the archaeologist's loose woman'. This disparaging view of the mosaicist's art obscures its genuine value. Yet its value is not just artistic: it also reveals to us a hidden chapter in the story of Roman and Gothic relations. The mosaics of this church, Sant' Apollinare Nuovo, have to be seen in person to be believed.

I arrived in Italy by plane from Frankfurt. The contrast of climates was all the more striking because of the speed with which a plane transports a person from one to the other. The sudden transition from the dark, windy and rain-soaked banks of the Rhine to the glorious sunshine of Bologna airport revealed another reason for the northern barbarian incursions into the Roman heartland – the weather. This is still what attracts hordes of German, British and Scandinavian holidaymakers to the beaches of southern Spain, France and Italy.

Who can doubt that some of the sombre and dark elements of the northern soul are the direct result of climate? My spirit was certainly lifted as I strolled for the first time around the streets of Ravenna. Replete with wonderful ancient buildings, as most Italian cities are, Ravenna has a particular connection with the aesthetic traditions of the barbarian king. The church of Sant' Apollinare Nuovo is unique in that it has magnificent mosaic decorations that date from two different periods, the early sixth century, the time of Theoderic, and the second half of the century when Ravenna was ruled by his Catholic successors. The Arian mosaics include a series of scenes depicting the life of Jesus. Although such scenes are standard in the Christian iconography of all periods, these particular examples show the tell-tale signs of the distinctly different Arian view.

There is no scene of nativity or baptism – clearly avoided by the mosaic makers who did not want to portray anything that might suggest the divinity of Jesus, which, as Arians, they did not accept. Although the Arians have gone down in history (a history almost exclusively penned by their enemies) as obscure and misguided heretics, the visitor to the church today cannot fail to admire the religious dedication embodied in the staggering work of this reviled sect. As my guide Manuela Farneti so elegantly put it, Theoderic's contemporaries must have felt they were entering paradise when they stepped into the church, which would have been lit by the flames of hundreds of candles and torches reflecting the light from the golden surfaces of the complex mosaics.

The memory of Theoderic was odious to those who came after him on two counts. Firstly, he was a foreign usurper and secondly, and more importantly from the point of view of the Church, he was the follower of what had by now become firmly a heretical sect – Arianism. Throughout history, new regimes have sought to rewrite history in their own image and this happened in a very literal way with the renovation works that took place in Sant' Apollinare Nuovo.

The mosaic panels of the royal palace that were commissioned by Theoderic are high above the floor immediately to the right as one enters the church. In an act of vandalism worthy of its namesakes, the cronies of the eastern emperor removed the images of Theoderic and members of his court and clergy that had once stood between the columns, replacing them with the curtains that can be seen today. Oddly, their hands can still be seen on the columns themselves. Why the revisionists left these disembodied hands is something of a mystery, but it has been surmised that they were left as a reminder to the faithful that the heretics had been conquered and destroyed. It was an act of censorship all too familiar from modern times – an ancient counterpart to the airbrushing of photos in Stalinist Russia.

There are other examples of the reworking of the original mosaics that have only come to light in our own era. To the right of the door is a mosaic portrait which had always been thought to represent the emperor Justinian, but restorers working in the 1950s discovered that the binder used behind the face and some other parts of this image was of a different composition to that used elsewhere in the mosaic. It is now thought that the mosaic was originally an Arian work and actually showed not Justinian but Theoderic.

The face, which survives from the original making of the mosaic, bears an uncanny resemblance to a medallion of Theoderic issued in the year 500 to commemorate the success of his reign. He never dared to have himself portrayed as an emperor, so a brooch and a purple robe, the imperial insignia that adorn the image that is visible today (and which are backed by a different binder), were additions of the Byzantine era. By this act Justinian sought to usurp the vision of Theoderic, to whom the real glory for the creation of this glittering work of light really belongs.

The mosaics of the two periods also show marked differences in their style of execution. Theoderic was deeply enamoured with Roman art and culture and yet succeeded in making something much more than a pale and lifeless imitation. He reworked these Roman influences in a fashion far removed from anything normally associated with barbarians. His highly skilled artisans represented the prophets in three-dimensional form. The artists made full use of the potential of their medium by using different stones and colours to evoke the three-dimensionality by the play of light on the mosaics.

The procession of saints by the Byzantine craftsmen is done in a very different fashion – flat, rigid and austere. The sensual and lifelike Gothic mosaics of the prophets were deemed too material and worldly for the Byzantine school, which strove to create images reflecting a more ascetic sense that they saw as more authentically spiritual. It is not without significance that the procession of saints is led by St Martin of Tours (to whom the church was later to be re-consecrated). St Martin was an early forerunner of the witch-finders, in that he led the persecution of those who were deemed spiritual enemies of the Church. He was the driving force behind the extermination of pagans and heretics in France.

The creation of these mosaic masterpieces was not the only major architectural expression of Theoderic's vision. He oversaw the construction of his own memorial. Work on his mausoleum began around the beginning of the sixth century a number of years before he died. There are no written sources concerning the architects who were commissioned by their lord – we do not even know whether they were Ostrogoths or Romans. Whoever the anonymous authors of this potent statement in stone were, they were surely the leading architects of their day.

At this time the coastline was much closer to the mausoleum than it is today. The choice of this site was anything but random – it would have been clearly visible from afar, not just from the city of Ravenna but also from the sea. The mausoleum was so dominant in the landscape that neither citizen nor visitor could ignore it. Not only was it designed to command the space around it but, as a memorial fit for a powerful leader, it was made to withstand the ravages of time. Unlike other contemporary buildings in Ravenna that were built of brick, Theoderic built in eternal stone. Some fifteen hundred years later it continues to hold pride of place in Ravenna, largely due to the quality of the workmanship involved. No mortar was used in its construction yet each stone was fitted precisely with no gaps.

His mausoleum is a unique monument that embodies both Roman and Gothic principles. It is, in some respects, modelled on the mausoleums of the Roman emperors, especially the lower of the two storeys which varies little from standard Roman imperial architecture. The upper storey (within which the sarcophagus lies) is something of a hybrid, combining Roman features with other, entirely alien influences. Much of the decoration on the outside walls of the upper level clearly echoes the patterns and motifs used in barbarian metalwork. It is a remarkable and successful synthesis, a concrete expression of the two traditions: a Roman basis (without mosaics and other finery) capped by a Gothic roof.

Remarkably, the roof was made from a single stone brought across the Adriatic Sea from Istria (present-day Croatia), which must have been a feat in itself. This single block is 11 metres across, a metre thick and weighs about 500 tonnes. The shape is highly unusual and, as Sauro Gelichi (a professor from the University of Venice who was kind enough to give me a guided tour of the monument) pointed out to me, is modelled on a yurt, a kind of tent used by nomadic peoples – undeniably showing that Theoderic, far from having forgotten his Gothic roots, was evoking the memory of his ancestors. What could be more fitting for his final resting place?

Visitors to the mausoleum today will see that this single mighty stone displays a large crack that scars its otherwise pristine surface. Catholic legend, with echoes of the story of the Tower of Babel, has it that God was angry at the arrogant work of Theoderic and meted out punishment in the form of a lightning bolt that caused the crack. A more prosaic possibility, and perhaps a more likely one, was that the crack occurred when the roof was set in place.

Although the building has survived to this day it has not survived intact. Around the whole of the upper level are a number of recesses. They are now empty but it is probable that each originally housed a statue. Whom these lost statues portrayed is a mystery, but it seems likely that they were prominent members of the Amal dynasty that linked Theoderic back to the primordial Gothic heritage. Some time after the demise of the Gothic regime the statues were unceremoniously removed and broken up for making cement. The survival of the mausoleum itself is probably only due to the fact that the upper part was reused as a chapel by the Catholics.

The sarcophagus was imported from Egypt. It was made of porphyry, no ordinary material, but one preserved for the exclusive use of emperors and their families. Theoderic would have been acutely aware of this, and his choice of porphyry for his sarcophagus is yet another instance of him announcing his quasi-imperial status. The sarcophagus was obviously set in place to receive the body of Theoderic upon his death.

On 30 August 526 Theoderic died suddenly after suffering severe intestinal pains. The cause of death is unknown. The fact that this was the very day on which the Catholic churches were confiscated by his order may well be no mere coincidence. The Catholics saw this as divine punishment, although the possibility that he was poisoned by an assassin for his persecution of the Catholics can hardly be dismissed.

It seems likely, although not certain, that his mortal remains were laid to rest in the mausoleum, but they did not rest for long as they were removed some time afterwards. Legends concerning the whereabouts of his body abound. Two versions of one legend survive, one Catholic, one pagan. In the first it is said that the devil himself, in the form of a large black horse, took the body down to hell. The other says that Sleipnir, the mythical eight-legged horse of Odin (or Wodan), the high god of the Germanic tribes, transported him to the warrior heaven of Valhalla.

There are also rumours that his final resting place may be within a stone's throw of the mausoleum, but this is a mystery that may never be solved. Even though he does not lie in its peaceful and austere embrace, the mausoleum is nevertheless a fitting architectural epitaph to the dual public persona of Theoderic the shadow emperor: a lover of all things Roman yet a man true to his Gothic roots. Stefania Salti and Renata Venturini wrote that 'anticipating history by 1,500 years Theoderic dreamt of a united Europe where different peoples could live together respecting each other's religious faiths and propagating their own cultures'. For all his faults, Theoderic was a leader of vision and his deep understanding of both the Roman and Germanic legacies undoubtedly resulted in the breadth of this vision. His defence of religious tolerance and multi-culturalism mark him as one of the prime movers in the shift away from the old Roman way towards the path to the development of the growing consciousness of being European.

Chapter Six

THE HELL'S ANGELS OF HISTORY

The first the occupants of a village or a fort learned of the arrival of a hostile force of Huns was a cloud of dust, followed by the sound of horses' hooves, followed by a rain of arrows.

Patrick Howarth, *Attila, King of the Huns*

On a high hill in southern Austria, amid an unexpected and swirling mist, I walked among the ruins of Theoderic's world. On the top of the hill two churches had once stood side by side – one Catholic and the other Arian. It was only a few metres from one to the other, and in Theoderic's day the hymns and prayers of one faith must have merged with the other. This poignant reminder of the short-lived tolerance that flourished in his time was one of two reasons that I had come to the village of Globasnitz, which, nestling at the foot of the hills, is some 30 kilometres from the Moravian border.

I stayed overnight at the only hotel in Globasnitz, and after lunch strolled across the village to have a look at the other reason for my visit. Just at the edge of the village, next to the main road, were the spoil heaps and other tell-tale signs of an archaeological dig. A large cemetery dating from the Dark Ages had been unearthed, and among the numerous human remains three highly unusual skulls were discovered. They were strangely deformed – more elongated than normal skulls. Scientific analysis of bone and tooth enamel samples suggests that their owners were probably not locals at all but immigrants from the east. Such deformed skulls are also known from other areas, including the north of Austria and Hungary, but until these three were dug up at Globasnitz archaeologists had never before found specimens south of the Alps. These skulls were not the result of some congenital disorder or pathological condition: they were deliberately elongated for cultural reasons.

The skulls from Globasnitz were sent for analysis to Professor Maria Teschler-Nicola, a leading anthropologist and custodian of the world's largest scientific collection of human skulls at the Natural History Museum in Vienna. The glass cabinets that line the walls display row upon row of skulls of all kinds, from the earliest stages in human evolution onwards. The vast majority of specimens are those belonging to *Homo sapiens*, and have reached these spectacular corridors from all over the globe. Anthropologists, explorers and scientists have brought the skulls of the world – from Tierra del Fuego to the Arctic, from New Guinea to North Africa – to their final resting place here in the heart of Europe.

To most of us, the differences in skull shape and size of these specimens are too subtle to discern, but the curious specimens from Globasnitz, being deliberately deformed, were unmistakably different – as I could see when I met the professor in the museum. She told me that the skull was deformed by being tightly bound with bands of cloth (about five or six centimetres wide) during infancy and early childhood. Such binding resulted in the skull not being able to grow in a normal fashion, and developing instead in an artificially elongated way. As most specimens (and the earliest of them) have been found in Asia, it seems safe to surmise that this is an eastern habit brought to Europe by a migrating people – the most likely candidate being the Huns. The Greeks also knew of this curious custom in the fourth century BC, describing the 'long-heads': a group of Scythians (the blanket term used by the Greeks to characterise the nomads of the steppe) living near the Sea of Azov. This region, as we shall see later, was thought in the Roman world to be the homeland of the Huns. (The custom of skull deformation, though, is thought to be much older than even the Scythians: a close colleague of Professor Teschler-Nicola, Erik Trinkaus, has suggested that Neanderthal man was the first to do it.)

We cannot be sure whether the deliberately deformed skulls found in Austria and also Hungary are those of Huns, or whether at least some of them belong to another ethnic group who may have copied this unusual custom from the Asiatic horsemen – perhaps as a mark of status. Among the Huns, both male and female skulls were deformed in this way, but most of the skulls unearthed alongside them are entirely 'normal'. If only a minority of Huns practised deformation, this suggests that it may have been a sign of high rank and restricted to the elite clans and echelons of the tribal confederacy.

But we do not know for certain what the meaning of this custom was for the Huns who practised it. It could well have been done for aesthetic reasons, as it was among some Native American groups of the north-west coast of Canada. Perhaps, in some ways, deforming the skull is a Dark Ages equivalent of the current obsession among certain people with body piercing. But, whatever the reason, it was an integral part of Hunnic culture and a dramatic, irreversible and permanent marker of identity. In the shadowy world of Hun history, the skulls provide another much needed clue to trace the movements and influence of these people.

Alongside the various nuggets of truth in the Roman accounts, there are many pieces of fool's gold that have duped generations of credulous commentators. The historian Ammianus Marcellinus, writing in or around the year 395 and relying partly on ill-informed hearsay, was clearly a victim of the effects of Chinese whispers when he tells his readers that the Huns made their clothes from the skins of field-mice! In fact, the Huns did make a significant sartorial contribution to the continent of Europe – but it did not involve a patchwork of rodent skins. They introduced a whole new style of dress by combining elements from their own cultural roots with ideas inspired by the dress codes of the Iranian nomads. High felt hats, baggy trousers with ornate belts and caftans and neck torques were the new haute couture fashion items for men. The spectacular garnet diadems worn by aristocratic women among the Huns no doubt inspired first envy and then imitation among the other barbarians.

The Huns also had their own distinctive hairstyles – cutting their hair in a circular shape. It may be that tightly binding the skull in childhood could have impaired the subsequent growth of hair, resulting in a hairline further up the head than would have otherwise been the case, although this can only be speculation. The Huns were also said to scar the faces of their children with swords. If they actually did this, it was more likely to have been a rite of passage (like circumcision or the scarification practices of some African peoples) rather than an act of sheer cruelty as the early report of the Gothic historian Jordanes suggests.

Probably the most popular of the anecdotes embodying misinformation on the Huns is that concerning their novel way of preparing food on the hoof. Ammianus tells us that they ate raw

meat, which they heated up by putting it between their horses'
backs and their saddles – a tall tale that was recycled in the time of
Tamburlaine as an unsavoury habit of the Tartars, another
nomadic society who were seen in later times as a threat to civilisation. It is only in recent times that the kernel of truth behind the
story has been revealed. The Huns most probably did put raw
meat under their saddles, not as a handy snack but in order to
prevent their horses' backs from being rubbed raw by constant
friction with the saddle.

The Huns were still being misunderstood in more modern
times. Half a century ago, one historian obviously thought that
their deformed skulls were a natural physical trait. He suggested
that this Hun characteristic has left its mark in the odd, distinctively Hunnic, shape of the skulls of the modern inhabitants of the
village of Pont l'Abbé near Quimper in Brittany. He claimed that
these people are the descendants of a small Hunnic community
that once lived in this part of Gaul. While the Huns may well have
reached this part of the world, their artificially induced skull shape
could not, of course, have been genetically transmitted.

No culture in European history has a more notorious reputation
than the Huns. Their infamous leader Attila was known as the
'Scourge of God'; he was seen as a divine punishment for sinful-
ness and an embodiment of demonic force. If we are to believe
ancient legends, then the Huns were the hideous offspring resulting from sexual intercourse between Gothic witches and evil spirits. The first signs of Huns lurking on the horizon must have
inspired fear in the same way that the dust clouds and roar of
motorbikes terrorised the inhabitants of small American towns in
the 1960s. They may have gone down in popular history as Hell's
Angels on horses, but we shall see that this is only part of their
story and that there was much more to Attila and the Huns.

Alien Invasion:
The Building of a Nomadic Empire

The alien customs of the Huns must have appeared strange to the writers of the time but underlying these exotic anecdotes were profound and very tangible differences in lifestyle. The settled and sedentary peoples of the ancient world – whether Egyptians, Greeks, Romans or Chinese – had cultures that were based on the twin pillars of agriculture and urban living. The whole lifestyle of pastoral nomads like the Huns was as foreign to the Romans as it would be to the city dwellers and farmers of today. Not only did the Romans see the culture of the Huns as different to their own, but they also saw it as inferior. The proudly independent Huns no doubt considered the Romans their inferiors too.

Who were the Huns and where did they come from? These are questions that can only be answered in the vaguest of terms. I was planning to go to Hungary in search of some tangible clues to this most elusive of barbarian peoples but, before doing so, I wanted to get a clear picture of them from the history books.

From the fourth to the sixth centuries they played a major role in European history yet they themselves left no written records of their exploits. For the details of their history and customs we rely purely on the accounts of foreign writers, many of whom were on the receiving end of Hun aggression.

The main region into which the Hunnic hordes poured was the great plain of Hungary that stretches across much of the country and must have been a home-from-home for the newcomers, rich in pasture and as flat as the steppe from which they came. These uninvited and unwelcome immigrants to Europe also reached the western part of the continent – even as far as Paris. When they first arrived on European soil in 375 the Huns probably numbered between 20,000 and 30,000 men, women and children. Whatever the catalysts, the direct result of this migration was the displacement of other barbarians in their wake – a domino effect that was to have great repercussions throughout the European continent.

Yet this was more than migration: it was a strident and, as it turned out, irresistible onslaught. The raw power of the Hun assaults was awesome. Patrick Howarth, a biographer of Attila, succinctly describes the colossal scale of events: 'When early historians wrote of the sky being dark with arrows they were scarcely exaggerating. Surprise and terror were of the essence of Hun tactics. Their whole strategy was, in a number of respects, a forerunner of the twentieth-century blitzkrieg.'

As the following chapter illustrates, their power lay in their symbiotic relationship with their mounts. With such a combination of equine and human capacities, the Huns were able to sweep aside other Iranian nomadic tribes such as the Alans and the Sarmatians in their push to the west. The Huns headed towards the territories of the Goths with their sights beyond them to the Roman empire itself. The next episode of the story of the Huns concerns their forcible entry into the Roman empire through Pannonia, the most vulnerable province on the eastern front. Today, what was Pannonia straddles Austria, Hungary, Croatia and Slovenia. Its eastern frontier was marked by the river Danube. Like the Vandals and their allies who crossed the Rhine a few years later, the Huns crossed the frozen Danube in 395. Rome had a new and powerful enemy on its doorstep.

The beginning of the fifth century is marked by the brooding presence of the Huns. Their leader Uldin is really the first historical 'king' of the Huns about whom we know something more substantial than just his name. He was not a king in the sense we would usually use the word; rather he was the military commander of a fairly loose-knit confederacy of tribes. In the year 400 he confronted Gainas, a Germanic leader who had fled with his followers from imperial forces across the Danube into what Uldin saw as his territory. After a number of clashes the Huns were decisively victorious and Gainas was killed on 23 December. Uldin sent his head in a package to Constantinople, the capital of the eastern empire. The head was displayed there on 3 January 401. Along with it was a demand for a 'reward' in the form of gifts, even though no bounty had been put on Gainas's head.

Among Uldin's other exploits was his crossing of the Danube and capture of a fortress in the Roman province of Moesia in 408 (directly to the south of Pannonia). This was achieved not just by sheer force of arms but by guile, as he had collaborators within the stronghold. Inspired by his success, he went on to invade Thrace (roughly equating to present-day Bulgaria and eastern Macedonia). The Romans sought to buy him off but in his arrogance he refused. This haughtiness backfired on him when many of his inner circle succumbed to Roman bribery and turned against him. He was lucky to escape with his life, and his remaining loyal followers, back across the Danube.

In 420 the Huns set up their capital – a sea of tents on the Tisza plains in what is now Hungary. It was to be during this decade that three Hun brothers rose to significance. One of these, Ruga (or Rua), was the military leader of the confederacy of Hunnic tribes along with another brother, Octar. The third brother, Mundiuch, does not seem to have shared power with his two siblings, yet *his* two sons – his elder Bleda and the younger Attila – were both destined to rule the empire of the Huns.

In 434 or 435 Ruga died and Bleda and Attila shared the reins of power. Not only did they continue the family business, they also expanded it. The eastern empire was forced to pay out even more than to uncle Ruga. The price of peace under the brothers' reign was increased to 700 pounds (about 350 kilograms) of gold per annum. Although company profits were up they still pursued a policy of hostile take-overs, ravaging numerous towns in the eastern provinces in 440. They were hugely successful and managed to triple the Roman tribute to 2,100 pounds (about 1,050 kilograms) of gold a year under the terms of an agreement known as the First Anatolian Peace.

Bleda was of very different character to his younger brother Attila. From the little history left to us, he seems to have been more gregarious and straightforward than Attila. One of the few anecdotes concerning him involved the Hunnic equivalent of a court jester in his retinue, a dwarf Moorish slave named Zerco, who would entertain his audience in a mixture of tongues – Gothic, Latin and the language of the Huns. Not satisfied with Zerco's natural disabilities (a stammer and a strange gait caused by deformity), Bleda felt the need to dress him up in a specially made suit of armour. While Zerco was a favourite of Bleda, Attila was indifferent to the ribald antics of the dwarf.

One day, Zerco and a number of other slaves escaped. On hearing the news, Bleda was completely unconcerned about the others but enraged at the loss of Zerco. Hun horsemen were sent out to track him down and he was brought back dejectedly in chains. Laughing, Bleda asked him why he had run away. Zerco replied that it was because his master had never supplied him with a wife and loneliness had made him reckless enough to risk escape. Bleda gave him a wife but, after the death of his master, Zerco was given away by Attila and as a result lost the wife he had temporarily gained.

After a successful partnership that lasted ten years, there was no brotherly love lost between the co-rulers of the Huns. Bleda died, most likely at the hands (or, at the least, at the instigation) of his brother. The empire that they had carved out of their European interests was now under the sole leadership of Attila, king of the Huns. Yet even the mighty Attila was not overlord of *all* the Huns; there were numerous independent groups of Huns and many who had long since signed up to auxiliary units in the Roman army. He was, notwithstanding, the most powerful Hun in history.

In the Presence of Attila

Our major source for the paltry biographical details we have of Attila is the *Byzantine History* written in Greek by Priscus of Panium (a town west of Constantinople, now Istanbul, on the coast of the Sea of Marmara). The fragments of this work that have survived down the ages give us an extraordinary if incomplete portrait of the great man. Priscus travelled with a diplomatic mission from the eastern emperor to the court of Attila in the years 448–9. He was probably the only writer from this age to actually have any in-depth experience of life among not just the Huns but any of the barbarian peoples.

The Huns were not by nature town dwellers and traditionally preferred life in tents to life in houses. In a large Hun encampment, Priscus laid eyes on the dwelling of Attila, a timber palace made from smoothly planed boards and encircled by a wooden wall. This wall, he tells us, was built less for defence than its elegant appearance. The Roman envoy gives an account of a banquet he attended in honour of Attila, describing the dramatic and poignant scene that unfurled before his eyes:

> *When evening began to draw in, torches were lighted, and two barbarians came forward in front of Attila and sang songs which they had composed, hymning his victories and his great deeds in war. And the banqueters gazed at them, and some were rejoiced at the songs, others became excited at heart when they remembered the wars, but others broke into tears – those whose bodies were weakened by time and whose spirit was compelled to be at rest.*

Unsurprisingly, Attila was not a man to be easily moved. Neither the gravity of the songs nor the light relief of the next act in the evening's entertainment received a visible reaction from the host. Priscus remarks on his indifference to the pranks of the jester Zerco and on his stony countenance that confronted all who came face to face with him; all, that is, but one. Having seen how coldly dismissive and contemptuous Attila was to even his own sons, Priscus was both surprised and intrigued when he saw his host warm as his youngest, Irnik (Ernac), came into the banqueting hall. Attila tenderly stroked his cheek in a rare moment of public affection. Priscus later found out that Hun 'soothsayers' (nowadays we would probably do better to describe them as Hunnic shamans) had predicted that Irnik would save the empire from ruin. Their prophecies were to come to naught.

On the other hand, Priscus did not find Attila's looks to be handsome, at least by Roman standards. He describes him as short and squat with deep-set eyes, a flat nose and a thin wispy beard. His foreign appearance was compounded by his enigmatic character. He was anything but ostentatious. At the banquet he held for Roman and other foreign delegations, guests would be served food on silver platters and drink from golden goblets, while Attila himself would eat from simple wooden plates and drink from a wooden cup. Both his own barbarian entourage and his 'civilised' guests were served rich dishes while he ate only meat. His men wore scabbards and boot fastenings adorned with precious stones, and their horses' bridles were equally ornate with gold and gems. Neither Attila nor his horse had any of these gaudy trappings – no amount of gold or jewels could outshine the sheer presence of the mighty leader. Priscus tells us that Attila embodied the rarest of attributes, for he 'was a man born to shake the races of the world. The proud man's power was to be seen in the very movements of his body.'

The Fading Power of the Huns

The Huns, like many other barbarian peoples, were more than willing to be mercenaries and trouble-shooters for the empire. Aetius, commander-in-chief of the Roman army in the west, had the unenviable task of keeping the western empire reasonably intact. He called on their aid to repel other barbarians from overrunning Gaul. The eastern part of the region was under threat from a people named the Burgundians, who were effectively suppressed with the timely arrival of the Huns. In 439 the southern part of Gaul was in danger of falling into the hands of the Visigoths, and the Huns were once more brought in to prevent that happening.

After years of working together, the mutually beneficial relationship between Aetius and the Huns broke down. In 451, with Attila at their head, the Huns invaded Gaul with the apparent intention of smashing the kingdom that the Visigoths had made for themselves in the environs of Toulouse. Aetius was very worried about the scale of the Hunnic army and joined forces with the Visigoths. A major battle between the two camps took place in the heat of July on the Catalaunian Plains near Troyes, to the east of Paris.

A whole host of other barbarian peoples were involved in the battle. Accompanying Aetius's own troops and the Visigoths were many who had made their home in Gaul – Franks, Bretons, Saxons, Sarmatians, Burgundians and Alans. On the side of the Huns were the Gepids and the Ostrogoths. Attila had sought the predictions of his shamans in order to know what the outcome might be. Through divining from the marks and lines on bones and the entrails of animals, they told him that the Hun forces would face major setbacks, even defeat. That was the bad news. The good news from their point of view was that an enemy general would fall in battle. Attila hoped this was a prediction that Aetius would be killed.

The night before the battle saw the first clash, between the Franks and the Gepids. Even if we allow for a great deal of exaggeration in the reports of the battle, this was no mere skirmish: 15,000 are said to have died before the battle had really begun. Around three in the afternoon the following day the fighting began on the 300 acres of flat, even battlefield.

According to one version of events, the Visigothic king Theoderic (not to be confused with the later Ostrogoth king of the same name), commander of the right wing of the Roman forces, was killed by a spear thrown by the Ostrogoth Andagis. The later Theoderic would look back on this battle and rue the conflict of Goth against Goth, describing it as fratricide. Another account says that he fell from his horse and was accidentally trampled to death by his own cavalry. Either way, the Hun shamans' prediction had come true even though the victim was not Aetius.

The battle was hard fought and exceedingly bloody: an estimated 165,000 died in addition to those who had died the night before the main conflict. The Huns were the losers and Attila, who up until this time had seemed invincible, suffered the humiliation of his first defeat. In the aftermath Aetius could have let the Visigoths pursue the Huns and effectively finish them off. He deliberately did not allow this to happen. Exactly what his motives were we cannot be sure, but it seems likely that he wanted to keep his options open. The Huns had been useful in the past and could well be useful to him in the future. The Visigoths, despite his temporary alliance with them, were a force that could easily get beyond his control – especially without the Huns to keep them in order.

In the fifth century the empire of the Huns encompassed a land mass reaching from the Rhone to the Urals. Despite his remarkable achievements Attila ruled his empire for only eight years. Legend envelops the death in the spring of 453 of the greatest leader the Huns had ever known. It is said that having gone to bed with a new concubine named Ildico he had died in the height of passion from a burst artery. Others claim that he was poisoned by this seductive and efficient assassin. Whether killed by a new concubine, or dying peacefully among friends as his funeral elegy claimed, Attila died in bed and not on the battlefield. His burial place has never been located; his grave remains one of the great unknowns of archaeology.

After his death his sons simply did not have the charisma and the power to hold the empire together as their father had done. Within a year Ellac, his eldest son, had died in combat with the forces of Ardaric, a barbarian leader of the Gepid people who had been living under the rule of the Huns. His second eldest son, Dengitzik, lasted far longer but died while fighting the armies of the eastern empire in 469. Attila's death was proving to be the beginning of the end, heralding the rapid disappearance of the Huns. They left the stage of history as abruptly and dramatically as they entered it. They would soon return again but their name would not. When the Huns came back they were to be known as the Bulrgar tribes.

Many of the barbarian peoples tried to emulate the Romans – the Goths, as we have already seen in earlier chapters, were enamoured of the empire and all its material and cultural trappings. The Huns were different. They spurned the chance to integrate, preferring to keep their own culture as distant as possible from Roman influence. Unlike the Germanic and Celtic barbarians, the Huns came from another cultural sphere altogether and left as quickly as they had arrived. They chose to live their own lives and returned to the steppe lands that placed them back outside the remit of written history. They were not an ignorant and backward people but had their own culture, alien to their European neighbours, but one with which they were as much at home as they were at home in the saddle.

Chapter Seven

ON THE
CENTAUR'S TRAIL

The nation of the Huns, scarcely known to ancient
documents, dwelt beyond the Maeotic marshes beside the
frozen ocean, and surpassed every extreme of ferocity.

Ammianus Marcellinus, fourth-century historian

In western Europe the memory of Attila lived on, albeit in a
distorted and limited form. He has gone down in history as an
arch-enemy of civilisation, a tyrant and a plunderer of the coffers
of Rome. Along with Genghis Khan and Hitler, he has been one
of the prime candidates for the role of Antichrist. The legend of
Attila also fuelled the western imagination through the media of
music and film. Among the high points are his starring role in the
Verdi opera *Attila*, Liszt's *The Battle of the Huns* and his appear-
ances in Fritz Lang's 1920s films based on the *Nibelungenlied*.
Perhaps rather less memorable is Jack Palance's Attila in the 1950s
Hollywood movie *The Sign of the Pagan*.

I came to Hungary to see what I could find out about the eastern European view of the Huns, to try for a more complete picture

of Attila and his people. (Despite the prominent position of the Huns in the cultural background of the Hungarian people, the name of the country itself owes nothing to the Huns. It was the Onungun tribes who entered what is now Hungary long after the Huns had disappeared who gave their name to the country.) On my first night in Budapest, the bridges that cross the Danube were floodlit to an unparalleled degree of brightness thanks to its use as a set for the latest Eddie Murphy movie. I checked into the Gellert Hotel, a gargantuan veteran that has seen the Communist era come and go.

I was aided in my quest to find out more about the enigmatic Huns by the Hungarian anthropologist and film-maker Janos Tari. He introduced me to Professor Peter Tomka, an archaeologist and specialist in Mongolian and other Central Asian tongues. Professor Tomka has spent his professional life tracking down the elusive Huns through their archaeological remains. It is difficult enough for archaeologists to assign the artefacts they find to a particular ethnic group, but it is doubly difficult when those people are nomads like the Huns.

In Hungary, the name of the most famous Hun leader lives on in road signs. Fittingly, I first met Professor Tomka one autumn morning in a cafe in Attila Street, Budapest. For the Hungarian citizen, this is taken for granted in the same way that the New Yorker would not think twice about the name Kennedy Airport or the Londoner Sloane Street. In Hungary and throughout eastern Europe the mighty Hun leader is not seen as a prime candidate for the job of Antichrist, but is honoured as a national hero in the same way as Genghis Khan is in present-day Mongolia. Attila is venerated as a hard ruler who sought to rid the Hun territories of Roman influence and to repossess the gold and other treasures plundered by the Romans. In this version of events, the reason he stopped short of ransacking Rome was that he had no desire to destroy the empire; his aim was simply to restore what he saw as

Hun land and Hun property. Having achieved this, he left Rome to its own devices.

The Hidden History of the Asian Huns

Through Janos Tari's able translation, Tomka began to communicate what he had learnt of the Huns. With the Huns, one has to start with the simplest questions to which there are no simple answers. I asked Tomka where they came from. As a wandering people, there was no one place that they could be pinned down to but somewhere in or around Mongolia was their homeland. Looking at a map gives one some idea about the size of this country – this can hardly be called pinning them down!

The writers of the ancient world who concerned themselves at all with the 'barbarian' peoples naturally did not have the same interests as those of the modern historian or anthropologist. In many instances their information is accurate and detailed and we can hardly criticise them for not writing to suit the requirements of our own era. While they do give us tantalising details of the customs and habits of these peoples, there are inevitably large gaps in our knowledge of Hunnic life.

The Huns seem to have given the Roman writers little in the way of information about themselves. This has been put down to their ignorance of their own origin and history – perhaps as a result of their migration over vast distances of the monotonous steppe from their unknown homeland. Yet it is hard to believe that any people could be so uninterested in preserving knowledge of their background. Furthermore, it is well known that even societies that have no recourse to the written word (and the Huns were such a people) have the means to preserve their heritage in great detail through the oral transmission of myths, legends and epic tales. We cannot reject the possibility of a certain reticence on the part of the Huns in telling the Romans the whole story.

The quote from Ammianus Marcellinus at the beginning of the chapter refers to the Huns' origin 'beyond the Maeotic marshes'. The Maeotic Lake was the ancient name of the Sea of Azov, a body of water north of the Black Sea to which it is attached by the Straits of Kerech. It was in this part of the world that the Huns first appeared on the horizon of Roman understanding.

To this day their ethnic and linguistic affiliations are poorly understood. Their language is usually thought to belong to either the group that includes Turkish, or the group that includes Finnish and Hungarian. I wanted Tomka's input on this question, hoping his expertise might be able to produce a definitive answer, a rare thing in the world of Hunnic studies. What of their language? He smiled and said that we do not know but, most likely, it was a member of the language family that includes Turkish and Mongolian (known as Altaic after the Altai mountains of Central Asia). Even some of the few supposedly Hunnic words that have come down to us via the history books may have been Gothic translations instead.

Jordanes, when writing of the Huns, may have altered the actual Hun words to suit the Gothic tongue. According to Professor Tomka, the very name Attila is the Gothic version of an unknown Hunnic title and translates as 'little father'. Others translate it as 'daddy'. That the most famous Hun of them all may be known only by a foreign name is another remarkable testimony to the enigmatic place of the Huns in the history of our continent. Linguistic comparisons have been made between the names of the Attila clan and other words given by Jordanes and words that made their way into the language of the early (pre-Slavic) Bulgarians. Based on the similarities found between the two tongues, a 'Hunno-Bulgarian' branch of the Altaic language family has been suggested as a way of pigeonholing the language of Attila and his people.

It will have become apparent by now that the Huns were not a people to be easily pigeonholed. It would be wrong to think of them as a single, unified society that was simply at odds with the dominant superpowers of the time – the Chinese, Persian and Roman empires. One cluster that splintered off the main body were the so-called White Huns who, finding the region to the north of Persia to their liking, gave up the nomadic lifestyle to settle there permanently. The rest of the Hunnic hordes kept on the move, not drifting aimlessly but resolutely westwards. Although literacy was a feature of the pre-Islamic Persian empire, the Iranian written sources concerning the Huns amount to little more than a few disconnected fragments.

If we go further to the east and into the cultural sphere of China, we find much more in the way of historical information that not only tells us about the life of the eastern Huns but also gives us the much needed background to their later arrival on the fringes of Europe and the Roman empire. It was first suggested in the eighteenth century that the Hsiung-nu, a nomadic and belli-cose people mentioned in Chinese sources from the Han dynasty, may be none other than the Huns who swept so dramatically into the European continent. Like most of their counterparts in the Greek and Roman worlds, the Chinese writers had no inclination to give a carefully balanced account of their war-like nomadic neighbours who lived beyond the Great Wall.

We have already seen what made the Goths a distinct group. It was not their language or their ethnic unity; it was their *name* (a banner under which a multi-ethnic society could come together) and the fact of their being under the leadership of a royal clan. The same is the case with the Hsiung-nu, the name given in the Chinese accounts to refer to the multi-ethnic state built up by the nomads. These people were ruled over by a royal clan of Huns that are called Lüan-t'i in the older sources and T'u-ko from the third century AD onwards.

By AD 48 the Hsiung-nu had split into two major divisions, rather like the Goths of Europe were to do. The southern branch settled down in the lands of northern China and in doing so accepted Chinese sovereignty. They retained a certain independence for a century and a half until their ruling Hunnic clan merged with the ruling class of the Chinese Han dynasty and then submerged into it in AD 216, thereby losing its own name and separate identity.

The Long Trail from Dzungaria to Hungary

Meanwhile, the northern branch of the Hsiung-nu kept their independence and the Hunnic name of the T'u-ko clan lived on, but unlike their southerly neighbours they were not able to settle down. In AD 91 they were pushed out of their homeland (now Mongolia) by their enemies, the Hsien-pi. This was to mark the beginning of a long westward migration of the Hun tribes from their traditional territory. They had to relocate, and their leader held court in the Ili Valley in what is now Dzungaria, the northern region of Xinjiang in China that lies between Kazakhstan and Mongolia. Their enemy took over vast tracts of land that had formerly been under the sway of the northern Hsiung-nu. By the middle of the second century AD the latter found themselves reduced to being merely the rulers of Dzungaria.

After the Chinese tell us these intriguing facts about the political fortunes of the barbarians on their borders, their records dry up. For during this time the Chinese too were losing territory, and their control over the western provinces of their empire waned; thus they ceased to share a common border with the Hsiung-nu. The trail of clues that shed a little light on the otherwise obscure westward migrations of the Huns can be picked up again over 200 years later, in the passing comments of an Armenian historian named P'awstos Buzandats'i. Writing in 380, he tells us that the king of the Maskut people has hired a considerable number of nomads as mercenaries to fight against the Armenians, among them being the Hon – clearly a reference to the Huns. The Armenian king he mentions as being the target of this mercenary force (Khosraw III) reigned from 330 to 338. Then, in the 350s, the Huns, fearless of the might of the Persian empire, entered one of its provinces and forced a treaty with its Iranian inhabitants.

In the latter part of the fourth century another Iranian people, the Alans, were to become the next victims of Hun expansionism. Under the leadership of a Hun king whose name is usually given as Balamber (but may better be written as Balamur, meaning 'the daring one'), the Alans were press-ganged into becoming the poor partner in an alliance with their new-found neighbours. According to the Gothic historian Jordanes, he was the first leader of the Huns to be deemed a real danger in the western world. It has been suggested that there is reason to doubt whether he was actually a real historical person, and that he may have been concocted by Jordanes. This seems unlikely, for the historian had nothing to gain from creating this Hun leader (who is said to have defeated Gothic forces as well as Alans) out of thin air.

We have now traced the Huns from their first appearance in history, on the periphery of the Chinese world, down to the time of Uldin and later leaders who were described in the previous chapter. The earlier and lesser-known phase in the history of the Huns began their migration across the vastness of Central Asia towards Russia, precipitated by the concerted Chinese campaigns against the northern Hsiung-nu. The shifts of power in the heart of Central Asia were to have a knock-on effect thousands of miles away, resulting in the Huns' appearance on the eastern fringes of the Roman world in the fourth century. There may have been another factor involved in the Huns' migration: their ever-present and pressing need to feed their horses and herds. Perhaps the climate on the steppe further to the east took a turn for the worse and the grasslands were unable to feed the countless animals of the Huns. Others have argued the opposite – that the favourable conditions of the time may have resulted in a population explosion among both man and beast, and that this was the driving force for their expansion. The lure of gold and other treasure undoubtedly played a role too, for the riches of the Roman empire were hardly a secret and attracted all the barbarian tribes without exception.

Whatever the factors, the story of the Huns is, in both time and space, of truly epic proportions. It is all the more remarkable in that none of our sources from either east or west were written by this enigmatic and powerful people themselves.

In the introduction to this book I remarked on how both the Roman and the British empires sought to understand the 'primitive', 'savage' and 'barbaric' peoples with whom they had contact. They were not always successful, especially when confronted by a very different way of life from their own. The cultures of nomads were based, as we have seen, on very different principles and concerns to those of the urban-based empire builders. The tension between the settled agricultural peoples and pastoral nomads undoubtedly has its roots in prehistory. Whether through trading or raiding, nomads have always relied on their more settled neighbours for grain and other foodstuffs which their own way of life usually does not allow them to produce. It would be wrong to assume, however, that because they were nomads they were constantly moving. Provided the local land could sustain them, they would simply rotate the pasture around them in a similar way to a farmer rotating his fields. But whether on the move or not, the Hun 'empire' was never anything remotely like the Roman empire, nor would it ever have developed along the same lines had it continued.

The Chinese also had difficulty in understanding the psychology of the nomads. To settle down and become farmers would have been living death to the Huns. They were not, as the archaeology shows, entirely averse to building settlements – it was just that they did not want to be tied down to them. Evidence of a Hsiung-nu settlement has been discovered at a site near Ivolginsk in the southern part of the Buryat region, north of Outer Mongolia. Only 10 per cent of the site has been excavated so far but already more than fifty houses have been discovered. Initial estimates place the population around the 3,000 mark. Other evidence reveals that through agriculture, the raising of livestock and a host of crafts and cottage industries (including metal and bone working as well as pottery), they were able to supply all the needs of a population of up to 13,000 nomads.

The market towns that grew up under the stewardship of the Hsiung-nu were only a part of their trading system. The Chinese sought to placate the nomads with sometimes lavish gifts. Chinese silk and rice wine were reported to be among the most prized goods among the Hsiung-nu. The mind-set of the nomads was very different to that of both the Chinese and the Romans. The chieftains and kings of the Huns did not simply want tribute payments and gold to stockpile in the same way that the sedentary city-dwellers might hoard their riches. A nomadic leader would often demonstrate his own power and prestige by giving away much of his own wealth to his followers. The more lavish and generous, the greater the leader. It was not simple greed for gold that motivated the nomadic leaders, material wealth was also a means to an end. One needs only to recall the austerity of Attila's clothing and simple wooden goblet and compare them to the rich trappings of his entourage to see this nomadic psychology in action.

There is an instructive anecdote in the account of Priscus concerning the Huns and the difficulties the Romans sometimes

ATILA FLAGELVM DEI

Attila, Scourge of God.

The deliberately deformed
skull of a Hun, from
Kerts, southern Russia.

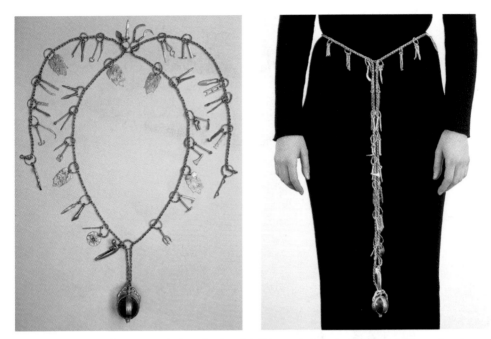

Barbarian jewellery unearthed at the site of Szilágysomlyó-Şimleul Silvaniei, Transylvania.

Mosaics in the church of Sant'Apollinare Nuovo, Ravenna, Italy.

A modern mosaicist at work in Ravenna.

Hadrian's Wall, marking a line between civilisation and barbarism.

The mausoleum of Theoderic, King of the Ostrogoths, Ravenna, Italy.

The sarcophagus inside the mausoleum of Theoderic.

The helmet from the Sutton Hoo ship burial, near Woodbridge, Suffolk, England.

The fallen warrior scene, a panel from the replica of the Sutton Hoo helmet made at the Tower of London armoury.

The reconstructed Anglo-Saxon village of West Stow, Suffolk, England.

An experimental replica of the Anglo-Saxon dwelling known as a Grubenhaus, *West Stow.*

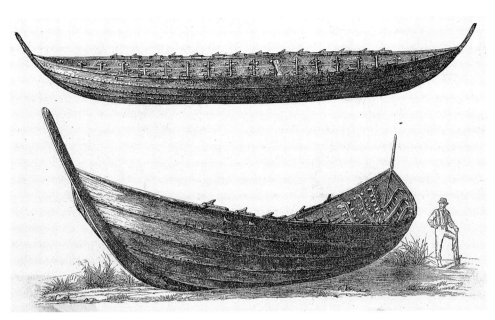

The fourth century Saxon boat found in the Nydam bog in southern Denmark in the 1860s.

Sæ Wylfing, *'the sea wolf's she-cub' half-scale replica of the Anglo-Saxon ship from Sutton Hoo, built by Edwin and Joyce Gifford.*

Kassai Lajos, horse archer, on the target range and outside his yurt, or nomad's tent, Kaposmero, southern Hungary.

had in understanding them. Two Romans were made prisoners of war, having been captured by the forces of Onegesius, Attila's second-in-command. In his previous life the first of them had been a prosperous merchant. Nevertheless, he accepted his lot and decided to take up the warrior lifestyle and, moreover, married a Hun woman. By going native he received the respect of his captors and gained not only his freedom but a good job in the military and as much wealth as he had before he had been caught. The second man to have been taken captive was a prestigious architect and oversaw the construction of a magnificent bathhouse for his new Hun master. Rather than being rewarded with his freedom, he was treated with disdain and demoted to the lowly role of being a simple attendant at the baths!

The lesson was crystal clear. Roman values counted for next to nothing in Hun society.

The Search for the Golden Bow

After my initial meeting with Peter Tomka, the whole Asian background to the history of the Huns' involvement in European affairs was unfolding before me. I decided to follow it up with a visit to Tomka in his hometown of Gyur in western Hungary. I wanted to see with my own eyes some of the tiny artefacts that marked the route of the Huns across thousands of miles of the flat, monotonous landscape of the steppe.

Gyur is a provincial industrial town, not without charm in the old quarter where Tomka works and studies. We headed for his museum, accompanied as before by Janos Tari. As we walked across a square around the corner from the museum, Tomka remarked in the most casual and offhand way, almost in passing, as if it were the most natural thing in the world, that this was the spot where he had found some deliberately deformed Hunnic skulls that had come to light while part of the square was being dug up.

The skulls that had first intrigued me in my quest to understand the Huns had resurfaced here in Gyur.

Once settled in Tomka's museum office, we began talking about the culture of the Huns again. Tomka answered one of my questions in his broken English saying, 'Bones not speaking.' But while the bones were silent, the skulls (at least the deformed ones) were one of the few indicators of Hun presence – or at least Hunnic influence. To find an archaeological signature of a non-literate people is not easy. One of the few characteristic artefacts that has been definitely linked to the presence of the Huns is a distinctive type of copper or bronze cauldron. Elongated and cylindrical, they are typically 50–100 centimetres high. They do not seem to have been ordinary vessels for everyday cooking tasks, and it may be that they were ritual objects used at funerary feasts. Over twenty such cauldrons have been found stretching across a huge swathe of land from the Ob river region in western Siberia to the battlefield of the Catalaunian Plains in France. The majority have been found in the military bases of the Huns in the Carpathian Basin and the Romanian plain.

Another way of tracing the trail of the Huns across Asia to Europe is by a scarce kind of small animal carving. One of these distinctive objects, carved from wood and covered in gold, was found in a Hungarian village among the artefacts recovered from a grave belonging to the Roman period. The peculiar way in which the ears, neck and head are crafted links it with others of the same type found over a vast region – Belarus, southern Russia, Kazakhstan and Tuva. The earliest of these carvings are those found to the east; the latest are those found in European sites. This shows that the people who made them originated in the east, and this fact makes the Huns the prime suspects for leaving behind these cultural sign-posts of their movements.

Tomka told me that, according to legend, Attila had found a mystical sword (echoes of King Arthur and the Excalibur story) that was said to impart to him dominion over the whole world. I jokingly asked him if he had excavated this sword. He laughed and said no, but he had found something that may have the finger-prints of Attila on it. I knew he wasn't talking about something we could take down to Scotland Yard but I was intrigued by what he actually meant. He went on to describe a very important find that had been dug up about half an hour's drive from Gyur in a place called Pannonhalma. In the corner of a field a hoard of golden treasure had been found by local peasants. Two golden horse bits and the other surviving horse decorations were identified by Tomka as undeniably belonging to the Huns. Similar pieces have been found elsewhere in Hungary and further afield in southern Russia, but this remains the richest hoard of Hunnic gold found in what was then the Roman province of Pannonia.

I was beginning to hope that some kind of picture of Hun life could be reconstructed from the few material remains that we could assign to their workmanship. Tomka, with the freedom from the beady eye of conservators that only the curator of a small museum can have, came back from the storeroom bran-dishing a 1,600-year-old sword. It was a metre long and had a very narrow blade – an eastern type clearly distinguishable from the shorter and lighter swords of the same age used by the Romans and the German tribes. He handed over the sword for my perusal then gestured to me to give it back, indicating that the best was yet to come.

Tomka explained that the sword was not the most important symbol of Hunnic military prowess. This singular honour went to the equipment of the horse archer. When he told me he was going to show me a golden bow, I was expecting something quite spec-tacular. I have to say that when he returned once more from the storeroom, this time with an old cardboard box, I began to have my doubts. He removed the lid with a dramatic flourish and withdrew from a mass of tissue paper some tiny fragments of wafer-thin gold leaf. Naively, I had been expecting something more dramatic – not a solid gold ornamental bow but certainly an artefact more substantial than that which lay before me on the table. But the treasure hunter in me soon subsided and I realised that, fragmentary as these remains were, their significance was as great as if the whole bow was right there in front of me. The delicate golden pieces that adorned it showed that the bow was not made for practical use – it was a symbol and, moreover, must have belonged to a very important Hun chieftain.

This discovery at Pannonhalma is rare but not unique. A handful of other finds of these small gold-covered bows shows them to be the clear insignia of rank in Hun society. It is no coincidence that the eastern emperor Marcian had a dream shortly before the actual death of Attila in which the demise of the enemy he feared so much was announced by an angel who showed him Attila's bow broken. The bow was the emblem *par excellence* of the military and political elite of Hun society.

The history books had conjured up scenes of the daily and court life of the Huns and had given them names. The deformed skulls and golden hoards provided a more tangible link to these most enigmatic of barbarian peoples but I still felt that I needed another way into their world. Tomka had a suggestion. If I really wanted to know more about the role of the bow in the culture of the Huns, then I should go to see the most accomplished horse archer in Hungary, a man as enigmatic and reticent as the Huns themselves.

A Meeting with a Centaur

The keys to the military power of the Huns were their horsemanship and their prodigious development of the bow as a weapon of war. The composite bow they used was very similar to that used by the Syrian forces whom the Romans employed far and wide in the empire (and, as recorded in Chapter 2, remnants of such bows have been excavated from the foot of Hadrian's Wall). The Huns were so close to their horses that they were likened to centaurs, man and beast seemingly one creature. The horses of the Huns were different to those of other contemporary armies in Europe. Stocky, incredibly strong and surprisingly fast, these steppe-bred horses were able to transport the Hun warriors over 100 kilometres per day.

The horse archery techniques of the Huns involved shooting a host of arrows in swift succession. The rider had to be able to manoeuvre the horse without the use of reins while accurately firing at a target, shooting backwards, sideways and forwards in a single manoeuvre. A Hun force of even a few hundred such archers would have been hard for any army – Roman or barbarian – to resist. The elite scouts of the Hunnic army were known as the Eagle Archers and were the Dark Ages equivalent of today's special forces: deadly, effective and widely feared.

Kassai Lajos is one of a very small group of practitioners of this little-known oriental martial art – the way of the horse archer. When I arrived at his home and headquarters in Kaposmero, a quiet backwater in southern Hungary, he was sitting on a bench by the side of a large pond drinking wine with a small group of friends and followers. After a rather stilted and awkward conversation designed to break the ice, his friends went on their way and then he simply got up from the bench and wandered off in the direction of his stables without a word. A short while later he reappeared in his austere black riding gear on one of his horses, carrying a Hunnic bow and quiver of arrows. He rode down to his target practice area and began his second training session of the day – another two hours of uninterrupted firing of arrows into the target. Manoeuvring his mount solely with his feet and legs, he fired eight arrows at the target on each ride: three arrows as he approached the target, two while he was level with it and three over his shoulder after he had passed it. He hit the target almost every time, seven out of eight being a poor score by his own standards and almost impossible by anyone else's.

The archer who uses the bow on foot can use a stronger, heavier bow but his horseback counterpart needs a lighter bow. My host estimated that in battle an adept Hun archer could shoot and kill either a man or a horse up to 300 metres away. It is hardly surprising that they put the fear of God into their enemies and victims.

The centaur description is apt: the grace displayed by Kassai Lajos on horseback echoed this symbiotic relationship that was at once practical and cultural – man and horse were two parts of a whole. Lajos explained that the horse was crucially important in a number of ways: it was not only the means by which the Huns moved from place to place and fought, it was essential to keep their herds of other animals under control. The horse was also eaten, or even shot and buried with its master.

Kassai Lajos is a man of action rather than a man of words and this demonstration of his mastery of the ancient art of horse archery certainly spoke louder than any words could. Later in the day when he had finished his training he seemed more relaxed and explained why he had dedicated his life to what to most people is an anachronistic and rigorous lifestyle. For him, identity can be realised only through contact with one's ancestors who, for him, are the Huns: to make contact with them, to share in their understanding of the world, means to do what they did, follow as literally as possible in their footsteps. His approach is Zen-like, and he was able to explain the core of his practice to me in English.

There are two worlds: the microcosm (or little world), the inner world or oneself; and the macrocosm (or great world), the outside world. The archer is the microcosm and the horse represents the macrocosm. When the two work in harmony, the arrows will hit their target; if they do not work in tandem, then they will miss. Successfully hitting the target is the proof of the attainment of harmony. The proof of the alignment of man and horse, microcosm and macrocosm, is in the archer's success.

Boiled down to its essence, Lajos's way is direct, simple and unequivocal. I asked him how he made connection with the past. He replied that the past makes the connection and not him, and he doesn't understand how it works. Isn't the connection made through the daily discipline of horse archery? In his words:

Yes... yes because have to do something and every day a step closer and closer and if... started do something what your ancestors did you can come closer, closer and closer. I think this is the point. If I don't use a bow and not sit on a horse, no contact... but I do every day, two times a day, it's a little bit closer and closer and I can thinking about the past. Make a fire, the same. Two thousand years ago, the people the same, shoot from the horse.

Lajos completes his reconstruction of the ancient way of the Hun with an authentic yurt (a type of tent used by the Central Asian nomads) that he has set up on a hillside on his land. He told me that he bought it from the estate of a Hungarian anthropologist who had brought it back from Kazakhstan in the 1960s. He, along with his pupils and his followers, often spend evenings gathered round the fire in the yurt reciting ancient stories, talking over the finer points of horse archery and conducting shamanic rituals. Outside the yurt stands a kind of Hunnic totem pole – a high wooden stake topped with a horse's skull and a mane of hair blowing in the wind.

Lajos is able to devote himself so wholeheartedly to his martial art by a mixture of selling bows made under his supervision and teaching pupils. In addition to his hardcore following of Hungarian students he has also taught others from further afield, including some Native Americans who came to Kaposmero to re-learn the skills of their own ancestors. Public events that include spectacles such as archery competitions (which he invariably wins), horseback drumming and other traditional musical renditions help bring his passions to a wider public.

Like those few others who dedicate their lives to rekindling the skills of ancient times, Kassai Lajos provides a way into the culture of the Huns that could never be attained through the written historical sources nor the artefacts of this lost civilisation of the steppes. Most professional historians and other academics may find little of use to them in the rigorous daily routine of training he undertakes. But can such scholars really say that the partial, incomplete and often incoherent texts and archaeological remains associated with the Huns can nullify the visceral impact of being able to witness living proof that man, horse and bow can be so intertwined? The legend of the centaur lives on in the fields of Kaposmero.

Part Two

SHADOWS
ON THE LAND

Chapter Eight

THE BARBARIAN HYDRA

*Mournful news arrived from Germany; that Varus
was killed, three legions cut to pieces, as many
troops of cavalry, and six cohorts...*

Gaius Velleus Paterculus, on the battle of Teutoburger Forest
(translated by John Selby Watson)

Leaving the centaur-like Huns, we can now turn to what may be described as another mythical beast: the many-headed hydra that was the Germanic people. Just as the east Germanic Goths and Vandals played a major role in the history of what were eventually to become Italy and Spain, so the various west Germanic peoples played an equally important role in north-western Europe. Their story takes them from the time they first appeared at the fringes of the Roman world, through to their settlements on both sides of the North Sea.

The Romans referred to these Germanic tribes as barbarians, and so they have been called in this book until now. The later

Christian chroniclers more usually called them pagans. Both terms denote exclusion: a barbarian is non-Roman and uncivilised; a pagan is non-Christian and ungodly. We will trace these people from their barbarian roots on the mainland to their encounter as pagans with a new God.

The Germanic Tribes

From the beginning of their interaction with the Roman world, the Germanic people were a force to be reckoned with. The south-ward migration of two Germanic tribes, the Teutoni (from which comes the word Teutonic, another epithet for the Germanic people) and the Cimbri, led in 113 BC to their sudden incursion into Italy. This rude awakening resulted in a number of serious conflicts between Roman and barbarian forces over the course of the next few years. Both these tribes were effectively kept at bay by the Romans.

Yet the Germanic peoples could be compared to the hydra of legend – cut the head off one tribe and another two grew up in its place. Julius Caesar was to come into conflict with the head of the Suevi tribe, a king named Ariovistus. The king already had an existing relationship with Rome and was considered a friend rather than a foe. This meant little to Caesar, who had to deal with him directly in the field. His forces drove the Suevi back across the Rhine from whence they came.

During the reign of the first emperor Augustus (27 BC to AD 14), plans were drawn up to expand the sphere of Roman influence. Augustus wanted to press beyond the existing frontier of the Rhine and secure the region beyond it, up to the river Elbe. A series of successful Roman campaigns seemed on the verge of adding Germanic lands to the list of imperial provinces, but an uprising on the south-east borders of the empire was sufficiently worrying to put the German question aside. A man whose name will always be linked to military disaster was left in charge of the Roman army in Germany – Publius Quinctilius Varus.

In AD 9 the barbarian hydra reared up again, this time in the form of the Germanic Cherusci under the leadership of Arminius (Hermann), also known as 'Hermann the German'. In a truly devastating ambush, the three legions under Varus's command were massacred in the Teutoburger Forest. Augustus never got over the defeat and it is said that he would shout at the dead Varus to give him back his lost legions. The defeat was heavy enough to keep the German homelands outside the empire for ever. The German people were to suffer defeats but they were never to be subordinated.

In various parts of this book I have had occasion to remark on the fact that the historical and ethnographic accounts of ancient authors need to be taken with large pinches of salt. Their reports concerning barbarian behaviour and beliefs are rarely their own observations. They are not even, as a rule, first-hand accounts told to the authors by third parties. Second-hand or third-hand information, rumour, tall travellers' tales and the like make up much of this ancient anthropology. We should not, however, dismiss it all as hearsay and nonsense for there are genuine observations alongside the more dubious anecdotes. It would be fair to say that we learn at least as much about the Romans from their biased accounts of other people as we do about the barbarians themselves.

Julius Caesar gives us a few interesting snippets of information concerning the Germanic people in *The Gallic Wars*. He notes among other things that they are not ruled by a priesthood like the Celts are ruled by their Druids. Neither are they particularly enthusiastic about observing sacrifices to the gods. This, along with the assertion that they have not even heard of any gods but the sun, moon and fire, cannot be accepted as a realistic portrayal. It was simply that the Romans were largely ignorant of the religious beliefs of Germanic people and so could say very little about them.

Caesar also tells us that they do not undertake much agriculture, preferring to tend their livestock, make cheese and hunt. Training to be warriors from a young age, they endure privation and hardship to toughen them up. They also say that it is a good thing for the young to avoid sexual relations for as long as possible. This practice is not based on prudery but on the belief that physical growth and power as well as the strength of one's sinews are increased through sexual abstinence. To have sex before the age of twenty is considered a despicable sign of weakness. Despite these restrictive recommendations concerning the health of young people, they nevertheless go in for mixed-sex bathing in the river with only the scantiest of skins or deerhide cloaks to hide their modesty. Caesar notes that such clothing still leaves them half-naked.

He also has something very interesting to say about the way that they order their society. The magistrates and headmen of the community have annual meetings at which each family and tribal division is allotted a tract of land that they are obliged to work on during the forthcoming year. The following year they are moved to another piece of land. There is a rationale behind this communal rotation: knowing that you will be moved on the next year prevents you from building your house too well – keeping out the cold and the heat is considered a sign of effeminacy. Similarly, the regular tilling of the same fields year after year may be habit-forming, and turn men into avid farmers and away from their desire for conflict and war. It may make them greedy too and encourage them to forsake fighting for riches. The accumulation of individual wealth is seen as a threat not just to the warrior ethos but also to the cohesion of society itself. Wealth creates inequality, inequality creates discord and envy, and these inevitably lead to civil strife.

There is a strange kind of logic to this way of running society, but how accurate a picture this is of ancient Germanic practices is hard to say.

The Tribes of Mannus

Julius Caesar's brief descriptions are intriguing, but the main account of the Germanic people was written somewhat later. Cornelius Tacitus wrote the *Germania* (or 'On the Origin and Geography of Germany' as it is sometimes called) in AD 98. It gives a wide-ranging picture of German life at that time, which is generally recognised as largely accurate. He was certainly an author with an agenda. He does not try to denigrate the barbarians (although he is scathing about them on occasions) – if anything, he does the reverse, for he uses the Germanic people as moral exemplars for the degenerate Romans of his day who have forgotten their own era of virtue. Tacitus does not let his moral message distract him from his central purpose, though: to provide a full and coherent portrait of a barbarian people. He does not simply provide a general overview, but names and describes the various Germanic tribes and their attributes to the best of his knowledge.

Tacitus begins his account by delineating the limits of the Germanic lands, which are separated from Gaul by the Rhine, and from Pannonia by the Danube; to the east they are divided from the Iranian Sarmatians by mountains – or, in regions where there are no mountains, by mutual fear! To the north they are surrounded by the ocean (in ancient geography the Baltic and the North Sea were believed to be part of the same expanse of water).

As to their origins and connections with other peoples, Tacitus remarks that they are indigenous and pure bred, having little to do with other races. Such comments were to be seized upon during the Nazi era to provide historical 'proof' of German racial purity and superiority. It is quite clear when reading Tacitus that such a view was not in his mind. For him, there were good reasons for this 'purity'. He goes on to ask the rhetorical question: who would want to leave the warmth of Asia Minor (present-day Turkey), North Africa or Italy to live in the inhospitable landscapes of Germany with its bad weather?

The Germanic people of Tacitus' time were not literate, but they passed down their traditions through songs. They worshipped a god of earth named Tuisto. The son of this god, called Mannus, they considered to be the ancestor of all the Germanic people. Mannus in his turn had three sons after whom three clusters of tribes were named: the Ingaevones, who lived near the sea (according to another source, the writings of Pliny, this group includes the Chauci, the Cimbri and the Teutoni); the Herminones, the interior or central tribes (which, says Pliny, include the Suevi, Hermunduri, Cherusci and Chatti); and the Istaevones, who consist of the rest of the tribes, especially those near the Rhine in Pliny's account.

Such is, according to Tacitus, the main Germanic myth of their origins and the relationships between the tribes. Other versions known to him claimed that other tribes also had a genuine and ancient heritage that could be traced back to the primordial ancestor Tuisto, among them the Vandilii (the Vandals). He also provides us with an explanation of how this group of tribes become collectively known as the Germani. Originally there was a single tribe known as the Germani (whose name had changed by the time of Tacitus to the Tungri), who were said to be the first of the Germanic tribes to cross the Rhine and invade the territory of the Gauls. In order to intimidate the Gauls, the Germani tribe began to call their fellow tribes Germani too. Soon other tribes began to accept this new title themselves, and diverse Germanic peoples had a name that unified them.

The stereotype of the physical appearance of a Germanic barbarian can be found in Tacitus. They are, he tells us, usually red-haired, well built and have fierce blue eyes. Although they are strong and can exert enormous energy on occasions, they are said not to be good at hard work and continuous labour. Due to the climate of their homeland and the poor soils, they can endure cold and hunger but not heat and thirst. Their clothing is simple, the standard dress code being a cloak fastened with a clasp or brooch (or failing that simply a thorn). Only the rich among them have the luxury of wearing underclothes; the rest have to make do with the cloak and furs and sealskins. Women wear basically the same as the men but might sometimes also be seen in linen garments with purple patterns.

Their leaders are of two types – kings and military commanders. Kings belong to noble stock and are powerful but not absolute rulers. Generals are selected on the basis of their valour and leadership skills; their social background is not considered very important. The priesthood also has a significant role in society, leading worship in sacred groves; totems and emblems from these holy places are even taken on to the battlefield to inspire and support the soldiers.

The people do not build temples to their gods, whose divinity makes the idea of trying to confine them to a building an absurdity. Nor do they consider it right to portray their gods in human form by way of paintings or sculptures. (Interestingly, the ancient Iranians, sometime easterly neighbours of the Germanic tribes, also had no temples or idols to represent their gods.) While gods such as Thor and Tiw (Tiu) accept animal sacrifices as sufficient, the rites surrounding the cult of the high god demand more, adding a more sinister element to their religious practices – using human sacrifices to propitiate the high god Wodan (also sometimes spelt Wotan or Woden – the Odin of Scandinavian tradition).

Different tribes practise their own rites and observances that often result in such offerings. Among the Suevi group, the oldest and most prominent of them are the Semnones (who have been identified by some historians as the people who were known by the third century as the Alamanni). This noble position they underline with a barbaric ceremony in a sacred grove, attended by delegations from all the tribes of the same name. The proceedings open with a human sacrifice and all visitors must enter the grove only if they are bound by a cord to symbolise their domination by the supreme god (presumably Wodan). If anyone happens to fall down while they are in this sacred place, they may not get up again but must crawl or roll on the ground until they are outside the grove. The grove was believed to be both a place where the presence of Wodan could be felt and the birthplace of their people.

Another group of tribes from Schleswig-Holstein and Jutland (including the Angles and possibly the Jutes) are described as worshippers of the goddess Nerthus or Mother Earth. They believe that she may ride out in her chariot, which is kept in a grove on a sacred island. The chariot is hidden from view by a cloth and only the priest may touch it. The chariot, accompanied by the priest, is drawn out of its shrine by cows and moves among the people. Days of rejoicing and celebration follow, public holidays in her honour when no conflict or fighting is permitted to take place. At the end of the festivities the cow-drawn chariot returns to its sacred place and then the chariot, its cloth and, so the story goes, the deity herself are washed in a secluded lake by slaves, who are drowned in the lake straight afterwards.

On secular matters affecting the community, the people hold assemblies at appointed times. Among the roles played by the assembly is that of judge and jury: offences of various types are heard and sentencing takes place. The death penalty is in force and the means of execution varies according to the offence committed. Deserters and traitors are hanged from trees while cowards and sodomites are pushed down under a wicker hurdle into bogs. The discovery of the so-called 'bog bodies' has provided archaeologists with a grisly confirmation of Tacitus' account. The reason for the different types of execution was based on the principle that crimes that directly affected public life should be punished in a way that was open and visible to all, while shameful acts should be hidden away.

Tacitus also describes the funerary rites. Prominent men are burnt on pyres, sometimes accompanied by their weapons and horses. They are buried under a mound of earth, the people not investing unnecessary labour by erecting stone monuments over the graves. It is not shameful for women to cry at funerals, but men are meant to keep their grief to themselves.

Tacitus was particularly impressed with the people's basically monogamous marriage customs which, he notes, were quite a rarity among barbarians. A few important men may have more than one wife, but this is usually because of obligations to seal alliances through the bonds of marriage than any other reason. Adultery is almost unheard of but, if committed, the guilty wife is punished by flogging and subsequently ostracised by the community. Tacitus clearly uses his account of barbarian marriage and fidelity as a means to an end – to criticise the decadence of his own countrymen. He rather haughtily remarks: 'No one in Germany finds vice amusing, or calls it "up-to-date" to seduce or be seduced.'

To limit the number of children – presumably a reference to contraception or other means of birth control – or to practise infanticide (at least of legitimate children) is not permitted. Germanic childcare also appeals to Tacitus, who cites with approval the fact that the children run around dirty and naked at home and so grow up to be vigorous and strong. He praises the women who, rather than leaving their children in the care of maids and nannies, all look after their own offspring and breastfeed them as well.

Even outside the domestic sphere, the womenfolk have a powerful role in Germanic society. In Tacitus' own words:

> *It stands on record that armies already wavering and on the*
> *point of collapse have been rallied by the women, pleading*
> *heroically with their men, thrusting forward their bared*
> *bosoms, and making them realise the imminent prospect of*
> *enslavement – a fate which the Germans fear more desperately*
> *for their women than for themselves. Indeed, you can secure a*
> *surer hold on these nations if you compel them to include*
> *among a consignment of hostages some girls of noble family.*
> *More than this they believe that there resides in women an*
> *element of holiness and a gift of prophecy; and so they do not*
> *scorn to ask their advice, or lightly disregard their replies.*

Divination and fortune-telling was a highly respected element of
their spiritual life. Tacitus describes the procedures involved in the
ancient art of prediction. A branch is cut from a nut-bearing tree
and cut into strips. Signs or markings are then put on these strips,
which are cast at random on a white cloth. If the query concerns
the public good, then a priest will say a prayer; if it is a private
matter, then the man of the house will say it instead. Then the
questioner (whether priest or father) will, while looking up to the
heavens, pick three of the strips, one after the other. He then looks
at the markings on these particular strips. These signs give him his
answer. If the answer is negative, then no further divination should
take place that day. If the answer has been affirmative but requires
further clarification, other methods of divining can be used (such
as seeking omens from the flight and cries of birds or the neighing
of horses).

There has been a great deal of debate about whether the casting of lots described by Tacitus refers to the runes or not. It was
once thought that the runes (the earliest form of Germanic writing) were not used at such an early date. Many people now believe
that runes did exist at this time and that therefore Tacitus is almost

certainly referring to them in this passage. The basis of this belief is that markings on what is known as the Meldorf brooch (found on the west coast of Jutland and dating from around AD 50) should be identified as runes – although other scholars would argue that this is open to question.

A less spiritual kind of lot-casting was enjoyed by the Germans in the form of gambling: playing dice games was a serious business. They were always willing to up the ante and would even stake their status as a free man and risk becoming a slave on the fall of a single throw of the dice. So high were the stakes that they would play only when sober – in marked contrast to other social engagements. Hospitality was an essential feature of ancient Germanic life: stranger and friend alike must be offered hospitality according to the traditional code. Celebrations were focused around the social institution of the feast. Wine and beer flowed freely on such occasions; heavy drinking was (and still is!) an integral part of the feast. Drunkenness was perfectly acceptable at such gatherings and such sessions would go on all night long. Arguments, brawls and sometimes serious injuries and deaths would occur in this rowdy and alcohol-fuelled atmosphere.

Whether they were staying sober and casting dice to let fate settle their future, or casting the runes to discover the will of the gods, the Germanic people retained control over their own lands: Rome had never succeeded in destroying this particular barbarian hydra. The offspring of Mannus continued to flourish.

Having viewed the story of the Germanic tribes and their origin through the pages of the history books, I shall now turn to the archaeological record. What do the relics from these 'dismal landscapes of Germany' – as Tacitus calls them – reveal about the unfolding story of the migration of its western tribes?

Chapter Nine

DWELLERS IN
THE MARSH

Those who wish for certainty in history and who
like to feel the ground firmly under their feet are best
advised to study some other period. For those who care to
venture into a quagmire, the archaeological evidence, and
the truly remarkable intellectual effort of archaeologists
to make sense of it, are of basic importance.

James Campbell, *The Anglo-Saxons*

Germanic roots are entangled in the fabric of English culture. To track down the ancestors of the Anglo-Saxons who lived in England, I travelled to Germany to see for myself their material remains in some of the key sites. My first port of call was the town of Bederkesa, which lies in a coastal area of northern Germany between the great Elbe and Weser rivers. The purpose of my visit was to see the collections of the castle museum where one of the curators, Dr Jorn Schuster, was able to show me artefacts from two crucially important sites for my quest: Feddersen Wierde and, the subject of the next chapter, Fallward.

The Manor on the Mound

Feddersen Wierde, which lies a few miles north of the major port of Bremenhaven, is the largest Saxon site found on the North Sea coast of Germany. Almost the entire settlement was excavated between 1955 and 1963, so a considerable amount is known about it. Today the sea has receded, leaving the site further inland today than it would have been in Saxon times. But even within the Saxon period, natural conditions changed dramatically.

The settlement started around the middle of the first century BC with a solitary farmhouse on what was then a beach ridge. Some time in the first century AD the sea-level began to rise and the inhabitants of the village were obliged to build an artificial mound to live on (the word *wierde* is used by German archaeologists for 'man-made mound'). This was by no means a desperate act or an act of survival. There was no problem with the seasonal flooding of their fields for, provided the waters receded again, the settlement was able to function quite adequately – more than adequately, in fact, because the ebbing waters left behind a very fertile silt. For a few centuries this was highly sought-after farming land. Agricultural experiments by archaeologists in the region showed that although wheat did not grow well in these salty areas, oats and rye flourished under such conditions. But there would come a time when even these crops could not endure the saline soils and they too would wither and die.

What had once been a tiny marshland village consisting of just four or five homesteads eventually grew at its zenith to having about twenty or thirty farms, with a total population estimated to be around 150 by the third century AD. The village seems to have been a peaceful place to live, for there are no signs of it being destroyed or badly damaged during its 500-year history. A few houses caught fire during the life of the village but even some of these were saved before they burnt to the ground.

The size of the community and its continuity over a number of centuries seem to indicate that a more intensive and successful agricultural regime had begun to emerge in this region. Tacitus, writing at the end of the first century AD, portrays the agriculture at the time to be much more basic: they change the arable land yearly and thereby do not strain the soil to yield too much. He adds that they do not want to put in the extra effort to plant orchards, irrigate vegetable gardens or fence off meadows; they prefer to simply plant grain and be done with it. Clearly, if we are to take Tacitus' account as an accurate picture of German agriculture at the time, a different, more intensive, system must have developed shortly afterwards.

This subsequent development involved elements of crop rotation and the use of livestock manure to replenish the soils. The end result of this seems to have been a significant rise in population. Although the inhabitants of Feddersen Wierde in particular were forced by the rising sea to move, in more general terms population increase in north-western Europe may well have been an impetus to migrate. In this scenario one can see similarities with the Gothic Wielbark culture, which expanded southwards from its origins in north-eastern Europe probably as a consequence of its burgeoning population.

Not all the buildings were of the same size. There was a cluster of buildings that seem to have belonged to a house much bigger than the rest, and which could be described as a manor house or *Herrenhof* as the German archaeologists describe it. On this basis, we can conclude that there was definitely a social hierarchy in this community. Most of the homesteads were not just for housing family members but also livestock; typically, the eastern parts of the houses would have served this function. It was different in the case of the manor house, because one of the luxuries enjoyed by these richer families was that they did not have to share their living space with their animals.

The kind of houses that these Saxon people built had much in common with those in the region both from earlier times (as far back as the Neolithic period, or New Stone Age) and continuing into the Middle Ages and beyond. One of the key features of their house construction was their inclusion of stalls in order that their animals could be kept inside in winter. When the Saxons and neighbouring peoples went to England, this feature of their house construction became less important as the climate was milder and did not require livestock to be protected from the elements.

It seems that there is an important lesson to be learnt from this. House building is one of the most fundamental aspects of any culture. The ethnic or cultural origins of a people do not seem to be as important as the natural environment they live in. That is why the same basic designs recur in the same place (in this case northern Germany) over a period of time, despite the fact that the population and its ethnic make-up may have changed. This is not to say that the Saxons did not take their own building traditions with them when they went to settle in England; what they did do was modify or draw on native designs in order to adapt their knowledge to a new environment.

Returning to the *Herrenhof* at Feddersen Wierde, there was also a dike (or perhaps a defensive rampart) along the north-east side of the manor, but it is not clear whether this was for keeping out water or whether it served some defensive purpose. There was also a palisade, the purpose of which is also obscure as it does not appear to have enclosed the perimeter of the house and so could have been of little use as a defensive measure. The possible solution to this problem that immediately springs to mind is that the dike (or rampart) was work in progress when the settlement was abandoned in the middle of the fifth century. However, this cannot have been the case as its construction dates to the second or third century – when the settlement was flourishing. Why it was unfinished therefore remains a puzzle.

It is not just the size of the manor that marks it out as different to the other farms of the mound village of Feddersen Wierde – it is also what the archaeologists found in its grounds. Earlier in the life of the village, Roman material was scattered throughout the settlement, showing that at its height (in the second and third centuries) the whole community had contact with the Roman world. But as the Roman twilight turned to a deepening dusk, imperial coins and other flotsam and jetsam of the empire are confined to the manor and its people. Whether it was only the rich who could afford to keep contact with the Roman world, or whether they simply took control over incoming goods, is unknown.

Local people from this region had been in Roman military service, as the material evidence from their graveyards proves. We should not think that these Saxon communities were populated by isolated country bumpkins without any knowledge of the outside world. Many men went off to the diverse regions of the Roman empire on military service, bringing back travellers' tales, trinkets, mementoes and perhaps, in some cases, even wives.

I asked Dr Schuster, my host at the museum, why the Germanic peoples in this time lived almost exclusively in villages. This was despite the fact that they knew all about the Roman towns and even the big settlements of the Celts. He suggested it could have been something to do with the Germanic psyche – a desire for autonomy, privacy and independence: things less easy to get in a crowded, bustling town.

Tacitus confirms that this was their preferred way of living. He tells us that in his day (around the same time that Feddersen Wierde was still a small village), it was well known that the people had no desire to live in cities and often did not even like their houses too close to those of their neighbours. To his Roman eyes, they selected their building plots at random, as the fancy took them. He remarks that each of the houses in their villages has open space around it (rather than being adjacent to each other as in the Roman way). Whether this is done as a fire precaution or simply through their lack of skill at building, he cannot say. We shall see later that the Germanic people were extremely adept woodworkers, drawing on thousands of years of experience in the craft. Tacitus was equally unimpressed with the rustic appearance of their wooden houses and remarks that they used neither stone nor wall tiles as a Roman would.

No doubt life in the village of Feddersen Wierde was very close-knit, despite the links with the outside world. There was another building in the village that archaeologists have identified as a public meeting place. It would have been used rather like a village hall is today, for important community events and discussions. Each freeman would have had the right to speak his mind. With farming conditions by the fifth century beginning to steadily and quite quickly decline, the main topic of conversation at the village hall would have been the very survival of the community.

Salt waters began to inundate the village farms all year round, making life increasingly difficult for the villagers. The waters that had once blessed the community by providing rich soil and pasture had now become a curse. The decline was painful but inevitable and finally, around AD 450, the Saxon farmers were forced to abandon their settlement and seek a life elsewhere. The sea that had sustained them for so long was now casting their community adrift.

We cannot be sure, but it seems likely that the villagers of Feddersen Wierde and their neighbours in this low-lying region set forth to seek new lands rather than simply moving further inland. They may first have travelled along the North Sea coast towards what is now the Netherlands and, from there, across the sea to England. The Saxon traders and soldiers would have already been well informed about the possibilities of starting a new life in

England. Many would have been there themselves. Their migration across the North Sea was not a desperate voyage into the unknown, but the result of a well-planned and well-informed decision.

The Well-groomed Saxon

One might have expected the Saxon inhabitants of a little marshland village to be fairly dirty and unkempt, but numerous finds at the site suggest otherwise. Among the familiar local crafts and industries – pottery making, metal working and so on – there were clearly a number of people making combs. Ornate combs made from bone are commonly found in graves at Feddersen Wierde and similar sites, showing they were important and widely used. The word *kempt* in modern German means 'combed', and this concern for their appearance was deeply rooted in the people's culture. It is said that when certain Germanic tribes took possession of a piece of land, they would mark the event by throwing their combs on to it to show that it belonged to them. This indicates that the comb must have been a very personal item – symbolising, as it did, its owner.

Tacitus mentions the long hair of the Germans he met, and it is perhaps not surprising that the comb was an important item to them. As Dr Schuster told me with some pleasure, the Vikings were singularly unimpressed with the hair care of the Saxons, dismissing them contemptuously as 'long-haired pansies'. Despite the impolite comments of the Norsemen, hairstyles were as important as cultural markers to the Germanic tribes as artificially deformed skulls were to the Huns.

The Suevi group of Germanic tribes had a way of showing themselves to be different from both their own slaves and other tribes – they combed their hair to the side and tied it in a knot. The so-called Suevian knot has been found on a 'bog body' found at Osterby in Schleswig-Holstein, near the German border with Denmark. This was the heart of the ancient territory of the Angles, the other half of the Anglo-Saxon equation (although we shall see below that many different ethnic units were to be described as Anglo-Saxons).

It was not only the western Germanic peoples for whom the comb was an important cultural icon. The Cernjachov sites north of the Black Sea, which mark the presence of the Gothic tribes in the region in the early centuries of our era, are full of combs made from bone. One particular site of an ancient village (Birlad-Valea Seaca) has revealed that a large number of huts there were used to make combs: examples of all stages of the comb-making process have been found. This not only shows us exactly how they were made but, even more importantly, it shows us that it was a thriving cottage industry.

The sheer number of combs that were manufactured in this small settlement made it impossible to believe they were solely for the villagers to groom themselves. It must have been a centre of bone-comb production that was supplying this essential item of Germanic kit across a much wider area. It is remarkable that almost identical styles of bone combs were made by Goths and Saxons as far apart as the shores of the Black Sea and the North Sea. We may speculate on the basis of this very wide distribution that this is a very ancient item of Germanic material culture, one that had a significance that was both practical and symbolic.

A Changing World

The decline and fall of the village of Feddersen Wierde over the centuries mirrors the wider changes that were happening throughout the Germanic world. The people who founded the village were probably the Chauci, one of a number of Germanic groups named by Roman historians such as Pliny and Tacitus. The latter describes them as next-door neighbours of the Frisians, but he also speaks highly of them, calling them the noblest of the Germanic tribes. He tells us that they maintain and secure their territories by justice rather than violence, living in peaceful seclusion, keeping themselves to themselves. Although they do not raid their neighbours or start wars, they are nevertheless perfectly willing and able to defend themselves as and when required. Tacitus remarks that it is this very preparedness that shows their moral superiority, for they do not uphold peace out of weakness of arms but in spite of their military strength.

Though praised by Tacitus, the Chauci disappear from the history books in the second century – at least under that name. By the third and fourth centuries they seem to have been assimilated into the group of peoples who became known simply as the Saxons. The original Saxons who are mentioned in the first and second centuries appear to have had their homeland north of the river Elbe. During the two centuries that followed, the Saxons seem to have expanded into the territories across the Elbe to the south, incorporating other tribes – including the Chauci – in a peaceful fashion. Saxon now became a name that was used to describe a much larger group of Germanic peoples than it had done in earlier times.

The Angles, close neighbours of the Saxons, were the Germanic tribe that was eventually to give their name to the country of England. They came from a land known as Angeln in what is now Schleswig-Holstein. Together, the Angles and the Saxons made up at least part of the immigrant people who were to be known as the Anglo-Saxons, although other tribal groupings such as the Frisians (who may or may not be the same people as the Frisians described in written sources from the first and second centuries) also played an important part in this story of migration. The Anglo-Saxons were a group of loosely related Germanic peoples who migrated to England, yet they never called themselves by this name. Almost all the ethnic names we have for the 'barbarian' peoples of this time come either from classical writers or from nineteenth-century scholars who had their own ethnic axes to grind.

Chapter Ten

GERMANIA RULES THE WAVES

*A larger fleet came quickly over with a great body
of warriors, which, when joined to the original
forces, constituted an invincible army.*

The Venerable Bede, on the arrival of Germanic invaders in England

The comb, as we have seen, was an important practical and symbolic object for the Germanic people right across the European continent. Another even more important item of Germanic material culture that also fulfilled these dual functions was the boat. For them, it was more than just a mode of transport, a way to get from A to B: it was also a vehicle to transport the deceased to the world beyond.

Just to the south of Feddersen Wierde is another important Saxon site, Fallward, excavated during the 1990s. Marshland is particularly useful from the archaeologists' point of view because organic materials that are usually completely destroyed in most

other conditions often survive. But even the optimism the archaeologists may have felt with such favourable conditions could not
have prepared them for what they were about to find. Unearthed
in the autumn of 1994, this was to be the most remarkable discovery they were to make: a fifth-century boat burial.

Although this was basically a farming community, the people also
lived on the coast. Boats were part of their daily lives, and one such
vessel was re-used for this very different purpose – as a coffin. In
much the same way as the manor house of Feddersen Wierde points
to the existence of a social hierarchy, the Fallward boat burial is an
expression of rank: of the 150 or so burials discovered in the graveyards of this area, only one man was buried in a boat. Whoever this
individual was, he was clearly an eminent local man. Evidence from
his grave in the form of a particular kind of belt buckle shows that he
held a high rank in the Roman army and so to have been buried with
full military honours. Very similar belt fittings have been found in
England, so it is quite possible that he may have actually served there.

The boat coffin measures 5 metres long and 1.3 metres wide
(16 feet by 4 feet 3 inches). The body was placed in the boat along
with a number of important items, and then planks were placed
across the top to seal in the body and the grave goods. It seems
very likely that boat burial was an important event, reserved for the
elite, and represented the symbolic voyage to the other world, the
deceased being accompanied by the most cherished of his personal
possessions. This was not a new custom, for boat burial was an
ancient element of Scandinavian culture that has been traced back
at least as far as the first century AD. The Viking ship burials of
future centuries were to be the final phase in this long tradition.

Accompanying the man's body in the Fallward boat burial was
an ornate wooden seat, which has been named the 'throne of the
marsh' by archaeologists. It is not a throne in the real sense of the
word but it was clearly the special chair of a man who was a big fish

in a small sea. The 'throne' itself and a carved footstool that accompanied it in the grave have very similar ornate designs on them, including swastikas. Both also show a definite Roman influence. Roman emperors are depicted on the coins of the fourth century sitting on a throne with their feet resting on a footstool. The message from the marshland is clear: this man was trying, in his own small way, to imitate the emperor.

Yet an independent spirit is undoubtedly present too in the Fallward artefacts. The footstool is adorned with runes, the early written characters of the Germanic peoples. Part of the Old Saxon inscription simply reads 'footstool'; more obscure is another runic phrase, next to a picture of a deer being pursued by a hound, which translates as 'deer killer' – perhaps a simple reference to his skill as a hunter.

The boat burial and its contents tell us something about the values of the Saxon elite at this time. Like the Goths, their Germanic cousins far to the east, they were clearly receptive to Roman civilisation and sought to mirror it after their own fashion. Yet they hung on doggedly to their own traditions (boat burial itself, for example), not just out of fear of being absorbed into the continent-wide melting pot of Roman rule but because they believed in its integral value. They were not about to give up the ways of their ancestors for anyone.

The Boat in the Bog

One of the most important of all continental discoveries from this time is undoubtedly the remarkable Nydam boat, built of oak. It was salvaged from the Nydam bog west of Sønderborg in southern Denmark, on 18 August 1863, during the course of early archaeological excavations; even after all this time, it remains the oldest and biggest seagoing vessel found anywhere in the whole of northern Europe. Today it is landlocked across the border in the

Archäologisches Landesmuseum in Schleswig, Germany, under the watchful eye of its curator, Dr Michael Gebühr.

The bog did not give up its secrets quickly, and more and more has gradually emerged over the course of nearly two centuries. The first finds from Nydam were brought out of the bog by a local farmer in the 1830s. These were swords and shields, and he gave them to his children to play with. Eventually news of the 'toys' found in the bog reached an archaeologist named Conrad Engelhardt, who undertook an extensive excavation from 1859 to 1863. He found an abundance of weapons and tools along with some pieces of clothing and, most dramatically, two clinker-built boats. Most of the weaponry (consisting of spears, lances, swords, shields and bows) was discovered underneath the remnants of a third boat, which seems to have been deliberately wrecked at the time that the weapons were thrown into what was then a lake. Over the years, this lake transformed into a bog, thus preserving the boat for posterity. As mentioned before, the wonderful preservation qualities of bogs are well attested by the dramatic and grisly finds of Iron Age 'bog bodies'.

All three boats, along with the weapons and other finds, had been deliberately deposited in the lake, not all at the same time. They belonged to the defeated forces of an unknown number of conflicts in the Dark Ages. Rather than keeping the boats and arms for their own future use, the victorious warriors chose to sacrifice them to a god (most likely to Odin, or Wodan). To our way of thinking today, this seems illogical and uneconomic. An incalculable number of skilled man hours went into the making of these weapons, and it seems wasteful (not to mention reckless during times of war) not to use everything you can. But the ancient mind did not work on such principles. They probably promised their god that if he gave them victory he would receive the spoils of war. It has not been just Odin who has benefited from this oath; so too have the archaeologists who can shed some light on this obscure period of history, based on evidence gleaned from the various deposits thrown in the lake during the period from AD 200 to 450.

Unfortunately, one of the two boats Engelhardt had recovered from its watery grave has not survived to sit alongside its fellow in the museum. At 19 metres (62 feet) long, this pine boat was slightly smaller than the oak boat that has been preserved. It was chopped up for firewood in 1864 during the German–Danish war by soldiers who were completely oblivious to its great historical value. The boats are those of the losers, and it is perhaps the case that the distant ancestors of the Germans and Danes who were fighting each other in the nineteenth century may have been protagonists in the original battle that took place so many centuries earlier. The lost boat that was meant to be permanently destroyed by the victors was, despite a brief respite in the attentive custody of the archaeologists, finally consumed not by water but by fire.

Sporadic excavations at the site continued until the beginning of the Second World War. Modern archaeological work at Nydam was undertaken from 1984 until 1997, and revealed a great deal of information about both the boat itself and the wealth of other finds. Based on the annual growth rings of the timber, the boat has been dated to around AD 320 – half a millennium older than its much more famous descendant, the Viking ship. It was built in a boatyard somewhere in the western or middle region of the Baltic and is thus unequivocally Scandinavian in both origin and design. It was sunk rather later, probably around the middle of the fourth century. Although it is generally considered that the Nydam boat itself was of Swedish workmanship, vessels of this type were made and used widely by the Jutes, Angles and Saxons. With its undoubted importance for the archaeologists of today and its remarkable state of preservation, this particular boat is unique to us – but to the people of the time it was one of many, a simple fact of life.

This type of long and narrow boat was designed more for warfare than for transporting goods, so high speed and manoeuvrability were its key features. It could have been used on the open sea, but was also useful for journeys along the coastline as well as estuaries and penetrating the inland rivers. What made it an optimal warship was the fact that it could be rowed in both directions. This was a feature of northern European boats since at least the time of Tacitus in the first century. He writes about a Germanic people called the Suiones who live on 'islands' out in the sea (he is probably referring to what is now Sweden), and describes their vessels thus: 'The shape of their ships differs from the normal in having a prow at each end, so that they are always facing the right way to put in to shore. They do not propel them with sails, nor do they fasten a row of oars to the sides. The rowlocks are movable, as one finds them on some river craft, and can be reversed, as circumstances require, for rowing in either direction.'

Such boats must have been the ancestors of the Nydam boat which, in turn, is an ancestor of the Viking vessels of later centuries. It embodies considerable woodworking skills, and its specifications demonstrate just how impressive it still is: approximate length 23 metres (75 feet 6 inches); width 3.5 metres (11 feet 6 inches); midship height 1 metre (just over 3 feet); water displacement 8.8 tons (including 1 ton ballast). It is clinker-built, with five oak strakes (lengths of planking) per side, joined together by iron clench-nails. Since the boat was salvaged from its watery grave, the wood has shrunk by approximately 15 per cent, so it would originally have been wider and therefore more seaworthy.

The oars measure between 2.2 and 3.4 metres (7 feet 3 inches to just over 11 feet); a steering oar (also called a quarter or side rudder) measuring 1.8 metres (nearly 6 feet) was discovered during the 1993 excavation season. The boat was built for fifteen pairs of oars, so a crew of about forty-five including thirty oarsmen seems like a reasonable estimate. There are no signs that the boat had a mast foot, and so it is almost certain that it had neither mast nor sail. Two recent and unprecedented finds were carved human heads on wooden posts nearly 1.5 metres (5 feet) long. It is thought that they were mooring posts attached to the bow. The Nydam boat that is on show in the museum today is, remarkably, 70 per cent original, the rest being a bold but successfully accomplished nineteenth-century reconstruction.

The boats were not the only find of interest. A great number of weapons have been pulled up out of the bog, including 100 swords, 370 lances and 40 longbows (ancestors of the English longbow). Estimates place the number of warriors whose weapons ended up in the lake to be about 500. That number would require a minimum of ten boats to transport them. Evidence from the weapons themselves shows that they were not only made to be offered as sacrifices but were made to be used. Many of the swords bear witness to the last battle of a defeated army – hack marks that have damaged the side of the blade. They are the only signs we have of the desperate struggle that took place. Archaeologists believe that the various weapon caches dumped in the lake would have belonged to the losers of battles with the local tribe of Angles.

There are a number of other major deposits of weapons that have been found in the bogs of southern Denmark dating from the latter part of the second century onwards. Like the Nydam example, these deposits of arms and other military paraphernalia represent the equipment of entire armies and not just a few soldiers. Again, like the Nydam deposit, many of them seem to have been deliberately damaged or disabled before they were thrown in as sacrifices to their god.

In one case, that of Ejsbøl Mose in southern Denmark, excavation has revealed a whole set of arms belonging to a third-century force estimated to consist of about 200 troops. Their equipment included spears, shields and lances and at least a quarter of them also had swords and knives. Many were also archers, as evidenced by nearly 700 arrowheads found by archaeologists. Twelve or more of the men had special equipment, and nine of these were on horseback. What emerges from this bog is a ghostly force that is clearly well organised, with a strict hierarchy and a wide range of military gear.

Half a century after the Nydam boat was deliberately sunk, the archaeological remains from the Schleswig-Holstein region all but disappear. Half the peninsula seems to have been like a vast ghost town – almost no settlements or cemeteries belonging to this era have been found. There has been a great deal of debate about what this drying up of artefacts actually means. Some archaeologists have voiced the opinion that perhaps the people of the region simply built houses and buried their dead in a different way from their previous practice, and in a way that has made it hard for archaeologists to find them. Much more plausible is the common-sense idea that if there is little that had been unearthed from this era in the way of graves, dwellings and objects, then it is probably due to the fact that many of the people left the region at this time. The Anglo-Saxon historian Bede also tells us that the homeland of the Angles who came to England was 'the country known as Angulus [his Latin version of Angeln], which lies between the provinces of the Jutes and Saxons and is said to remain unpopulated to this day'. Where did they go? The obvious answer is that they went to England.

The population starts to wane around 400, and traces of what appears to be the presence of Saxons and other Germanic tribes appear in England around the beginning of the fifth century. Michael Gebühr, the curator of the Nydam boat, believes that this vessel and others like it could have crossed the North Sea and reached England safely. Other kinds of boat would have been better for such a voyage across open seas, but the Nydam style of boat would have sufficed.

Computer simulation studies that Dr Gebühr has overseen led to the conclusion that over a period of only nine years, even fifty such boats could have easily transported 30,000 people from Schleswig-Holstein to England. In just under a century the whole population could have been moved out using boats of this kind.

Objections have been raised against this reconstruction of events. Placenames are often used as a way of discerning links between different regions or countries. In the part of Germany that includes the sites of Feddersen Wierde and the Fallward boat burial (Lower Saxony) there are many placenames that are similar to those in England. This has been used as evidence to suggest that people moved from there to England. In Schleswig-Holstein there are almost no placenames that correspond with English ones. This has led some to suppose that there was little migration from this region (usually believed to be the homeland of the Angles) to England. Dr Gebühr begs to differ. He argues that so many people left the region that it was almost completely abandoned and therefore the placenames given by them to their settlements in Schleswig-Holstein were almost all forgotten. They were replaced by new names, which seem to be of later, Viking, origin.

If Dr Gebühr is right and a whole population of Angles left during these times, what was their reason for abandoning their home-land – a decision they would surely have not taken lightly? The reason may lie with climatic change. Not far to the south lay the marshlands dotted with Saxon villages such as Feddersen Wierde, which started to suffer environmental decline from 400 onwards (the same time as the exodus of the Angles seems to have begun). Did the Saxons' more northerly neighbours find they too could not grow enough to feed a population that was probably expanding rapidly?

The vast number of weapons that were deposited not just in the Nydam bog but in many others such as those in southern Denmark tell us that these were difficult and violent times. The Ejsbøl Mose site mentioned above shows that these armies were full-time and organised hierarchically, so they must have had a considerable civilian population supporting them with food and supplies. Such armies could not have made up even 10 per cent of the total population. Counting up the weapons from the numerous bog finds makes one realise that tens of thousands of people at least were caught up in the war zone that affected much of the Baltic region.

These wars could have been the result of there simply not being enough good arable land (and therefore food) for everyone when the population rose and the climatic conditions worsened. Migrations and warring parties further south in the Germanic world may also have cut the supply lines by which luxury Roman goods reached the region. Local chieftains and kings needed such goods not just for their own pleasure – their status depended on the ability to distribute largesse among their own entourages. The only solution was to get such goods from other tribal units, which meant a proliferation of local conflicts.

This scenario of climatic decline followed fairly rapidly by social decline could have been the major spur to numerous chiefs to take their people to new lands. England was well known to many who had served in the Roman army there (among them perhaps the Fallward Saxon chief) and would have been an obvious choice. Being an island probably made it all the more attractive, in that those who went there would be more likely to be safe from their enemies on the mainland. Boats such as that from Nydam made it all possible.

Another pointer to fairly large-scale migration to England is language. The Germanic tribes migrated all over the continent, yet nowhere did their presence have a fundamental effect on the indigenous language. Their effect on the language spoken in England was far more dramatic, suggesting that a major cultural transformation took place. Such a change would have needed significant numbers of immigrants to this new island home.

Chapter Eleven

THE LAND OF TWO DRAGONS

*The barbarians drive us into the sea, and the sea
drives us back to the barbarians. Between these, two
deadly alternatives confront us, drowning or slaughter.*

Bede, quoting a letter from 'the wretched remnant of the Britons' to the Romans

As the Angles and the Saxons, leaving their environmental problems and warfare behind them, set sail for England, we go ahead
of them to look at the Britannia on whose shores they will soon
arrive. The Celtic world in what is often called the Dark Ages was
very different to the Germanic world. And the archaic traditions of
the Celts were tenacious – they were not to let either Roman or
Germanic influences subsume their essential culture.

We have the partisan account of a man named Gildas, who
wrote his book *On the Fall of Britain* in Latin around the middle
of the sixth century as a Christian priest and as a Briton (a British
Celt). By the time he was writing, Anglo-Saxon power was in force
over much of the island, and of the pagan immigrants he has, not

surprisingly, little of a positive nature to say. Before assessing his and other early chroniclers' views about them, it is important to consider how Britain functioned once the Romans pulled out their troops, never to return.

The Red Dragon's Story

After about four centuries of Roman domination, the Celtic people were able to reassert their own cultural values. It would be wrong to think of this as merely a reversion to life as it was before the Romans. The world had moved on, and not just because of the changes wrought by Roman influences. Christianity took hold among the Celts at an early date and many of them had been converted by the time the Anglo-Saxons arrived. Long before the renowned community at Lindisfarne in the seventh century, the Celts were successfully establishing monasteries throughout the British Isles.

One crucially important contributor to this was the son of a Celtic chieftain from Carlisle. This was Ninian, who, after being ordained by the Pope in Rome, returned to set up a monastery at Whithorn in Galloway, Scotland, which by his death around 432 was widely known. This is also the year in which St Patrick (himself probably a native of Carlisle) is believed to have returned to Ireland as a bishop to begin his successful conversion of its inhabitants. He had initially gone to Ireland as a 'guest' of Irish raiders. It was through the Christian faith that Latin was kept very much alive. Christianity was second nature to the Celts, while the Saxons, Angles and other Germanic tribes were still wholeheartedly pagan.

The departure of the legions inevitably made life easier for Saxon pirates and other barbarian marauders, whose raids were no longer intercepted by a strong defensive force. The other marauders were basically the Picts (Celts who lived in Scotland north of the Forth–Clyde line) and the Scots (who were actually inhabitants of Ireland). Yet, according to Gildas, the inhabitants of Britain enjoyed a time of prosperity after the Romans had left. There are few historical sources available concerning this time and so we can be sure about very little.

It seems that the Celtic tribal system never really died out under the Romans – it simply lay under the grid of Roman admin-istration that had been superimposed on it. Many chiefs and local kings of the British Celts were allies of the Romans and as such were tolerated. Peter Berresford Ellis, who has written a number of books about the Celts, has compared this to the state of affairs that existed under the British empire in India where numerous Indian princes who accepted British rule were tolerated.

When the grid of Roman rule was removed, Britain became once more a cluster of interlocking petty kingdoms ruled by Celtic chieftains. It is sometimes claimed that there was an indigenous central authority that ruled at this time. The truth is that the evidence for this period is so scanty that we simply cannot be sure whether this was or was not the case. The sources, such as they are, mention one Ambrosius Aurelianus in respect to this question. Gildas tells us that his parents had 'worn the purple', a term that may suggest they had some kind of imperial status in post-Roman Britain. An early-ninth-century Welsh source, a work completed around 830 and attributed to a man named Nennius, says that Ambrosius was 'king among all the kings of the British people'. Some see in this shadowy figure the legendary King Arthur, a Celtic hero who fought against the Saxon invaders.

Britain clearly did not fall apart immediately the Romans left. True, the use of coins all but died out in the 420s and the large-scale pottery industry set up by the Romans collapsed – people were forced to turn once more to their own resources and make their own pots at home. Villas and other substantial buildings continued to be built for a while but the trade routes with the

European mainland were routinely cut by Saxon pirates who intercepted the shipping trade. Yet despite this the economy held together, and there is no evidence of agricultural chaos. Whatever system of government was in place after the Romans left was sufficiently well organised to defend the land against the various enemies from the west, north and east. This ability of the inhabitants of Britain to defend themselves single-handedly did not last long. The call for help was to end in disaster.

Just how the Anglo-Saxons came to overrun a substantial part of Britain in the course of the next few generations is not known for certain. One explanation of the unfolding of events is given by Gildas, and further details are supplied by later sources such as Bede in the eighth century and Nennius in the ninth. The story is plausible and, while no doubt containing fictitious elements, may well be a fairly true rendition of what happened.

According to these accounts, Vortigern became the king of southern Britain around 425 and reigned for some thirty years. This suggests that he was a popular ruler, but he has gone down in history as the Judas of the British Celts, the man who sold them out to the Germanic invaders. His task was not an easy one – he was fighting back the Irish raiders and the Picts as well as the troublesome continentals who had almost certainly started small colonies of settlers on the North Sea seaboard of England. He simply could not fight them all off at once, and decided to use a policy that had worked for the Romans under the empire: set one barbarian group against another. The fierce Germanic warriors would make fine mercenaries, and he decided to hire just such a force.

The mercenaries he hired were led by two brothers named Hengist and Horsa. Bede tells us that they were Jutes rather than Angles or Saxons. The homeland of the Jutes is generally thought to be Jutland, directly north of Schleswig-Holstein. The exact date of their arrival is uncertain, but it was probably towards the last years of the 440s; their first down payment was the Isle of Thanet. The mercenaries proved to be effective against the Picts and Irish forces as well as their own Germanic brethren, the Saxons and the Angles. Everything seemed to be working out well for Vortigern, but he grew reliant on his mercenaries and as their number grew so did the cost of paying them. Overtaxing his citizens seems to have been the only solution he could think of, and this made him deeply unpopular.

A rather tall episode of the story concerns the background to the Jutes' claim on the whole of Kent, their number having outgrown the Isle of Thanet. It is Nennius who tells us that Hengist managed to justify his claim through tricking Vortigern, organising a feast ostensibly in his honour. Having got the king drunk, Hengist's daughter – who was said to be very beautiful – began to weave her seductive spell on him. In his drunkenness he agreed, through his official interpreter Ceretic, to share his kingdom with her if she would be his wife. This is said to be how the Jutes justified their attempt to take Kent for their own. Interestingly, Nennius continues by saying that after the marriage Hengist sent for more ships to bring his countrymen over, so many in fact that the islands from which they came were left uninhabited. This seems to be supported by Michael Gebühr's idea that the inhabitants of Schleswig-Holstein and Jutland abandoned their homeland *en masse* around the same time.

Vortigern's star was definitely on the wane: he was losing his grip on power as his mercenaries became increasingly dominant. Around 450 they are said to have turned against him, rallying their fellow Saxons and Angles and raising a rebellion. The result of this was widespread carnage and the destruction of many British towns, if we are to believe the lurid prose of Gildas:

All their inhabitants, bishops, priests and people were mown down together, while swords flashed and flames crackled.

Horrible it was to see the foundation stones of towers and high walls thrown down bottom upwards in the squares, mixing with holy altars and fragments of human bodies, as though they were covered with a purple crust of clotted blood, as in some fantastic wine-press. There was no burial save in the ruins of the houses, or in the bellies of the beasts and birds.

The Germanic attacks were by no means a total success. Vortigern had his son Vortimer lead the counter-attack. We are told that he succeeded in pushing the Jutes back to the Isle of Thanet but only at the cost of his own life. The fate of his father is rather hazy. One version of events has the shadowy figure of Ambrosius Aurelianus deposing him and becoming the focus of British military resistance to the Germanic forces. Nennius says that there was a prophecy that the red dragon (representing the British Celts) would one day overcome the white dragon (the Anglo-Saxons). Many people would still argue that modern Britain is still a land divided between these two dragons.

After this brief glimpse of the Celtic version of events, we can now turn to the story of the white dragon, although we will often have to lean on Celtic and hostile sources to do so. We can also temper these accounts with hard evidence from the ground in the form of early Anglo-Saxon burials and artefacts.

The Story of the White Dragon

Every English person must have heard the dismissive Scottish term 'sassenach', though not many may know how it originated. Variants of it exist in the different Celtic tongues: *sasanach* in Irish, *sasunnach* in Scottish Gaelic, *sais* in Welsh, *saws* in Cornish, *sostynagh* in Manx and *saoz* in Breton. In all these languages the word simply means Saxon. What the Celts meant by Saxon was, however, not exactly straightforward. For them it was a generic term for all the west Germanic peoples who came over to Britain. In addition to the Saxons themselves it was also used when referring to the Jutes, Angles and others – much as we do today when we talk about Anglo-Saxons in a historical sense. The people themselves certainly did not use that term; it started to be used at all only in the eighth century. In a later period, the time of King Alfred in the ninth century, when the Anglo-Saxons were merging to become a cohesive whole, we can see it has become a word essentially meaning the English.

When, where and who are the big questions concerning the arrival of the Anglo-Saxons on the eastern shores of Britain. Bede, writing in the eighth century about that earlier period, divides the colonisers into three: Saxons, Angles and Jutes (modern historians and some other early sources would add others such as the Frisians). The Jutes colonised Kent, but their descendants also lived in the kingdom of the West Saxons opposite the Isle of Wight and on the Isle of Wight itself. The Saxons (who Bede says came from Old Saxony) were the progenitors of the East, West and South Saxons. The Angles came from the country Bede calls Angelus, which according to him (as we have seen earlier) remained deserted from that time to the present. This country he places in between the land of the Saxons to the south and the Jutes to the north. Today this is the region that includes Schleswig-Holstein, where the absence of archaeological remains from this time supports his statement about its abandonment. These Angles are the direct ancestors of the East Angles, Middle Angles, Mercians and Northumbrians (by which is meant all those peoples who inhabit the area north of the river Humber).

One of the best archaeological clues concerning the migration of the German Saxons to England is the style of pottery. In the fifth century, the two regions basically had the same kind. Pottery linked to that found at Feddersen Wierde has been identified at sites such as Mucking on the Thames, and also at West Stow (which is visited in the next chapter). The English form has been described as 'baroque' as it shows a degree of extravagance in decoration that is missing on the continental pots. It is often the case that when people leave their home and set up in new lands, they feel a need to assert their cultural values and, in doing so, often exaggerate them as if to underline their difference from the native people who surround them. It is a mechanism for cultural survival.

Despite this, however, a certain amount of caution is needed because not all of these English pots were necessarily made by or for Saxons. They would have been first brought to England from the continent, but the local Britons may have found them attractive and started to make and use them. The case is similar to that of the deformed skulls of the Huns – a practice spread by the Huns and then taken up by other barbarians. In short, we can discern Saxon origins of pottery and Saxon influence on it, but it does not always mean that all the people who lived at the place where the pottery was found were necessarily exclusively Saxon.

To find traces of the earliest Anglo-Saxons in England, I visited some of the key archaeological sites that have shed light on the shadowy world of this migration. One of the more unusual sites in England lies in the midst of what is, for all intents and purposes, a small American town: RAF Lakenheath in Suffolk. It has been a USAF base for more than half a century, yet has hardly become integrated into mainstream British culture. It is a home-from-home for the USAF, with its shopping malls and fast food restaurants where you can spend dollars or pounds.

A good place to live is a good place to live whatever the era, and the site of the air base was first settled in the Stone Age. Long before the first planes or even the invention of gunpowder, the site had military associations. In the Iron Age, Celtic warriors watered their horses at what is now the base's pond. Roman legionnaires were garrisoned nearby and evidence of a Roman villa has been found at what is now RAF Lakenheath High School. While F15s and other state-of-the-art fighter planes roar across the skies above Lakenheath, below the ground lie the remains of the cultures of the past.

The name Lakenheath is said to come from the Anglo-Saxon place name Lokenhyte, meaning 'the landing place of Laka's people'. The true nature of the Anglo-Saxon connection came to light in the late 1950s, when some new buildings were being built. Archaeologists discovered the remains of an ancient cemetery, excavating thirty-three burials that appeared to belong to the Early Anglo-Saxon period (which comes after the Roman period). Along with the human remains were rich deposits of grave goods: spears, shields, daggers, brooches and beads. With intermittent demolition and construction work taking place, new parts of the ancient site were revealed in the 1960s, 1997 and most recently 2001. Many more human remains and artefacts have come to light over the years, giving us shafts of light into the murk of the Dark Ages.

Until very recently, it was thought on the basis of the excavations that the Anglo-Saxons at this site were mercenaries who had been brought to Britain just after the Roman period, in the early to mid fifth century; they had stayed on and died here. Now more accurate dating techniques show the burials to belong to the late fifth or early sixth century, which would probably make them part of a later wave of Anglo-Saxon immigrants who came from the continent to actually settle permanently in Britain. It has not been possible to pinpoint the date of many of the finds, but the material found so far at Lakenheath spans the time from the fifth to the seventh centuries. The archaeologists reckon that most of the objects discovered at Lakenheath belong to the middle of the Early Anglo-Saxon period.

In 1997, while the base's Softball Field No. 1 was being dug up to make way for a new dormitory block, the local archaeologists who had been employed to oversee the project called a halt to the work when pieces of human bone came to the surface. These few fragments turned out to be the tip of the iceberg, and by the end of the archaeological investigation about 170 Anglo-Saxon graves had been excavated, making it one of the largest cemeteries known from this period. No evidence of Christian burials has been found, so this is assumed to be an entirely pagan cemetery.

One particularly dramatic find made in the 1997 season caused a minor media sensation – an Anglo-Saxon warrior buried with his horse and his weaponry. Examination of the man's skeleton showed that he was 5 feet 10 inches tall and in his early thirties. The horse seems to have been pole-axed, killed in order to accompany its master to the grave, a practice of many barbarian peoples including the Huns. His sword was a fine weapon embodying the skill of its maker. Nearly eighty metal strips had been used in the subtle alchemy of the swordsmith to forge a single blade. The warrior was obviously someone of high social standing, perhaps a member of a noble clan, and certainly belonged to the military elite.

To date, about a hundred iron spearheads have been found in male graves at Lakenheath. It would be hasty to conclude that this is clear proof of a warrior-based society; studies of the numerous human bones from the site has not corroborated this. Despite the greater hardships and risks of day-to-day existence then compared with now, there are surprisingly few instances of traumatic injuries or deaths. No clear and incontrovertible proof of fighting has been found. This has led archaeologists to conclude that the spear was more of a status symbol (revealing the social standing of its bearer) than a regularly used weapon.

Other kinds of weapons are scarce. A number of iron bosses are all that remain of the wooden shields used by the Anglo-Saxons. There are a couple of axes, some arrowheads and the odd high status sword. The scarcity of swords suggests that only the top men would have been buried with this kind of weapon. There seem to be three kinds of male burial: men who had swords, men who had spears, and men who had neither; this suggests that there may have been three social classes. But it is always dangerous to jump to conclusions and we cannot be sure of this. However, there were three distinct classes elsewhere in the Saxon world: the *nobiles* (nobles), the *ingenui* (freemen) and the *liti* (the dependent). There was a taboo forbidding the three social classes from inter-marrying; transgression was punished by death.

There are also a few cases of small children being buried with spears, but most infant graves contain small pots, perhaps meant to hold food or milk for the afterlife. These pots are embellished with very distinctive Germanic stamped decoration. Pots containing food were also found in adult graves. Brooches are among the most popular grave goods found in the burials of women. They belong to a style that is also found on the continent and their discovery in Suffolk, Norfolk and up the north-east side of England marks them out as a type that is distinctly Anglo-Saxon.

So the weapons, everyday pots and the jewellery discovered at Lakenheath all reveal the recent continental origin of those people who made and used them. The pottery is probably the clearest indicator. The shape and decoration of their pottery link these people with continental Europe and it is completely different to the Romano-Celtic pots that precede it. For archaeologists from both England and Germany, the pots clearly bear the undeniable signatures of their Saxon origin.

Although they were recent immigrants, their behaviour reveals that they did not see themselves as unconnected with the past peoples of Britain. Among the most recent revelations made at Lakenheath, in the summer of 2001, was the reason for the Anglo-Saxons choosing this particular place to bury their dead. In the middle of their cemetery lie some Bronze Age burials. In Anglo-

Saxon times this area would still have had the prehistoric burial mound pretty much intact and, by deciding to place their dead near those of the earlier people, they seem to have been making a conscious and concrete link with the past. They sensed that this had been a holy place in earlier times than their own. This was not the only Anglo-Saxon site that was selected because of its earlier, prehistoric occupation, as we shall see later in the case of West Heslerton in Yorkshire. Of course, in a later period, churches were routinely built on sites of pagan significance although in these cases the motive was rather different – to obliterate the memory and the power of the pagan deities.

Overall, the archaeological evidence definitely points to the strong influence of Germanic cultures, but whether the people of Lakenheath were themselves all continental or included Britons who were copying and using continental products we cannot be certain. There is no evidence from Lakenheath that indicates a violent and dramatic invasion by the newcomers, so the most likely explanation is that the migrants integrated fairly peacefully with the natives. This seems to contradict the violent storyline of Gildas's account.

Perhaps we have not only a Britain split in two – one half Celtic, Christian and 'civilised', and the other Germanic, pagan and 'barbarian' – but also two very different stories: one from the writings of Celts and Christians, and one from the material remains of the Anglo-Saxons of Lakenheath. Evidence from other early sites also shows a more peaceful world, one that existed in a sleepy village in Suffolk: West Stow.

Chapter Twelve

RECONSTRUCTING THE ANGLO-SAXONS

West Stow is a constant reminder of the debt we owe the past, particularly to those early Anglo-Saxon communities who laid the foundation of society today.

Stanley West, excavator of West Stow

The Anglo-Saxon site of West Stow is in the same county as Lakenheath – Suffolk. It is set on a small hill on the banks of the river Lark a few miles to the west of the town of Bury St Edmunds. After its excavation, it was decided that an attempt should be made to reconstruct, as authentically as possible, the old village. This was a large-scale and long-term project in experimental archaeology. The idea was to try to make things (buildings in this instance) in the way that they would originally have been made. The durability of buildings naturally needs to be monitored over a number of years, and the reconstruction of the material culture of the Anglo-

Saxons of West Stow has been on-going since the early 1970s. It is the realisation of this project that greets the visitor today.

West Stow is open to the public, who can get a flavour of what life in a typical Anglo-Saxon village might have been like. Some days it is populated by members of Angelcynn (Old English meaning 'the English people'), a re-enactment society who not only dress the part but seek to recreate the cuisine, the crafts and many other aspects of Anglo-Saxon culture. As they are part-time dwellers at West Stow, actually using the village as their living space, the Angelcynn also have some interesting ideas about how the village might have been used. They understand it in a way that perhaps the archaeologists and other visitors are unable to do. One of the members told me that it was almost as if each building worked rather like one room of a large dwelling. The largest of the reconstructed buildings at West Stow acts as a lounge-cum-kitchen-cum-dining room. It is the 'room' where the main socialising goes on. The weaving house on the site is like a workshop off to one side, while other buildings would have played the role of bedrooms.

Rebuilding the Anglo-Saxon Past

The story of the excavation of West Stow begins in the middle of the Second World War, when the archaeologist Basil Brown (who had made his name as the excavator of Sutton Hoo, about which more in later chapters) discovered a couple of pottery kilns from the Romano-British period. Stanley West joined Brown in the study of these remains and it was soon realised that there were shards of Early Anglo-Saxon pottery strewn across the site. After a number of years digging elsewhere, West returned to dedicate himself long-term to the study of West Stow.

The site of West Stow was first used by Stone Age hunters and fishermen, who left their flint tools behind them. Somewhat later, in the Neolithic period (New Stone Age), a number of people were cremated at the site, and one burial with a solitary stone bead was found. These modest finds from remote times were not the only signs of human activity before the Romano-British evidence. In the Iron Age there were a number of loosely connected farmsteads with enclosures and ditches. By AD 60 the Iron Age occupation was over, and replaced by a cluster of kilns used in the manufacture of a wide variety of quality ceramics during the first and second centuries.

In 1849, only 400 metres from the West Stow site, an Anglo-Saxon cemetery was discovered; about a hundred graves were excavated, along with some 150 miscellaneous objects. These were variously dated from the fifth to the early seventh century, and the village itself dates from the same period. (After it was abandoned in the seventh century, the site was not used again for another 600 years.) This was one of the earliest villages of the Anglo-Saxon settlers, and the remains from West Stow allow the archaeologists to see three distinct phases of the settlement over this time. The initial phase is basically the fifth century; the second phase is sixth century; and the third covers the late sixth and early seventh century. With the present state of knowledge, it is not possible to be less vague than that.

The excavations revealed that there were seven 'halls' (buildings constructed with rectangular settings of post holes) and seventy 'houses', which the archaeologists prefer to call 'sunken-feature buildings' (SFBs for short), as this is a more neutral term that does not commit one to saying what their use might have been. SFBs of similar type have been discovered in England and on the continent, and used to be called 'pit-houses', 'sunken houses' or *Grubenhauser* (the German for 'pit-houses'). The SFBs may be divided into various types, but for our purposes we need only treat some of the key features of interest. All of them have a roughly rectangular pit over which they were built – hence the name 'pit-house' that was given to them.

Five of the seven halls were built along the central part of the hill, and all the indications are that this is a sign that the community was well organised. The other two halls break with the original plan of the village: one is off to the north and the other to the south. More is known about two of the halls (Hall 1 and Hall 2) than the others. Calculating from the centre of the post holes, Hall 1 would have been 7.9 metres (26 feet) long and 4.1 metres (13 feet 6 inches) wide. There appear to have been two doors, one in the east wall and one in the south. The eastern doorway (if, indeed, that is what it was) was about a metre (just over 3 feet) wide; the southern doorway a little narrower.

Hall 2 is not only one of the largest of all the West Stow buildings but it also commanded a position at the very hub of the village. It was 9.75 metres (32 feet) long and 4.27 metres (14 feet) wide. It was also the only hall to have an internal partition, which gave it a separate room at the east end measuring 2.44 by 4.27 metres (8 by 14 feet). Hall 2 appears to have had a doorway 1.8 metres (6 feet) wide. Both halls had large hearths in the centre of the building. The largest of all the buildings is Hall 7, which once stood on the northern slope of the hill. It was approximately half as big again as Hall 2.

A certain amount of detective work is needed to understand how the settlement developed and how it functioned. Stanley West believes that there are three plausible scenarios. The first is that each SFB was a family house, and that there was only one hall in the village at any given time. In this case, a single hall would have been the focal point of the whole community; it would have functioned pretty much as a village hall does today. In this respect, it would seem to echo the use of a similar building on the Feddersen Wierde site. The experimental building of a hall showed that a life-span for the building before it subsided or totally collapsed could easily have been more than a quarter of a century. The seven halls would then have succeeded each other over a period of roughly 200 years, which approximates to the life of the Anglo-Saxon village.

So far, so good – but there are weaknesses inherent in this reconstruction of the organisation of the village. Firstly, it means that we have to accept that the hall is constantly moving its location in the village; secondly, that some of the SFBs that are contemporary with each other seem to have been used regularly and intensively for specific activities. This suggests that one family probably used more than one building.

The second scenario holds that there were three (extended) family units in the village, each with its own group of SFBs and a central building in the form of a hall. There are a number of problems with this concept too, not the least of which is that it means some of the individual halls would have had to remain in use for the best part of a century – a lot to ask from a timber building of this type, based on the experience gleaned from trying to build one. The third possibility is that there were two rather than three early centres. In this case two groups of SFBs would have clustered around each of the co-existing halls.

There are pros and cons with all these scenarios, and we cannot really be sure which is the most likely. It is also difficult to be sure how many people lived in the village at any one time. We can estimate that a single hall along with eight to ten SFBs could accommodate an extended family of around thirty.

The previous designation of SFBs as 'pit-houses' reflected an idea that had been present among both continental and British archaeologists since the nineteenth century – that the 'primitive' Anglo-Saxons would have been quite at home in what was thought to be their chosen way of making a house. It was thought to be little more than a pit that had been dug in the ground and covered with a bivouac type of thatched roof. It was believed to have no planked floor, and the refuse found in the pits was used as confirmation that these people wallowed in their own filth. Barbarians were supposed to have lived in this fashion through their ignorance of anything more comfortable or technically accomplished. Today, this view of Saxon housing sounds completely ridiculous.

Stanley West admits that something along these lines was what he had in mind when he began excavating West Stow in 1965. Apart from a few sporadic instances of pit-houses discovered in England, almost all the work had been done in Germany. It was Germany's own archaeologists to whom this prejudicial view of the Germanic peoples' technical capacities can ultimately be traced. The work of West and others at the village site has done much to destroy this erroneous notion.

In 1975–6 a reconstruction of the old view of the *Grubenhaus* was made. It was soon found that apart from the practical difficulties of living down in a pit, there were other problems – particularly with the rapid decay of the part of the thatched roof in contact with the ground. A different reconstructed *Grubenhaus* had also been made at the site. It was based on the hypothesis that the early Anglo-Saxon house basically had a floor at ground level and a pit beneath that. Over time it became clear that this latter was a much more convincing reconstruction than the more primitive one envisioned by earlier generations of archaeologists working purely from theory. In this instance, the reconstruction of early Anglo-Saxon buildings was also a rehabilitation of Anglo-Saxon abilities and cultural sophistication. They were not the ignorant savages that they had been portrayed as being for far too long.

Wood was the material *par excellence* in the northern tradition of house building. The 'poor' Anglo-Saxon housing was for a long time perceived as a real Dark Ages fall from the grace of Roman building techniques. This is simply to misunderstand the nature of

the northern technological traditions. Wood was the most plenti-
ful and practical building material, and it is absurd to think that
after using it for countless generations the northern people who
became the Anglo-Saxons did not have a mastery of this material,
and could construct only draughty and rickety buildings. The
Nydam boat shows the high degree of practical skill that existed in
the northern shipyards. If they could make boats of this technical
level they were hardly likely to lack similar abilities in the building
of their own dwellings and workshops.

The surviving evidence indicates that the various crafts and
industrial activities that took place in and around the village (weaving, pot-making, bone-working, smithing and so on) were all for
servicing their own needs. They were probably not entirely self-
sufficient and were certainly not cut off from the outside world.
Exotic goods of various kinds found their way even to this quiet
Anglo-Saxon village. Cowrie shells from the Red Sea or the Indian
Ocean and brooches in the Frankish style were among the
women's fashion items. The ubiquitous Germanic bone comb also
inevitably turned up among the material remains from the village.

West Stow must have been integrated into a loose-knit skein of
villages, all probably under the jurisdiction of a local chieftain to
whom the villagers would literally pay tribute. This in turn would
have linked it to the much wider network of the kingdom of East
Anglia. There is little in the archaeology to suggest that these were
violent times for the villagers. Stability is demonstrated by the
continuous occupation of the same site for 200 years or more.
Two of the most complete pictures we have of the world of the
early Anglo-Saxon people in England come from Lakenheath and
West Stow. The picture that is emerging is not one of violent and
savage destruction but of technical ability and stable and secure
village life. Another site much further to the north tells us even
more about the lives and deaths of the Anglo-Saxons.

West Heslerton: Virtual Landscape of the Angles

Like Stanley West, who excavated at West Stow on and off for a quarter of a century, Dominic Powlesland spent many years directing excavations at the site of West Heslerton, on the edge of the Vale of Pickering, North Yorkshire. For both archaeologists, a single site proved endlessly challenging and fascinating, changing every time something more was unearthed, something new understood. In Powlesland's case, he went on to study the computerised data base, creating a virtual West Heslerton that is as useful for reconstructing the Anglo-Saxon past as the houses and other buildings put up at West Stow.

Powlesland is one of the archaeologists who maintain that the standard picture of the Anglo-Saxons is a long way from the truth. Just as the Romans and other imperial powers denigrated their contemporaries as 'barbarians' or 'pagans', so archaeologists of the past were mostly members of the Establishment and as such tended to project their prejudices back into the Dark Ages. They were particularly dismissive of the pagan Anglo-Saxons, believing paganism to be a sign of a primitive cultural level. In contrast, they exalted the Roman era in Britain as a Golden Age of civilisation and learning. Yet, as Dominic Powlesland put it in conversation with me, the Romans weren't that golden and the pagans weren't that primitive.

One of the problems with the Anglo-Saxons has been that although numerous cemeteries have come to light, few associated settlements have been found. Much more is known about the way they died than the way they lived. But among the sites that can show us both aspects of their culture, West Heslerton is one of the most important and certainly the most meticulously documented. Using the most sophisticated computerised system of recording the data from the site, Dominic Powlesland has created a state-of-the-art model for future archaeologists to emulate. It is, by his own admission, the most sophisticated use of computer technology in archaeology anywhere in the world.

The north of England has been seen as the place where the Angles rather than Saxons or other Germanic peoples chose to settle. The Anglo-Saxon (or Anglian) cemetery and settlement at West Heslerton was found by accident, as so many sites are, as a result of industrial quarrying. During the autumn of 1977, sand was being quarried when a burial became exposed. Luckily, Jim Carter, the quarry worker who found it, had previously worked on other archaeological digs and informed the local archaeology unit. Work then began at the site and continued until 1987. It is the most complete settlement and cemetery of an Early to Middle Anglo-Saxon period to have been excavated in England. The whole site turned out to be over 8,000 square metres (86,000 square feet), of which 6,000 square metres (64,000 square feet) were thoroughly excavated; the rest of it lies under the A46 trunk road that bisects the site.

Long before the Angles came to this part of the world, the site was used as a ceremonial centre by people of the Late Neolithic and Early Bronze Age periods. It will be remembered that the Bronze Age burial mound at Lakenheath was incorporated by the Anglo-Saxon community into their cemetery. The choice that the Angles made at West Heslerton may indicate that they too wanted to associate themselves with the indigenous past. For whatever reasons, they identified more closely with the prehistoric rather than the Roman past.

In prehistory at least ten people had been buried and three cremated in what was for its makers a sacred zone. The Anglian cemetery was founded in the late fifth century in the midst of this prehistoric ritual complex consisting of barrows, an enclosure and a number of round barrows. The Anglians continued to use the cemetery until the early seventh century. West Stow and West

Heslerton were therefore contemporary. Dominic Powlesland and his team excavated and documented 201 burials, mostly inhumations but also some cremations. Study of the physical remains has revealed two distinct physical groups: the majority were shorter and of stockier build while the minority (about 20 per cent) were taller and gracile and were buried with their weapons.

It seems that the taller people were of southern Scandinavian origin and were therefore Anglians, while the rest were indigenous Britons. Whether the evidence from the cemetery indicates a small force of Anglians dominating the local people, or whether it actually shows small groups of Scandinavian migrants integrating themselves with the locals, is impossible to say. Invasion and violence are not indicated by the human remains. None of the many burials contains evidence that the deceased had suffered a violent death or traumatic injuries likely to have been caused by warfare.

What is clear is that the material culture from the site is unequivocally Anglian, with strong links to Scandinavia. Numerous brooches, beads, pendants, buckles and belt fittings gave the archaeologists plenty of material to compare with finds from both elsewhere in England and on the continent. Powlesland is very keen that people do not jump to premature conclusions when looking at the artefacts. He makes an analogy with our own times: just because you use a Japanese computer does not mean that you are Japanese. If you took the number of Japanese computers in England today as an indicator of the presence of Japanese people, then you would conclude that there were many living here, whereas in fact the percentage of Japanese people living here is very low. If you accept things too readily at face value, false conclusions are not far behind.

We can also add to this example of the computer. Not only does the widespread presence of Japanese computers in England not automatically demonstrate the presence of Japanese people –

neither does it show that those who use the computers have any knowledge of the Japanese language or even have even the remotest interest in Japanese culture. People use Japanese computers for utilitarian reasons, not because they are Japanese themselves or wish to adopt Japanese ways.

The computer is of course a different kind of object from a brooch. The first is mainly practical, the second is mainly decorative. However, wearing a brooch of Scandinavian origin does not necessarily mean that you are trying to become Scandinavian in a wider cultural sense – you may simply like the brooch. Yet whatever the reason, it is clear that the inhabitants of West Heslerton, including the indigenous people, preferred Anglian dress, fashions and designs. They also adopted their burial practices. In life and death the Anglian influence was paramount. Some of the burials turned out to be a big surprise.

Some of the burials that have items typically found in male graves have female remains in them. The discovery of a woman buried with two spears is certainly not the norm at West Heslerton, and it raises some interesting questions by challenging our stereotypes. We cannot say with certainty that she was an Amazon, or female warrior. The weapons, like many that are found in graves, do not seem to have seen much action. They may be better explained as symbols of rank rather than arms as such.

There are also some unusual burials of men with objects traditionally found in female graves – brooches, beads and items that are usually described as purses but which Dominic Powlesland says are really more like large handbags. Shamans have been known to dress in the clothing of the opposite sex, though a modern interpretation might be tempted to consider transvestism. Which of these is the most likely is an open question, but the fact that these burials (both the woman with spears and the men with handbags) were in the main cemetery with the more ordinary burials shows that these individuals had not been spurned by their communities. Had they been outcasts, surely their mortal remains would have been deposited beyond the boundaries of the community.

The settlement was probably a fairly typical Anglian village in its time, and the excavation has done much to change archaeologists' views about Anglo-Saxon villages. The reconstruction work at West Stow has helped to show how knowledgeable the people were at building in wood. Even as recently as twenty years ago the view was that a typical Anglo-Saxon settlement consisted of a few shifting farmsteads that gradually evolved then moved on to a new location every few years. This preconception seems to echo what Tacitus says about the shifting farming practices of the ancient Germans. West Heslerton shows that their villages were large, well-organised and stable communities. There is no sign whatsoever that they were eking out a miserable living any more than they were living in holes in the ground. The population was probably around a hundred, which is what the present-day village of West Heslerton (just down the road from the site) would have been about twenty years ago. A village population of a hundred people would have consisted of probably something like six to ten extended families. Only one or two of these would have been of Scandinavian origin. Overall, the population of the Vale of Pickering and the number of villages in it was probably the same in Anglo-Saxon times as it is today.

The village community in some ways echoes that of West Stow. It was well organised and there are no real signs of great differences in wealth or status among the inhabitants. But, as seems to have been the case at West Stow, beyond the confines of the village there was probably some regional leader to whom they paid homage. There are two main types of buildings: the *Grubenhaus* type of continental origin and post-hole buildings (rather like the 'halls' at West Stow) that seem to be a local development.

There is a surprising degree of uniformity in the buildings from the various excavated Anglo-Saxon settlements. The buildings from sites in Hampshire, Suffolk or Northumbria could almost be pulled out of the ground and placed in the post holes at West Heslerton. There is a fairly limited range of standard designs and these appear regularly throughout England. As Dominic Powlesland says, 'It's almost as if there's an Anglo-Saxon Mr Wimpey or Mr Barrett out there who has a book of building plans and you choose whichever one you like. It's interesting enough that it occurs on this site. But it's quite remarkable that it occurs throughout early Anglo-Saxon England.'

The combined evidence from West Stow and West Heslerton paints a far more complete and rosy picture of the early Anglo-Saxon communities of England. We know from West Stow how sophisticated their building and woodworking traditions were. The buildings from West Heslerton and other sites show us that it was not just a sophisticated tradition but one that was standardised. This suggests that the various communities, far from being isolated, were in touch with each other and drawing on common traditions and cultural practices. The old reconstruction of pit-dwelling Anglo-Saxons who were primitive pagans – violent, savage and unsophisticated – has been demolished by the evidence from West Stow and West Heslerton. Its debris should be cast in the rubbish pit of history.

Chapter Thirteen

THE LEGACY
OF A
LANGUAGE

*If you look at the countryside of England, the
pattern that we see, of villages, of churches, of parish
boundaries, county boundaries, the major towns, the roads,
the whole map – particularly the map as it was until the
Industrial Revolution – is a map that was created
and developed in the Anglo-Saxon period.*

Dr Catherine Hills, a specialist in the Early Anglo-Saxon period

The archaeological evidence presented so far demonstrates that the
Anglo-Saxon contribution to the cultural history of England was
far more significant than previous generations had believed; it still
influences the land and the people today in many very different
spheres of life. The maps, the language, the literature and even the
characteristic sense of humour of the English are all stamped with
the unmistakable signature of the Anglo-Saxons. It is not just the

name of the country of England that comes from the name of one of the Germanic peoples, the Angles. It is also the political entity of England that can be said to have emerged out of the actions of the Anglo-Saxons.

The Seven Kingdoms

The writings of men of the Church, most notably the Venerable Bede in the eighth century, supply us with details of the various kingdoms of southern Britain as they were organised in the seventh century. By this time, the so-called Anglo-Saxon heptarchy (that is, seven kingdoms) was in place: Wessex, Sussex, Kent, East Anglia, Essex, Mercia and Northumbria (the last of these consisting of two parts – Deira and, further to the north, Bernicia, representing the Anglian presence north of the river Humber).

In reality, the picture of the vying kingdoms was even more complicated than these seven units might lead us to believe. There were other regional rulers, subordinate maybe, but nevertheless referred to as kings – the king of the Isle of Wight and the king of Lindsey (the region between East Anglia and Deira), to name but two. Elsewhere in Britain there were still independent Celtic kingdoms: Dumnonia (Cornwall), Dyfed, Powys and Gwynedd in Wales and others in Scotland.

The more powerful kings of the late sixth and the seventh centuries were able to extend their rule beyond the confines of their own kingdoms. Bede gives a list of these that includes Aethelbert of Kent, Raedwald of East Anglia and Edwin of Northumbria. Such kings are described in a later source (the ninth-century *Anglo-Saxon Chronicle* – a composite work based on earlier sources) as *bretwaldas*, a word meaning 'ruler of Britain'. This information cannot be taken simply at face value. The shifting tides of power in Britain at the time make it a mistake to envisage anything approaching 'national unity' or a stable political map.

There were clearly kings who were able to dominate the neighbouring kingdoms for a few years, but that is all.

England and Britain as a whole still had a long way to go before the countries into which it is divided today came into being. However, many of the county and other regional names of England have their origin in the Anglo-Saxon kingdoms. East Anglia, not surprisingly, got its name from the Angles, while it was also felt necessary to distinguish the north folk and the south folk – hence the county names Norfolk and Suffolk. The Saxon presence also left its mark: Wessex (the land of the West Saxons), Sussex (South Saxons) and Essex (East Saxons).

Anglo-Saxon Word-play

We can equally say that the Old English language, spoken by the Anglo-Saxons, had a long way to go before it became Modern English. When we consider the strong influence of both Roman and, later, Norman culture on England, it is rather surprising that the language that evolved is not Latin or French but a Germanic language: English – rooted in the Dark Ages, and not in Roman or Norman times.

For the Anglo-Saxons, spoken language was not just a means of everyday communication: in a mainly non-literate society, it was also a means of learning about the past and the outside world – as well as a vehicle of artistic expression and amusement. The reciting of poems and the telling of stories in the evenings played the same kind of role as television does in the homes of today. One of their great delights was the posing and answering of riddles. This was not just a matter of fun; it was also one of the chief forms of cultural expression. The ambiguity that is an integral element of the riddles of the Anglo-Saxons captured the imaginations of the whole community from children to kings. Here is an example from a collection of riddles translated by John Porter:

I saw a beast breasting the waves,
it was strangely stuffed with wonders.
It had four feet beneath its belly
and eight upon its back;
had two wings, twelve eyes
and six heads. Say what it was.
It flew over oceans but was no bird,
yet showed some likeness to
horse and man, hound and bird,
and women's beauty too. You will, if you know
how to, tell the truth about
the way in which this creature moves.

The answer to this particularly abstruse riddle is a ship. The four feet represent the four oars, the eight feet belong to those of the four rowers on board, the two wings are sails and the six heads belong to the four oarsmen and the figureheads at either end of the ship (the twelve eyes – eight human and four on the figureheads). This love of circumlocution, analogy and double meanings was not just limited to their riddles and rhymes. This feature is also found elsewhere in their culture. Brooches, as we have seen in the sites of Lakenheath and West Heslerton, are one of the material indicators of the presence (or at least influence) of continental ideas. A study by David Leigh of a particular type of this kind of artefact, the square-headed brooches made in Kent during the fifth and sixth centuries, has shown that visual tricks were a common feature of the designs. What appears to be an animal from one point of view, if turned ninety degrees, suddenly appears as human faces. This seems to have been much more than just a clever illusion. Something deeper is also communicated by this recurrent theme in Anglo-Saxon art. As the riddle is a serious play on words, so the brooches are a play on images; the eye and the tongue can both deceive and be deceived.

The fact that such ambiguous images are found on expensive items of jewellery shows that many of them clearly belonged to the upper echelons of society, and were designed to last. Ambiguity was a recurrent theme of such art and is therefore unlikely to simply be a trivial and meaningless device. The use of images which, when seen from one angle, appear to be animals and, when seen from a different perspective, appear to be human may well be an expression of the theme of human–animal transformation that is fundamental to the theory and practice of shamanism. Although shamanism is normally associated with Siberian and Native American peoples, it was also widely practised in prehistoric and pagan Europe. One of the skills attributed to shamans is their ability to understand the animal world and, on occasion, be able to change themselves into a bird or other type of animal.

The shamanic god *par excellence* among the northern deities was called Woden in England (Wodan or Wotan in mainland Europe, equating to the Viking Age Odin). The myths and stories concerning him give him a number of shamanic attributes. We have little direct information about the Woden of the pagan Anglo-Saxons but it is likely that many of the attributes of Odin were shared by his west Germanic counterpart. The *Prose Edda* (one of the primary sources of Norse mythology) tells us that Odin was a shape shifter. He is said to be able to transform into a dragon, a bird, a beast or a fish at will. His 'vehicle' by means of which he travels to the other world is his eight-legged horse named Sleipnir. This supernatural steed is the equivalent of the shaman's mount that takes him down to the underworld or up to heaven. Oddly enough, among the Buryat, a people who live to the north of Mongolia, female shamans were said to ride eight-legged horses.

It has been suggested that the steed's four pairs of legs might simply represent the fast speed at which it travels, but the most convincing explanation is that put forward by Hilda Ellis

Davidson, one of the leading scholars of the northern European myths. She notes another instance of a reference to an eight-legged horse as far from northern Europe as the Buryat example given above. Among one of the numerous tribal peoples of the Indian sub-continent, the Gonds, the bier of a dead man, carried by four men, is explicitly compared to an eight-legged horse. The carrying of the deceased on a bier in the northern world could have led to the descriptions of Sleipnir, particularly as it is said to carry its rider to the land of the dead. The creature can now be seen to have developed out of the very tradition of ambiguity that has already been identified: four men carrying a bier seems to be the answer to the riddle that is Sleipnir.

We can see this delight in ambiguity not just in the riddles and jewellery designs of the Anglo-Saxons but on a far more basic level, in their sense of humour. Here is another riddle from the same collection:

Strangely hangs by man's thigh
below his lap. In front is hole.
Is stiff and hard, stands in good stead
when the man his own skirt
over knee hoists, wants that known hole
with his dangler's head to greet,
fill it as he filled it long and oft before.

Despite the deliberate attempt by the riddler to mislead by means of the heavy sexual connotations, the answer is actually a key. Ben Levick, one of the mainstays of the Angelcynn (the Anglo-Saxon re-enactment society), told me that he believes the Anglo-Saxons are the source for the sexual *doubles entendres* that have survived in such elements of popular English culture as the 'saucy' seaside postcards and the bawdy *Carry On* films of the twentieth century.

It is something that resonates through the whole culture from top to bottom, and from the ridiculous to the sublime. It has many applications, from vulgar humour to communicating the esoteric language of the gods.

Beowulf: a Hero Immortalised

Another of the core members of Angelcynn is Ben's father, whose Anglo-Saxon name is Dodda. He explained to me, by way of an anecdote, how he felt his society brought back to life the traditions of the past one night at West Stow:

> *There was an evening we had a couple of years ago when we were in the hall building. We simply got together a crowd of people who were to do with West Stow. We had a young lady as a member of the group whose main subject at university had been Old English, and we had a meal. We were sitting around drinking by firelight and she was telling the story of Beowulf in Old English. My son, who is her partner, was actually giving the modern English translations and there was one point when suddenly it sort of ceased for a moment and I think that everybody when we spoke afterwards was aware that the original inhabitants could almost have been there.*
>
> *It was just one of those moments. I don't think it could have happened if the building wasn't on the site of one of the original buildings. And you get moments like that and they are absolutely wonderful.*

Beowulf is the most famous of all works written in the language of the Anglo-Saxons, Old English. Its unique status has made it an enduring monument in the landscape of English literature. The poem, 3,182 lines long, has become an institution. Its very stature has made it less approachable, yet it still has a resonance and a power to move that has not diminished through time. J. R. R. Tolkien, best known for *The Hobbit* and the epic *The Lord of the Rings*, was also Professor of English at the University of Oxford. In the 1930s he wrote a study of *Beowulf* that criticised the dry approaches to the poem that had surrounded it with a stale and academic air. He helped to resurrect it as a work of art and imagination – he breathed life back into it. The poet Seamus Heaney, himself a recent translator of the saga, has said that while its narrative belongs to an age long past, 'As a work of art it lives in its own continuous present, equal to our own knowledge of reality.'

Only a single manuscript copy of the work is known and is now ensconced among the treasures of the British Library. The date of its composition is still hotly debated, but lies somewhere between the middle of the seventh and the end of the tenth century. Most commentators would place it in either the seventh or eight century. Where it was composed is as contentious a question as when. The kingdom of Mercia during the reign of King Offa (757–96) has been suggested, on the basis that there is a section of the poem that sings his praises. Others have suggested that it was much more likely to belong to the world of seventh-century East Anglia as there are echoes of the world of *Beowulf* in the archaeological discoveries from the site of Sutton Hoo, the subject of the next two chapters of this book. Its author is unknown. Over a millennium or more the English language has changed dramatically and the reader of modern English cannot simply pick it up and read it. There have been a number of translators who have taken on the onerous task; Seamus Heaney has compared it to 'trying to bring down a megalith with a toy hammer'.

The poem tells the heroic story of Beowulf, leader of the Geats (a people of southern Sweden), and his deadly encounters with three supernatural foes. He travels over the sea to the land of the Danes to confront the first two, the monster Grendel and his mother. He defeats them both and returns home to be made king and reigns for half a century. His last foe, a treasure-guarding dragon that has been plaguing his own country, he kills only at the cost of his own life. The poem begins and ends with a funeral, first that of Shield Sheafson, a great warrior king of the Danes, whose body is carried by his warriors on to a ship in the harbour. He is laid out on the deck, which is then piled high with treasures from far and wide. The ship is then set adrift on the icy seas and seen no more. The funeral recounted at the end of the poem is that of Beowulf himself.

The dying king instructs his warriors to build a mound on the headland of a coast. This will serve as a permanent reminder of Beowulf to both his subjects and all who sail by in their ships. His body is burnt on a pyre and his ashes then transported to the heart of the mound. In death he is surrounded by helmets, shields, armour and other trappings of war along with gold, jewels and other treasure. Twelve mounted warriors ride around the mound, singing dirges in honour of their lost king.

Whether a real Beowulf ever lived we do not know, but he has been immortalised in this poem. And for those who read the poem out loud at West Stow it provides a link with a rich and powerful tradition that evokes the spirits of our Anglo-Saxon ancestors.

West Stow gave us some idea of what life for the average Anglo-Saxon villager might have been like. The most famous of all the Anglo-Saxon sites is not far from the peace and quiet of that ancient village. It tells us about the other end of the social scale: it was a final resting place fit for a king – the Sutton Hoo burial ground. The world that *Beowulf* conjures back to life is evoked once more by the archaeological treasures unearthed from this site.

Chapter Fourteen

THE BURIALS OF SUTTON HOO

The message of the cemetery, like that of Beowulf,
*is heroic and international; in praise of enterprise,
achievement and fame, of a life that is memorable even if
short, rather than one that is long and virtuous or boring.*

Martin Carver, *Sutton Hoo: Burial Ground of Kings?*

What were once places of great significance in the past are often now just quiet backwaters far from the centres of contemporary power and influence. Today's Sutton Hoo lies in the peace of the Suffolk countryside outside the small town of Woodbridge. The Sutton Hoo of the seventh century was a place of regal power and a prominent feature of the political landscape. Then, the river Deben that flows past the ridge upon which the burial mounds were built was the route to the estuary that led to the North Sea. From there, ships travelled across to the river Rhine and into the heartlands of Europe. In Anglo-Saxon times, the rivers and the seas, far from being a barrier, were the arteries of communication and trade.

The Secrets of the Mounds

To the visitor, Sutton Hoo has none of the immediate impact of either the earlier Stonehenge or the later castles built by the Normans. Here there was no statement written in enduring stone, yet it marks one of the turning points in the history of Britain. A cluster of grassy mounds is all that is visible today, but what has been unearthed from inside them has shone an unexpected and dazzling light on the Dark Ages. Three major archaeological campaigns took place: the first in the 1930s; the second the British Museum dig in the 1960s; and the excavations that took place in the 1980s. The combined discoveries have resulted in a vast amount of hitherto unknown aspects of Anglo-Saxon life.

There was an unsuccessful attempt to rob the mounds in the sixteenth century. Queen Elizabeth I herself, desperate for loot to melt down for bullion, reportedly gave Dr John Dee (an antiquarian and her personal astrologer) permission to dig in East Anglia. Whether he was actually involved in the failed attempt is not known. The story of the rediscovery of this long-lost part of our heritage begins in 1926 when a Colonel Pretty bought an Edwardian mansion and the land around it that included a strange series of mounds. His wife Edith gave birth to a son in 1930 but, sadly, the colonel died when the boy was just four years old. The grief-stricken widow sought solace in the company of a medium. Her interest in spiritualism seems to have had a bearing on her decision to initiate the excavation of the mounds. There were strange stories of ghostly sightings at Sutton Hoo – reports of spectral visions of a man on horseback, and claims of phantasmal figures wandering the mounds at night. Furthermore, Mrs Pretty's nephew, a keen dowser, believed (rightly as it turned out) that gold was present at the site.

Whatever influence the supernatural aura of Sutton Hoo had on Mrs Pretty's decision to dig there, it would be a mistake to see her as simply a mystically inclined individual. She also had her feet firmly on the ground and had witnessed her own father excavating elsewhere near her childhood home. She went to the local museum at Ipswich and was put in touch with an enthusiastic archaeologist named Basil Brown, who was later to be connected with the initial work at the village of West Stow. One of Brown's contemporaries was to characterise him rather rudely as a ferret-like man in a trilby hat, but one of Sutton Hoo's later excavators, Martin Carver, was to describe his work at the site as an 'excavation of genius'.

The work began in 1938, on the biggest mound of all – known as Mound 1. Preliminary digging also took place on Mounds 2 and 3. The following year further excavations at Mound 1 took place, and around noon on 11 May one of Brown's assistants dug up a small piece of iron. It turned out to be a rivet from a ship. More rivets were unearthed and Brown was quick to understand what they had found. He realised that the rivets were all that had survived of a ship, which, being made of wood, had long since decayed. The position of the rivets in the mound marked their original position and so the whole shape of the vessel had been preserved. They had truly found a ghost ship that had left its shadow in the sandy soil. This was no modest boat like the one that the Fallward chieftain had been buried in – it was about 27 metres (90 feet) long.

News of the discovery did not take long to spread, and the archaeological establishment descended on Sutton Hoo. The gold that Mrs Pretty's nephew had predicted to be at the site soon came to the light of day. A curator from the British Museum was met at the local railway station by one of the expanded team of archaeologists, who showed him a buckle, one of a number of pieces of jewellery that had emerged. It belonged to a type well known to both the curator and the excavators – it was clearly Anglo-Saxon and had been made in the seventh century.

Then a shield, a large silver dish, a bronze bowl of east Mediterranean origin, more silver bowls, gold and garnet shoulder-clasps, a sword and a mysterious sceptre – the cultural treasures of the Anglo-Saxons came thick and fast out of the mound. In what must have been one of the most hectic periods of excavation in the history of British archaeology, over 263 artefacts made from numerous materials were found over a period of seventeen days.

The mound had revealed many of its secrets. A large ship had been buried in its midst and in the ship itself a trove of Anglo-Saxon riches of unparalleled beauty and craftsmanship. In later times the Vikings buried the great and the good in ships and covered them with mounds. Mound 1, belonging to an earlier period, seemed to foreshadow this tradition but there was something missing: a body. Initially, this led some observers to believe that there had never been one and that the site, rather than marking a burial, was actually a memorial to a person who had died elsewhere. Perhaps it commemorated someone who had been lost at sea.

The senior archaeologists who had been excavating Sutton Hoo in 1939 thought otherwise. Sandy soils having a high acidic content (like that at Sutton Hoo) often tend to destroy all traces of skeletons, and so the absence of evidence was not evidence of absence. The British Museum gave the onerous responsibility for publishing the reports concerning Sutton Hoo to Rupert Bruce-Mitford; these would eventually run to nearly two and a half thousand pages. Bruce-Mitford left no stone unturned in his efforts to track down any possible traces of a body in the mound. He even went to the Pathology Museum of Guy's Hospital in order to look at the evidence of a victim of the notorious killer John George Haigh. By putting her in a bath full of acid, Haigh had attempted to destroy all traces of his victim, a Mrs Durand-Deacon, and only her heels survived. Bruce-Mitford concluded that something similar, but less sinister, had happened to a body in the mound. The interminably slow effects of the acidic soil had completely disposed of all traces of the body except a slight but recognisable difference in the level of phosphates in one area, which would have been where a body would have once lain.

Naming the King

It is now universally accepted that this was indeed a burial and obviously that of a highly important person – a great ship, full of treasure and fit for a king. The next question was inevitably to try to identify who it was who had been buried. Hector Munro Chadwick had an incomparable knowledge of the Anglo-Saxon period, and when he visited Sutton Hoo on 18 August 1939 he immediately gave his verdict: this was the final resting-place of King Raedwald, who had ruled East Anglia from about 599 until he died in or around the year 625.

Bede tells us that he was a powerful ruler who once controlled the whole region south of the river Humber. He was a king at a crucial time in history. England was on the cusp of conversion to Christianity. Some of his contemporaries had already gone over to the new religion, while others held tenaciously to their pagan traditions. These dual forces of tradition and innovation pulled Raedwald first one way, then the other. While he was visiting the court of Aethelbert of Kent, which had already succumbed to the Christian faith, he was persuaded of the virtues of the new religion. His 'conversion' was to be short-lived, though. On his return home, both his wife and his advisers dissuaded him from his new-found faith. He wanted to have the best of both worlds, and set up twin altars in his place of worship: one to the old gods and one to the Christian God. This compromise must have proved to be untenable – his pagan followers would have disapproved and the Christians certainly would not have accepted that their God would share power with what they saw as evil spirits and effigies of idolatry.

What evidence is there to support Chadwick's emphatic selection of Raedwald as the focus of the Sutton Hoo ship burial? Martin Carver has summarised the key arguments in favour of this identification. Firstly, the contents of the burial chamber are the richest treasure to be found from this period, and so it is fitting to link them with a royal grave. Sutton Hoo is in East Anglia, therefore a king of East Anglia would be the most obvious candidate. The artefacts from the mound were indisputably seventh century in date, and so a seventh-century king would obviously fit the bill. The burial was in Mound 1, the largest of the mounds at the site and so likely to be the resting-place of the most powerful king of the time. Raedwald as controller of much of England again seems the most logical. The artefacts seemingly displayed both Christian and pagan symbolism – both of which, as we have already noted, appealed to him.

Concerning the dating of the burial, there was still some fine tuning to be done. Various exotic items in the treasure would help to establish it more accurately. An impressive silver dish was marked with a stamp of a Byzantine emperor named Anastasius I, who reigned from 491 to 518. This meant that the burial could not be earlier than 491. Radiocarbon dating of a piece of wood and a lump of wax gave, with its usual margin of error, dates that were not precise enough to pin the date down accurately enough.

A number of Merovingian coins that had been minted in France seemed like a better bet. At first there was some confusion and they were dated to somewhere between 650 and 660. This was accepted for some time and seemed to put Raedwald completely out of the picture. But in 1960 a French coin expert corrected this by stating that the latest date that could be put on the coins was around 625 – the date of Raedwald's death. It is because of the very convincing nature of these numerous arguments in favour of Raedwald being the man who was buried in

Mound 1 that this identification has been generally accepted. We cannot be 100 per cent sure, but the odds are very strongly in its favour.

Mound 1, the biggest of the mounds and the location of the great ship burial, dominates Sutton Hoo but there are another seventeen mounds of various sizes at the site. It is believed that they were raised in order to bury other prominent members of the Anglo-Saxon aristocracy. They are a far cry from the more modest burials of most cemeteries of the time. Most of those buried at Sutton Hoo were men, but at least one wealthy woman and a few children were also laid to rest there. Mound 17 contained the remains of the burial of a young man laid to rest with his horse. A young person who was buried in Mound 5 had suffered a violent death, the skull cut by repeated blows from a sword. There was even another ship burial inside Mound 2, although on a smaller scale – the vessel was about 20 metres (65 feet) long. A number of the mounds remain deliberately unexcavated, the archaeologists having chosen to leave this task to future generations who will have many new kinds of scientific techniques unknown and unsuspected by their counterparts today.

It is quite probable that the other mound burials once contained the bodies of other members of the lineage of Raedwald and his close associates. It has been suggested that leaders both before and after the time of Raedwald may have been buried at Sutton Hoo. From the middle of the sixth century the East Angles had been ruled by the Wuffinga dynasty. The first ruler of East Anglia in this line was Wehha, whose son Wuffa gave his name to the dynastic house. Descent from the god Woden was also claimed by these pagan kings. It has been surmised that Mound 5 contained the mortal remains of Wehha, Mound 6 Wuffa (died 578), and Mound 7 Wuffa's son Tyttla (died 599).

Certainly there was no shortage of sudden and often violent deaths during and after the reign of Raedwald. The clashes between kingdoms were often bloody. Aethelfrith, the king of Northumbria, ejected a troublesome prince of a rival royal house named Edwin from his kingdom. After wandering through other kingdoms, Edwin found his way to the court of Raedwald in East Anglia. Aethelfrith regretted letting Edwin go and was now anxious to put an end to his potential rival for the Northumbrian throne. He tried to both bribe Raedwald with silver and gold and coerce him with intimations of war in order to have Edwin handed over.

Raedwald decided that the best course of action was simply to attack Aethelfrith – and to do so rapidly. Caught by surprise, Aethelfrith was killed and his forces defeated, and Edwin was installed as the new king of Northumbria. But this change of power was not gained without Raedwald paying a heavy price, as one of his sons died in the conflict. After Raedwald's own death another of his sons came to power, only to be murdered soon after. Raedwald's son (or perhaps stepson) and nephew were both killed while fighting the forces of Penda, the king of Mercia.

There would have been little problem in filling the cemetery at Sutton Hoo, but it seems that the time around 650 marked the shift away from pagan burial, and subsequent kings of the dynasty were buried in churches or Christian graveyards.

The Death Throes of a Pagan World

The sheer size of the ship and the wealth exhibited by the treasure from Mound 1 makes Sutton Hoo one of the most remarkable finds to have been unearthed in Britain. But what does it all mean? Why had the king been buried in a boat and why had so many things been deposited in the ground? Martin Carver has suggested that in a society that was not literate, such as the one that buried its dead at Sutton Hoo, this was one of the ways they could make statements that a literate people would have written down. The various mounds and their contents are statements that would have been read as easily as later peoples would read a book. The language of the mounds and the material culture they contained would have been well understood at the time. Today we cannot read it so easily, but it is not entirely unintelligible.

The single most obvious feature of the Mound 1 burial is the presence of the ship. Boat burial, as we have seen, was also practised at Fallward but the centre of such a tradition is further to the north. As far back as the Bronze Age, the people of Scandinavia would bury their dead inside a group of upright stones in the shape of a ship. Long after Sutton Hoo the Vikings would continue the ancient traditions of boat burial. The Britons before the Anglo-Saxon era do not seem to have done so, and we can see Raedwald's burial as a statement aligning him with Scandinavia.

Carver also makes analogies between the time of Sutton Hoo and our own era. Britain still finds itself in two minds concerning greater integration with the rest of Europe. It is surely no accident when the British sometimes refer to continental Europe as simply Europe, almost as if we are outside it. The desire for autonomy and the maintaining of long-established tradition vies with the advantages of new trading possibilities in a changing political landscape. For Raedwald and other leaders of the time Christianity offered the chance to forge new alliances with continental leaders and all that went with that. Paganism offered the sense of security that the familiar provides. His vacillations on this issue eventually cost him and his ilk dear. As Carver put it:

> *Whether or not the occupants of East Anglia were Scandinavians in body, they were Scandinavians in soul, members of a North Sea culture for which Christianity meant ideological conquest by France and a political wrong turn.*

Politically the people of East Anglia were North Sea people, adherents to free enterprise and small trading settlements as opposed to the urban network and the state. This was and still is an area of profound political controversy in northern Europe. Archaeology is beginning to suggest some of the pagan mental strife which has gone unrecorded by documents largely composed for Christians by Christians.

The actual funeral must have been a great drama in itself. The preparation of the mound, the inviting of guests from near and far to pay their respects – some of the foreign items found in the burial chamber may have been brought to Sutton Hoo by foreign allies and envoys. To the archaeologist, the Sutton Hoo ship burial is as important a testimony to the richness of Anglo-Saxon life as is *Beowulf*. The poem spoke of the sumptuous trappings of a king buried with his treasure under a mound visible from the sea. Before Sutton Hoo was excavated, it was still believed that the Anglo-Saxon world that followed that of the Romans in Britain was a squalid, primitive period that deserved to be dubbed the Dark Ages. Sutton Hoo showed that there was much factual as well as poetic truth in *Beowulf*. Treasures described in the poem, which had so long been put down to poetic licence, were not just the product of a rich imagination – they were buried in the mounds of Sutton Hoo. The Scandinavian links are there both in the poem and the site. Not just the tradition of ship burial itself, but many of the objects from the chamber, bear the unmistakable hallmark of Swedish influence.

Bold, spectacular and even ostentatious, the great theatrical statement of Sutton Hoo was a final fling, the death throes of a pagan dynasty. For about a hundred years this royal and aristocratic cemetery was a centre of power and a focus for the glamour of the regime that came to be buried in it. Paganism was on the wane and it would soon be consigned to history.

Chapter Fifteen

TREASURES OF A WARRIOR KING

Many archaeologists maintained the belief that after the Romans left northern Europe the material culture of the barbarians plummeted... the discovery of a royal grave at Sutton Hoo, packed with a magnificent range of possessions, had a startling effect on the interpretation of Anglo-Saxon culture.

Angela Evans, curator of the Sutton Hoo treasure

At Sutton Hoo, each of the items in the incomparable trove of heathen treasure was a testament to the complex nature of the period. The regional and international connections that Raedwald maintained are recorded by their very presence in his burial chamber. Each has its own story to tell concerning the technical abilities, the artistic power and the aspirations of late Anglo-Saxon paganism on the verge of extinction. Besides the ship itself and the magnificent sword – such important symbols that they are merit the following chapter to themselves – a host of other objects that make up the finds from the burial chamber highlight the numerous roles that this Dark Ages king would have played: the warrior-king, the bountiful host in his great hall, the civic and ceremonial leader of his subjects and, more sobering, as simply a man.

A Man of Many Parts

Many of the objects from Sutton Hoo are on display in the British Museum. Angela Evans is the curator in charge of the artefacts and, as such, she has inevitably given much thought to what this remarkable collection of Anglo-Saxon objects might have meant in its own time. She believes that while we may view it as an inventory of all the things it was believed that the king might need in the afterlife, it also had a very worldly statement to make. It was an expression of disposable wealth: the means by which the Wuffinga dynasty to which he belonged could very publicly demonstrate their power and their continuing potency: 'The king is dead – long live the king'. It was a material sacrifice that they patently believed they could afford. It was worth its political weight in gold.

The most important object that manifests the king's status as commander of his armed forces and a warrior in his own right is, of course, the sword. Other weapons were placed in the burial: six spears, three barbed throwing spears known as angons, and an unusual iron instrument that combined the attributes of an axe and a hammer. His defensive equipment consisted of a coat of mail, a shield and a magnificent helmet. The mail was strong but flexible. It was made of links a mere 8 mm (a third of an inch) thick and strengthened with copper. The lime wood shield, badly damaged, is thought to have had a diameter of a little less than a metre (3 feet). In style and manufacture, it has been linked to

Swedish workmanship. It was fitted with ornate trapping, suggesting that it was more for show than use.

The helmet has become perhaps the best known of all the objects from the burial chamber. When it was excavated, it was in a very poor state of repair and it is only through the great skill and ingenuity of its restorers that its full glory has been brought back to the light of day. The cap was made from a single piece of iron, to which were attached two iron side flaps and a neck guard at the back. On top of this iron core there was a layer of a mixture of tin and bronze, which gave it a silvery colour. The restorers believe the inside of the helmet was probably lined with leather for comfort. A steel replica was made by the Armouries of the Tower of London. Angela Evans told me of a rather unexpected aspect of the helmet. At a conference in the 1970s, Rupert Bruce-Mitford wore the replica helmet and, despite his having a very soft voice, a booming and stentorian sound emanated from it. It must have been a very dramatic sound in Anglo-Saxon times.

The helmet was divided into a number of panels that were decorated with four different designs. One of these is known as 'the fallen warrior scene'. It depicts a warrior on horseback with his spear and shield trampling on an enemy clad in mail who is stabbing the horse with his sword. This scene is by no means unique to this helmet, but is a traditional northern European motif that dates back to an earlier period. This motif, along with some of the technical features of its making, have led to the helmet being linked to Scandinavian and, more specifically and in line with the shield, Swedish influences.

One of the most complex and beautifully crafted examples of the Anglo-Saxon love for the ambiguous image is to be found on the front part of the helmet. The iron crest is in the form of a snake inlaid with silver, and is finished with animal heads in gilt bronze, the eyes of garnet. The eyebrows also terminate in gilt-bronze

heads, this time being those of boars. These features in conjunction with the cast bronze nose and moustache make up another
co-existent image – that of a bird in flight. The tail is the moustache, its body the nose, its wings the eyebrows, and its beak
confronts the mouth of the serpent descending from the top of the
helmet. Today we can only admire the workmanship and artistic
power of this composite image. In its own time it surely had many
meanings that we will never be able to grasp.

Other artefacts from the burial show the importance of feasts
and hospitality in the Anglo-Saxon world – the king certainly
entertained in style. Three cauldrons were found in the burial
chamber; the largest, made from a single piece of bronze, had a
diameter of 70 cm (28 inches) and held about 100 litres. It hung
from a wonderfully wrought chain nearly 3.5 metres (11 feet 6
inches) long, which was replicated in the 1970s by H. C. Landon,
a master blacksmith who, with the help of his brother, completed
a complex and demanding task few in his trade could have
managed. This was no plain and simple chain: it had different
elements, each with its own intricate and distinct patterning. The
length of the chain gives us an idea of the height of Raedwald's
hall. The chain would have been attached to a cross-beam that
must have been at least 5 metres (about 16 feet) from the ground.

More ostentatious than these robust cauldrons and chain was
the sixteen-piece set of silver that came from the workshops of the
eastern Mediterranean. Angela Evans has surmised that they may
have been a diplomatic gift. The largest piece, the silver dish with
the stamp of emperor Anastasius I, has a diameter of just over 72
cm (28 inches). It is possible that a meal might have been placed
on this dish as part of the funeral ceremony. Two silver spoons
found among the king's effects have been seen as evidence of his
dabbling with Christianity. Both have crosses on them and Greek
inscriptions reading respectively *Saulos* and *Paulos*. It is believed by

some that this is a reference to the conversion of St Paul on the road to Damascus.

Beside these imported wares were two drinking horns, objects that epitomise the age-old traditions of the Germanic peoples. Yet these were not simply a pair of rustic vessels but elegant objects decorated with silver-gilt depictions of animals, birds and human faces. A set of bottles of maple wood were found alongside the horns; these were also adorned with finely decorated silver gilt. What their contents were is unknown. Part of a finely made maple-wood lyre also survived, along with a few hairs identified as the remains of a beaver skin bag that once contained it. This six-stringed instrument may once have played music that accompanied recitals of poems and tales such as *Beowulf*.

Along with the sword, the sceptre is perhaps the most enig-matic and fascinating object of them all. It was a symbol of royal power, but much of the subtle symbolism eludes the modern observer who cannot read it in the way it would have been in Raedwald's day. There are four heads at each end; some are bearded, while others are not. It seems clear that these are meant to be the faces of individuals rather than simply uniform heads. They may be representations of earlier members of the Wuffinga lineage. If this is so, then the sceptre has a totemic quality and openly expresses the king's right to rule – his dynastic origins and the tacit endorsement of his ancestors. Between the two sets of heads is a whetstone with four sides. It bears no sign of ever having been used, which strongly hints that it was purely symbolic. Sword-sharpening was a symbol of the king as warrior and his ability to summon his men to arms. At the top of the scep-tre there is a bronze stag with antlers. The sceptre as a whole is a unique item and may represent a fusion of diverse styles of barbar-ian art. It owes nothing to Roman influence. Whetstones with carved heads at the end are known in the Celtic art of Britain, but the other features of the Sutton Hoo sceptre make any direct comparisons impossible.

There are yet other wondrous objects: a matching pair of shoulder-clasps that would have been used to fasten a front and a back leather plate together; a so-called 'purse-lid'; and a large gold belt buckle (weighing over 400 grams/14 ounces). All were part of a set and made to match, wrought as they were from gold, the first two also adorned with garnets. These objects can truly be said to be the work of master craftsmen producing unique and especially commissioned pieces for a very wealthy and powerful client. They are part of the collection on display in the British Museum, and visitors can appreciate for themselves the technical perfection of the craftsmen and the excellent taste displayed by their designs.

For the king and his ilk throughout the ages, personal adornments are one of the best ways to impress subjects and other leaders. These showy items were not ornamental jewellery in the strict sense, as they all had a practical function as part of what seems to have been the king's ceremonial regalia. The lack of wear and tear (including the fact that all the pieces are still mechanically sound) strongly suggests that these items, and by implication the leather and textiles which would also have made up the costume, were used only rarely. This would imply that only on important days or at special events would the king have been dressed in this garb.

Inside the leather purse that was once attached to the 'purse-lid' were thirty-seven small gold coins, three gold blanks and two small bars of gold. As mentioned earlier, all were Merovingian coins from Gaul. This group of coins had clearly been hand-picked for inclusion in the burial as each and every one had come from a different mint. A historian, Philip Grierson, came up with an ingenious explanation for their presence. According to classical mythology, it was necessary to pay the ferryman Charon a small coin (known as an obol) to take you safely across the river Styx to Hades, the land of the dead. For Grierson, the peculiar coin collection from Sutton Hoo had a very similar other-worldly purpose. The thirty-seven coins and the three blanks, making a total of forty, represented the payment to be given to the forty ghostly oarsmen who were to row him to his final destination. The two small bars were likewise to be given to the pilot and helmsman.

As if to remind us that we all have to pay the ferryman, among the great number of exotic, superbly crafted and hugely expensive objects that went into the burial chamber there was a small collection of more humble items. A rough iron lamp containing beeswax and a small clay bottle seem a little incongruous alongside all the ostentatious accoutrements of royalty, but there must have been a reason for their inclusion. Perhaps they had sentimental value to the king who, for all the pomp and circumstance that inevitably ruled much of his life, was on one level a man like any other.

Other less fortunate individuals were to find themselves buried here after the main story of Sutton Hoo, that of the mound burials, was over. The excavations were to reveal the presence of another cemetery on the site that made its way into the archaeological reports as a macabre appendix to the tale. The bodies were not the mass of skeletons and broken bones that are usually found – in fact, only fragments of bone survived. They were encased in sand which, it was soon realised, outlined the shape of the flesh. These were bodies replicated in sand. The postures in which the people had died were bizarre. Martin Carver describes the scene as the excavations of the 'sand bodies' took place:

> *One was kneeling, head to the floor of the grave; one stretched out, hand above the head; another folded forward, another folded back, another sideways; and, strangest of all, one*

splayed out in a hurdling position, accompanied by a wooden object that seemed to belong to an ard or primitive type of plough. Every burial seemed to be different... most... indicated some special abuse of the individual.

Burial 24 had his head at right angles to the vertebral column, and teeth, hand and wrist had survived to give a tableau that was both ghastly and sad. Those who saw it all came to a similar conclusion and it was soon being referred to as 'the hanged man'.

It seemed that these grisly finds could be evidence for the heathen practice of human sacrifice. The eleventh-century churchman Adam of Bremen reported that the Vikings in Uppsala in Sweden hung bodies of both animals and men in trees as sacrifices to their pagan gods. Might not something similar have occurred at Sutton Hoo? A large pit was discovered and it was surrounded by a number of post-sockets. The archaeologists realised that they were looking at the traces of an ancient gallows. Radiocarbon dating exonerated the pagans: the victims belonged to the Christian era.

The graves had been hastily dug during the eighth to eleventh centuries, by which time the site had become an execution ground. The Christians who succeeded the pagan elite had no reverence for this burial ground, and reduced its once high status to that of a common place of execution. Sutton Hoo, sacred to the pagans, was unhallowed ground to the Church. Perhaps persistent pagans who refused to accept Christianity were done away with here, when folk memories of its now despised pagan background were still rife.

Chapter Sixteen

LAST RITES OF A PAGAN WORLD

No ship have I known so nobly dight
with weapons of war and weeds of battle,
with breastplate and blade...

Beowulf, from the Prelude (translated by Frances B. Grummere)

Of all the marvellous artefacts found in the burial of King Raedwald at Sutton Hoo, which help us in our attempt to enter this pagan world, the two most significant are the ship and the sword. The ship contained both the body of the king and all his most prized worldly possessions, while the sword is the very symbol of his kingship.

The King's Ship

We have seen in the story of *Beowulf* that the ship was the means by which the dead hero or king is transported to the other world. The ghostly traces of the Sutton Hoo ship that were left in the depths of the mound remind us that not only the king but his vessel have long gone to that shadowy realm. The ship not only served the king as his vehicle in death, but there is clear proof that it had also been used in life. Even though no timber from the ship survives, the archaeologists could tell from the pattern of the rivets that one or two parts of it had been repaired.

It was the king's own vessel, and Richard Darrah, an expert on Anglo-Saxon woodworking (who helped in the reconstruction of the village of West Stow), has aptly described it as the Air Force One of its day. It was Darrah who explained to me the importance of understanding the role of wood in Anglo-Saxon times. The building of ships was part of a wider woodworking tradition which it is important to understand first.

Wood, as a material, pervaded Anglo-Saxon life. It was used not only to build houses and ships but also to make fences to keep livestock from wandering off, bowls to eat from, and shafts for spears. Almost every element of life needed wood in some form or another. Stone, on the other hand, was not an important or frequently used material in early Anglo-Saxon times. Since wood, unlike stone, seldom survives for archaeologists to discover, the remains of their culture seem impoverished – not due to their own shortcomings but merely because of their chosen material. As we have seen, this has affected the way that the Anglo-Saxons have been perceived by creating the false impression that they were less able than other cultures.

One way to gain an insight into their woodworking traditions is by means of experimental archaeology. This involves trying to reproduce some of the objects that people have made in the past in order to understand their techniques and skills – an aim amply demonstrated by the West Stow reconstruction. Richard Darrah, as a skilled woodworker, obviously understands his material. When he studies some of the Anglo-Saxon wooden objects that have survived, he is able to tell, purely by the tool marks on the pieces, how the ancient carpenters achieved their results. He told me that, for him, it is as easy as reading a letter. He can tell the difference between the work of a competent and patient woodworker and a lazy or careless one.

He can also interpret aspects of the Sutton Hoo ship even though no timber from it has survived. The dimensions can be worked out by the rows of iron rivets that remained in place for 1,400 years. The gaps between the rows of rivets are approximately 30 cm (12 inches), which means the planks used must have been about 35 cm (14 inches) wide. A large tree (over 5 metres or 16 feet) would be needed in order to dress down such planks to the required degree of flatness. Large trees were extremely important economic assets and it seems certain that the wealthy and the powerful would have been in control of such timber reserves. Cutting down trees did not just need an axe (the Anglo-Saxons of this time did not have saws), it also needed the permission of whoever owned it.

Even after obtaining a sufficiently large tree, plank after plank would have had to be laid down and all of them would have had to be curved over their length to make the actual shape of the ship. Building such a boat is, in Darrah's opinion, like doing a three-dimensional jigsaw puzzle. It is all the more skilful in that no paper plans of any sort would have been used by the Anglo-Saxon boat builders. The whole enterprise would have been impossible without great craftsmanship, organisation and experience. The Sutton Hoo ship was no ordinary vessel – it was almost certainly a royal vessel and as such would have been one of the best boats of its time. It is possible to calculate its length as just under 27 metres (90 feet); its width was 4.5 metres (14 feet). It would probably have been able to carry a hundred people.

Just as the house-building techniques of the Anglo-Saxons have been under-valued, so too have their ship-building skills.

Edwin Gifford, a retired engineer, naval architect and expert on sailing technologies, and his wife Joyce have long been of this opinion. Despite the indisputable fact that the Anglo-Saxons arrived in Britain by boat, there has been a tenacious prejudice that they were not great seafarers like the Vikings of later times. This is a belief that the Giffords have found hard to uproot. They saw the Sutton Hoo ship as the means to demonstrate the nautical skills of the Anglo-Saxon period.

The practical capacities of the vessel had originally been considered by a naval officer, Lieutenant-Commander J. K. D. Hutchinson, who had been assigned by the Science Museum to lead a team to work alongside the archaeologists in the original excavations. Due to the outbreak of war in 1939, he had to abandon his research before it was complete and written up in its entirety. Unfortunately, he died in the war and much of his work was lost. As a consequence, no one with the necessary expertise was to study the Sutton Hoo ship for many decades to come.

It seemed that the Anglo-Saxon boat builders were to remain in the shadow of the Viking longships that were better known and better understood. It was thought that the Anglo-Saxons were incapable of sailing and that all their vessels were essentially rowing boats. To the trained eye of Edwin Gifford, there are certain differences between the fourth-century Nydam boat from southern Denmark and the Sutton Hoo ship of the early seventh century that can shed light on this debate. As a rowing vessel, the Nydam boat has a steering paddle which is not strongly mounted and stern frames that are not strengthened. The Sutton Hoo ship has heavy framing at the stern, which is necessary only for a sailing vessel. Its powerful mounted rudder would also have been superfluous on a rowing boat. The very shape of the Sutton Hoo ship also indicated to Gifford that it was a vessel that could be sailed as well as rowed. Its leaf-like shape is more generally associated with sailing vessels rather than a simple rowing galley, which typically has nearly parallel sides.

Despite all these strong arguments, there is no concrete material evidence to prove that the early Anglo-Saxons had sailing ships. Neither sails nor masts survive, yet there is no reason to think that the Anglo-Saxons did not sail even before the time when the Sutton Hoo boat was made. John Haywood, another expert on navigation in the Dark Ages, cites a number of Roman sources that mention Saxons and sails in the same breath. One such source is a letter written by Sidonius Apollinaris, a Roman aristocrat who lived in Gaul, and dating from around the year 473 in which he mentions the Saxons unfurling their sails as they set out on their voyage home.

Some of the Saxons and other Germanic tribes were considered highly dangerous pirates by the Romans. They raided in a similar fashion to their later cousins, the Vikings. Despite their long interaction with the Roman world, the Anglo-Saxons not only built their houses according to different principles but they also built their ships in a different style. Their tradition developed somewhere in the southern Baltic region among their own Germanic people and owed nothing to the Romans.

The Giffords decided to build a half-size replica of the boat to test its capabilities and to demonstrate that it had been designed by its makers as a sailing ship. The resulting vessel was named *Sæ Wylfing*, which translates as 'the sea wolf's she-cub'. The ship was rigged with a square sail of a Roman type that would have been familiar to the Anglo-Saxons. The ship has reached speeds of over 7 knots and in smooth water can achieve one and a half knots direct to windward. It has been shown to be more than capable of being navigated in shallow waters.

It is 12 metres (40 feet) long and so even though it is considerably smaller than the original Sutton Hoo boat it is perfectly at

Garnet and gold shoulder-clasp.

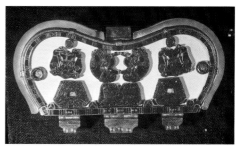

The 'sceptre' found in the burial
mound, symbol of royal power.

*The 'purse-lid', made of gold,
garnets and millefiori glass.*

The imprint of the Sutton Hoo ship in the sand, as found in the 1930s.

*Lindisfarne,
or Holy Island,
Northumberland,
England; a view
across the water
from a 1904
postcard.*

*Illumination from
the Lindisfarne
Gospels, page
facing the Gospel
of St. John.*

Viking ship in a boat shed, Oslo, Norway, 1914.

Oseberg ship burial finds, Viking Ship Museum, Oslo (clockwise from right)*: 'Baroque' animal head post; wood-carving of a man's head on the Oseberg cart; monstrous animal wood-carving from a sleigh.*

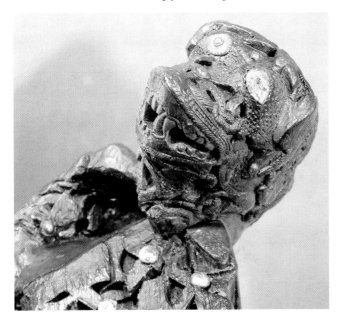

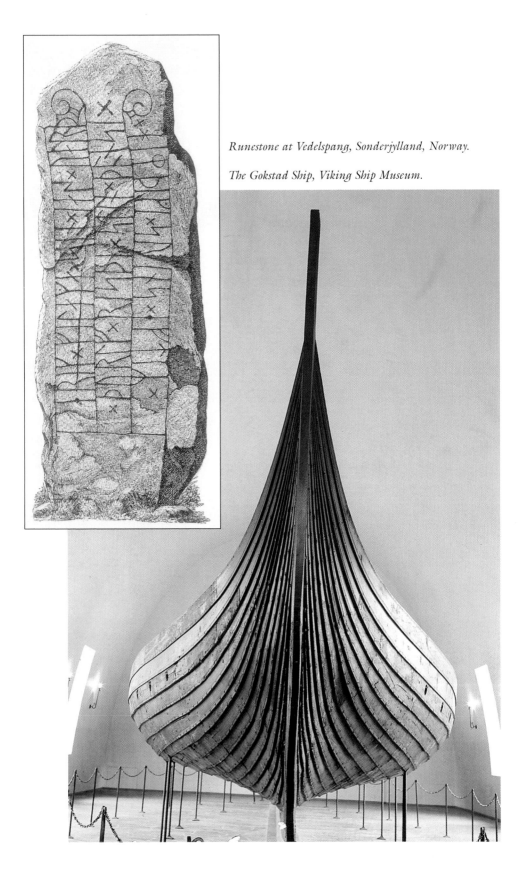

Runestone at Vedelspang, Sonderjylland, Norway.

The Gokstad Ship, Viking Ship Museum.

Viking burial sites with stones forming the shape of a ship at (top) *Runsa and* (left) *Blomsholm, Sweden.*

The author with the crew of a replica Viking ship in Gotland.

Picture stone, a memorial depicting scenes from this life and the afterlife, found under the floor of Ardre church, Gotland, Sweden; date 700-800 AD.

Sixth or seventh century bronze statuette of a Buddha (8.4cm high) from northern India, found in Helgö, Sweden.

The biggest Scandinavian example of an artefact known as a bracteate, suspended from the neck and worn on the chest as a magical amulet, Asum parish, Skåne region of southern Sweden.

Arab astronomers using scientific instruments to measure angles.

The ancient mosque at Cordoba, now a Catholic cathedral.

ease in rough weather. Some Finnish friends of the Giffords sailed her across the North Sea in three days without any problems. Gifford himself estimates that a journey from Sutton Hoo to the north of Sweden would have taken three weeks, allowing for some days waiting for good weather. The crew would have kept themselves insulated from cold by rubbing animal fat on their bodies.

Gifford took me out on the Solent and showed me just how efficient and elegant she was when sailing or being rowed (by his crew of suitably attired members of an Anglo-Saxon re-enactment society). He proudly refers to his ship as a thoroughbred and rightly so: its manoeuvrability, speed and reliability make it a great vessel to sail in – and so, by association, would the original Sutton Hoo ship have been. In the course of their various trials, the Giffords also discovered how to land properly in the surf. If everyone on board simply moves aft just before you land, then the boat will sail right up the beach and you arrive dry shod. This turned out to be very simple as was demonstrated when we landed. It dispels the cliché that such crews had to wade up to their chests in water before engaging in battle.

The replica enabled the Giffords to reach this conclusion about the Sutton Hoo ship and the similar vessels that must have existed at the same time:

> *They were not at an intermediate stage of development by shipwrights searching blindly in the Dark Ages, but were fully resolved designs, difficult to improve upon even with today's knowledge. This programme of building, sailing and testing of half-scale models has expanded our understanding of their performance and seaworthiness from an intuitive appreciation to a conviction based on measurement, which must substantially change the generally held views on Anglo-Saxon seafaring.*

According to calculations by Edwin Gifford, the full-scale original could have travelled at speeds of between 10 and 12 knots. At such speeds, the king and his entourage could leave a place one day and be 150 miles away by the next. They, if not their crew, could arrive refreshed and ready for whatever task lay ahead, whether fighting or diplomacy. The same journey on horseback overland would not only have taken far longer but it would also have been much more tiring. It is easy to agree with Richard Darrah's description of the ship as the Air Force One of its day.

The Giffords' replica has allowed reasonably accurate estimates of journey times for the Sutton Hoo original. Suffolk to Canterbury was a half-day trip, as was Canterbury to France. From Canterbury up to York was a two-day journey. The key role of boats in the Anglo-Saxon world should not be underestimated. Places that were readily accessible by boat (whether up the east coast to the north of England or over the sea to the low countries) were more likely to be part of the political and economic landscape than places far inland and to the west. The speed of Raedwald's vessel may have had a bearing on his surprise attack and defeat of Aethelfrith in Northumbria, and was most probably the means by which he travelled to Aethelbert's court in Kent where he was tempted to become a Christian. The rivers and the seas played a greater role in Anglo-Saxon life than the roads that had once been so important during the Roman occupation of Britain.

The Cutting Edge of Anglo-Saxon Technology

One of the king's most precious and personal belongings was his ornate pattern-welded sword that would have been placed by his side. The blade itself was made from bundles of iron rods twisted left and right by a master swordsmith to create a distinctive herringbone design. The blade would have been kept bright and clean by the oiled lamb's wool lining of its wooden scabbard. The hilt and the scabbard were adorned with gold and garnets, two precious materials that were used to make other objects which were also part of the king's regalia.

Archaeologists can only tell us so much about this magnificent sword. I was fortunate enough to gain a very different perspective on its significance from a modern exponent of this art who can read a sword like a book. Hector Cole was commissioned to make an authentic replica of the Sutton Hoo sword in his Wiltshire forge. Not only was he required to make a finished product as close in appearance to the original as possible, but also to make it using traditional techniques like those the Anglo-Saxon smiths themselves would have used.

He classes himself as a mere novice in comparison to the Anglo-Saxon swordsmiths, maintaining that when he travels to see their works on display at the British Museum he comes away feeling like a rank amateur. Only when you have seen him at work can you understand how hard he is being on himself – his skills in this field today are highly sought after.

Much of his work involves being commissioned by archaeologists to reproduce as precisely as possible artefacts from various periods. The replica of the Sutton Hoo sword that he has made is one of the many objects he has reproduced from the original work of Anglo-Saxon smiths. When undertaking such work, he is always careful to record everything. He records the weight of the material before he starts, the number of times it goes in the fire, the amount of fuel used, the debris from both the anvil and the forge and the time taken for the completing of each part of the process. This way, the archaeologists get a full record of what happens when someone makes an Anglo-Saxon sword.

Hector Cole embodies the truth that the ironworker has to have an affinity with the material. Control of the fire is one of the keys to the art. A smith is able to 'read' the different kinds of sparks that the fire gives off; they tell him when his material is ready to weld. Making a blade requires skill and concentration, as the slightest mistake can result in failure. The heat has to penetrate to the core of the metal, but the danger for the smith is that the cutting edges will burn away before the centre is hot enough to weld. If that happens, then the blade has been ruined and the metal has to be recycled for some lesser use like making spears.

Most men in Anglo-Saxon times had a knife and a spear but not a sword. The sword was a high prestige weapon because it was so expensive to make. It was not just the amount of high quality metal required in its making that made it beyond the reach of most Anglo-Saxon men. It was also the time that it would take even a master sword smith to make a single blade. An Anglo-Saxon sword blade uses four different types of iron, each with its own specific function in creating the finished product. It was long thought that high-quality steel was unknown to the Anglo-Saxons, but more recent studies and experimental sword making has challenged this assumption.

The quality of the Anglo-Saxon swords has, in Hector Cole's expert opinion, been grossly underestimated (as we have seen was also the case with their house- and ship-building abilities). He believes that they were making blades of the same quality 600 years before the Japanese Samurai blades. The essence of a sword blade is that it will not break but will take a sharp edge. The Anglo-Saxon blade was fearsome – when sharpened, it could literally cut a man in two. There is one recorded example of someone cleaving his opponent from his collar bone right through to his hip.

The swirling patterns of the best Saxon swords are an aesthetic by-product of the technological improvements sought in the ceaseless quest for a stronger and more effective weapon. In folding over the metal, a stronger blade is forged and also there is a pattern that emerges as a consequence of this twisting of the metal.

The herringbone design of the Sutton Hoo sword is one of a number of possible finishes known from the Anglo-Saxon world.

Despite their great cost, swords were often buried with their owners, as at Sutton Hoo. Rather surprisingly, there is little or no evidence that they were dug up again by thieves. In ancient Egypt many of the pharaohs' tombs were looted within weeks if not days of being sealed despite numerous precautions. Some belief or taboo seems to have prevented the Anglo-Saxons from such grave robbing. Unlike most other weapons, swords were sometimes believed to have almost an identity of their own; they were very personal pieces of equipment and were often given a name – an earlier chapter mentions the legend of Attila's sword and the broad parallels with the Excalibur story. As swords were often surrounded by a supernatural aura, it was perhaps fear of the consequences that let the swords and their owners rest in peace.

The smith, like the alchemist, was himself the stuff of magic and legend. In later times skilled smiths were rumoured to be in league with the devil and their forges seen as miniature infernos. I asked Hector Cole whether he thought the old smiths themselves saw any spiritual significance in what they were doing. He replied:

> *I don't think that the smiths would give it such a significance but the general populace would because it's magic. You see something that is, to most people a very resilient material suddenly become plastic. It is being shaped at the will of the smith. Then it becomes a rigid piece again. Then to have the patterning in it as well – you know that's magic, isn't it? You see the pattern come out, you'll see it is magic.*

Not all swords were buried with their owners. The quality of some blades meant that they continued to be in service generation after generation, while their hilts changed according to need or fashion.

Some blades that were made in the eighth and ninth centuries have been found in swords with hilts from the eleventh or twelfth century. The average Anglo-Saxon village blacksmith would have been able to produce the various utensils and other prerequisites of daily life – knives, axes, nails, chains for hanging pots above the fire, shears for fleecing sheep, needles for sewing, and so on. But the making of a sword required much greater expertise and specialist knowledge. The makers of the Sutton Hoo sword and other masterpieces from the Anglo-Saxon forges must have been highly sought after and highly valued in their societies. Like the master shipbuilders they were the most skilled exponents of their craft.

When Raedwald took his precious sword with him to the afterlife, borne in his great ship, much of the pagan independence of the Anglo-Saxons died with him. Many of his contemporaries had already converted to the Christian faith and the rest would soon follow in their footsteps. Yet the force of pagan northern Europe was not yet spent. The Scandinavian influence that we have seen both in *Beowulf* and at Sutton Hoo was to come to the fore again with the Vikings, whose world we will soon explore. The arts and crafts of the Anglo-Saxons were also to be retained and not lost in the process of conversion to Christianity. Many of the achievements of the pagan era were not obliterated but transformed under the sign of the cross.

Part Three

NORTHERN
LIGHTS

Chapter Seventeen

THE TWIN MONASTERIES

*The holy man had deliberately chosen 'anti-culture' –
the neighbouring desert, the nearest mountain crags.
In a civilisation identified exclusively with town
life, the monks had committed the absurd –
they had made a city in the desert.*

Peter Brown, *The World of Late Antiquity*

A new kind of force was sweeping across the northern world. Men with neither weapons nor wives were threatening the very survival of kings and warriors. They were Christian monks who saw themselves as wounding the body of Satan every time that they put pen to vellum. They truly believed that the pen was mightier than the sword. Their goal was to destroy the heathen and barbarian world with the teachings of the Bible and the 'civilising' force of the written word. These poor and celibate monks must have seemed very strange to the barbarians. Their extreme asceticism had no counterpart in a pagan Anglo-Saxon world. In order to understand how monasticism exerted a powerful influence on both the sovereigns and subjects of Britain, we must seek out its origins.

Monks and Missionaries

It is to Egypt in the latter part of the third century AD that the beginnings of monasticism can be traced. Who the first person to follow this path was we do not know, but St Anthony (*c.* 250–355) has gone down in history as its founding father. Anthony was immortalised by his biographer Athanasius, the patriarch of Alexandria, who wrote his life's story shortly after he died. By the time Anthony was eighteen years old, both of his parents had died. On hearing the gospel, he took literally the admonition to give up all one's worldly ties to follow in the footsteps of Christ.

As Christ had gone into the wilderness, so Anthony decided to live in a tomb at the edge of the desert and afterwards in a derelict desert fort where he spent twenty years in self-mortification. He then went back to Alexandria to attempt martyrdom in protest at the persecution of Christians, but when the persecution subsided he returned to the desert to die, supposedly at the age of 105. He had spent over seventy of those years in the wilderness.

Despite his desires, Anthony found himself confronted by the problem that was to plague other pious hermits in the future. His very piety and example inevitably attracted followers eager for his guidance. The further he moved into the solitude of the desert and the more extreme his privations became, the more attractive an exemplar he became. Anthony, as an uncompromising hermit, did not want to formally organise those who were anxious to follow him. He took on only a handful of disciples.

Other spiritual guides such as Pachomius (younger than Anthony but his contemporary) were willing to organise their fellow seekers. Soon groups of up to two or three hundred men were living in villages of their own making. The ideal was that each would, when sufficiently spiritually prepared, go off into the desert on his own to seek salvation. Yet many of the aspirants remained in these villages which were, to all intents and purposes, monastic communities. The members of such communities were under the strict control of a man designated as their spiritual father or *abba*, from which the term 'abbot' derives.

The urban-based civilisation of Roman Britain had not, as we have seen, been simply taken over by the incoming Germanic peoples. The pagan Anglo-Saxon communities had, in the main, their own centres in a world more concerned with communication by river and sea than by road. When the monastic ideals of Egyptian origin reached England, they too were not to be cast in the old Roman mould. A new network of monasteries began to dot the landscape. They were often founded at places seemingly far from the centres of power and influence. But soon these monastic communities themselves became the hub of a new order disseminating their message far and wide. Remote monasteries in Britain became the northern equivalent of the original monastic communities that made up 'a city in the desert'. The monastic way of life was therefore no more dependent on the old Roman system of social organisation than that of the barbarian Anglo-Saxons.

As we have seen, Britain after the Romans was not left entirely at the mercy of the pagan immigrants from the continent. Celtic communities in both Britain and Ireland kept Christianity alive before the conversion of the Anglo-Saxons took place. This provides the background to the founding of the famous monastery of Lindisfarne dealt with in the following chapter.

The conversion of the Anglo-Saxons is thought to have begun in 597 when, with papal approval, Augustine and his forty-strong entourage arrived in Kent. Aethelbert, the king, fearing sorcery, had agreed to meet them only out in the open where their magic would be less baleful. The missionaries were armed with a silver cross and icons of Christ and they chanted in Latin. Soon realising that he had nothing to fear from the Christians, Aethelbert gave them free rein to expand their mission throughout his lands.

Whether to become a Christian was not just a matter of belief for the various Anglo-Saxon kings – it was also a decision that had political ramifications. It meant a dramatic break with tradition and possibly the loss of some pagan allies, but it also offered a number of benefits. To become a part of the Christian Roman Empire meant that one was joining an ever more powerful network that was threatening to engulf older, independent polities. The conversion of all the various Anglo-Saxon kingdoms was inevitable despite some wavering and even backsliding in some parts of the country. In 627 Edwin, who had been crowned king of Northumbria thanks largely to the intervention of Raedwald the pagan king of East Anglia, gave up his heathen ways and was baptised on 12 April, Easter Day. The quote from Bede on the dedication page of this book is said to be a faithful version of the words of one of Edwin's chief advisers, words that convinced the king to become a Christian.

Re-opening the Roads to Rome

The following year, 628, saw the birth of Benedict Biscop into a noble family in Northumbria. Few people today have heard of Benedict Biscop, yet his role in the history of England should not be overlooked. According to Bede, he was an old man in a young man's body and his sober nature disinclined him from the world of sensual pleasures. He grew up to be a valued member of the Northumbrian court and was favoured by the then king Oswiu. Yet he yearned after the spiritual life and decided at the age of twenty-five to give up his status and career and make a pilgrimage to Rome in order to visit the tombs of the Apostles.

Biscop's first port of call was the Roman Christian stronghold of Kent. It was there that he met a fellow Northumbrian noble named Wilfrid. Wilfrid had been a monk at Lindisfarne where, at this time, the Celtic church still held sway. He was dissatisfied with their interpretation of Christianity, which was the very reason he had relocated to Kent. Yet he, like Biscop, wanted to go to the source. It was only the concerns for his safety voiced by the Kentish king Erconbert that had so far prevented him from making what was then the long and hazardous journey to Rome. The king, reassured by the arrival of Biscop, gave his blessing to the two would-be pilgrims to make their way there together.

One of the first places they stopped was Lyons, where the local archbishop convinced Biscop's companion to stay for about a year. Wilfrid later went on to Rome and returned home triumphantly with a copy of the much sought-after *Benedictine Rule*, probably the first to reach the shores of Britain. Biscop decided to press on alone. The route that he took across Europe is not clear but he arrived safely in Rome in 654. He spent about a year there before returning to Britain where he eagerly shared his experiences and new-found knowledge with his Christian brethren. We know next to nothing about the next ten years of his life, but it is likely that he travelled around Italy and Gaul, staying in a number of monasteries and absorbing everything he could. He reappears in the history books in 664, by which time he was back in Northumbria.

Almost straightaway his restless and inquisitive spirit led him to set out once again for Rome. One of the main aims of these early monks was to collect as many books as possible. Books were the lifeblood of the monastic network that stretched across much of Europe. In a Britain that was only just emerging from the non-literate traditions of the pagan kingdoms of the Anglo-Saxons, books were a genuine novelty. Yet they were far more than that. Books opened up a whole new way of transmitting and recording knowledge, not just about the Christian faith and the codes of conduct that monks were expected to follow, but they also provided a window into the classical heritage that had long been obscured. Fuelled by the books and the learning they embodied, the monks from Britain had returned to their homeland and set about changing the intellectual and spiritual landscape for ever.

On his way back from his second trip to Rome in 664–5, Biscop decided to visit a monastic community that had achieved widespread fame for its leading role in the intellectual world which was being formed. Like so many other monasteries, that of St Honorat was deliberately founded far from the centres of commerce and political power. It was built on the small Mediterranean island of Lérins off the coast of Provence. It was there that Biscop finally committed himself for good to the monastic life and received the tonsure. He also decided to call himself Benedict as a mark of respect and allegiance to Benedict of Nursia (*c.* 480–550), the author of the hugely influential *Rule* bearing his name.

Rome called him for a third time in 667, where a twist of fate was to change his life. An entourage had been sent to Rome by Oswiu and Egbert (the new king of Kent). At its head was a man named Wighard who was to be consecrated Archbishop of Canterbury by the Pope. His royal patrons had given Wighard the job of reconciling the Celtic and Roman factions within the English Church. It was only three years since the Synod of Whitby had begun the healing of this divide. Fate decided that Wighard was not to live to see this happen. Both he and his companions died of the plague shortly after arriving in Rome. The Pope sought a replacement for the post of archbishop and selected Theodore of Tarsus as the most suitable candidate. He would, however, need an interpreter to help him in his mission, and Biscop's reputation and experience made him the ideal choice. The two arrived in Canterbury in 671.

Having helped install Theodore, Biscop found himself free again and went off to Rome for a fourth time. Book-buying was still one of his main priorities and he collected numerous volumes on his travels. Before the era of printing, books were not easy to come by. Yet Biscop was part of a vanguard who realised just how important books would become and he managed to obtain many works that would become prohibitively expensive for his counterparts in the next generation. In 673 the great traveller Biscop was back in Northumbria tirelessly pursuing his goal. The new king Egfrith agreed to give him some land on the north bank of the river Wear (Wearmouth) to found a monastery, which was to be named St Peter's. Today Wearmouth is known as Monkwearmouth and is in the heart of Sunderland.

With his king's approval, a monk named Ceolfrith was made prior of St Peter's. Biscop wanted its church to be made of stone, but by this time there were no masons available – when the Romans left Britain they took their building technology with them. So Biscop went off to Gaul to find some, and shortly arrived home with the necessary craftsmen. No sooner was their work under way than he went back again, this time in search of glaziers whose art, known in Roman times, had also been lost in his home-land. The stained glass that was the result adorned the small church windows. It was almost certainly the first glass to be made since the Romans had left Britain.

He made sure that these foreign craftsmen taught the English to work in stone and glass so that future projects could be undertaken by native workmen. Work on the monastery proceeded quickly, allowing Biscop to go back again to Rome, this time with Ceolfrith at his side. In 681 they returned laden with books and all kinds of religious objects for adorning their church – relics, pictures, priestly apparel and icons. He also brought back one of Rome's most distinguished cantors, who taught the monks of Wearmouth how to chant and sing in the Roman style.

The library he had so enthusiastically amassed was the inspiration for the scriptorium, the part of the monastery in which books were written and illuminated. Among his prize possessions were a number of books that he had obtained from the library of a famous Roman monk named Cassiodorus. These works in particular were a major influence on the output of the Northumbrian scriptorium. The most famous is the *Codex Amiatinus* Bible, which now lies in a library in Florence. J. A. Vaughan, a writer on Biscop's life and achievements, describes this mighty tome: 'It is an enormous work, ten inches thick, weighing seventy-five pounds, and requiring two men to carry it.'

Even for the bibliophile of today who has the luxury of being able to admire books from across the globe, it is a timeless work that is truly world-class in its stature. The technical and artistic magnificence of this manuscript was thought to be due to its Italian origin – until just over a century ago. Only careful analysis revealed that while it was greatly influenced by Italian works it was, in fact, made in Britain. It was on its way from Jarrow to be presented to the Pope but it never reached its intended destination. What had misled people for so long was the dishonesty of some Italian monks into whose hands it fell. They rubbed out the original inscription (which revealed its origin) and replaced it with an Italian one.

King Egfrith continued to support the Northumbrian church and endowed it with more land, this time on the south bank of the Wear at Jarrow. A twin monastery and a church, St Paul's, was built in 681, and Ceolfrith was made abbot. Biscop employed his cousin as a co-abbot for Wearmouth, and then set out on his sixth and last journey to Rome. He was to spend four years abroad; when he finally returned he was told that his cousin and many other monks had died of the plague.

After an eventful and fruitful life, Biscop suffered from a debilitating condition that left him bedridden. Despite the fact that he had given his cousin such a prominent post, he could not be accused of nepotism. He left strict instructions that his brother should not take over as abbot of the monastery as he was not sufficiently advanced on the spiritual path. Biscop decided instead that Ceolfrith should be abbot of both the twin monasteries. Shortly after, on 12 January 690, he died.

Biscop had not only set up the twin monasteries and the best library in northern Europe, he had also made them famous far and wide. The organisation of the monasteries was based on the rule of St Benedict and became a model for many others both in Britain and beyond. He had re-established the Roman world in Britain – albeit a different Rome. One thing he cannot have foreseen was that his twin monasteries were also to count among their brethren one of the leading intellectuals of the age, a man who was to be known as the Venerable Bede.

The Father of English History

The life of Bede was very different to that of the widely travelled and tireless Biscop. He was born in 673 in the environs of the monastery at Wearmouth. At the age of seven he entered Biscop's monastery to begin his education. Later in his youth he moved over to the newly founded Jarrow where he was looked after by Ceolfrith. At nineteen he became a deacon, and a priest at the age of thirty. The long-distance travels and worldly experience of Biscop were not to be emulated by Bede who, it seems, travelled no further south than York and no further north than Lindisfarne in his whole life. His whole work was to be wrought in the confines of a 10-foot-square cell and the monastic library.

By 716 the twin monasteries housed about 600 monks and were a thriving centre for learning. Bede established himself as an extremely gifted scholar and eagerly pursued his studies, using the magnificent library that had been so painstakingly founded by

Biscop. The library was well stocked and not just with biblical commentaries and the works of the church fathers. There were texts by diverse classical writers – Pliny, Virgil and Homer among them. There were also works by anonymous Irish scholars which gave Bede access to the records of the Celtic Church. He could read not only Latin but also Greek and Hebrew. His main works were written in Latin but he also wrote poetry in Old English and was even working on a translation of the Gospel of St John into his native language when he died in 735.

In the modern world, the sheer quantity of knowledge breeds specialists. Bede stands by way of contrast as a polymath not only with a firm grasp of many fields but also the added ability to contribute something lasting to many of them. He is best known for his work as a historian, but he had many other talents. Many believe him to have been the most learned man in the Europe of his time. Bede's interests were wide-ranging and his writings include biblical commentaries, translations of the lives of saints, his own biography of St Cuthbert, works on the calculation of time and his most famous work the *Ecclesiastical History of the English People* written in 731 at the height of his powers.

Bede was foreshadowing events that were still a long way in the future when he wrote his *History*. England as a country was not to achieve unity until the tenth century. An English Church and an English people existed in his mind before they existed as political and social realities. His vision of history was to have a lasting impact on how the English viewed themselves and their own past. His most famous book was to have an immediate impact and copies of it were in demand across Europe. It was, in its time, the equivalent of a best-seller and even today it shows no signs of ever going out of print.

In the Britain of Bede's time it was usual to refer to dates by the year of a king's reign, but with so many regional kings this made for a very unwieldy system poorly suited for a history on the scale that Bede was writing. He decided to use the then little-known Anno Domini system of dating that had been developed by Isidore, bishop of Seville. Bede was not only the first English historian, he was also the first to use the AD dating method for the writing of history. Today, of course, this is taken for granted, but at the time Bede's decision to use it was bold and highly innovative. It was also a considerable labour, as the historical sources he was using were obviously not using this chronology and he had to convert the numerous dating systems. This meant not only a host of Anglo-Saxon sources based on years of a king's reign but also Roman ones based on the reigns and periods in office of assorted emperors and popes.

Like all historians, Bede was not impartial: he had a very clear idea of what he wanted to write. His *History* was not merely a disordered collection of data that he had accumulated as a result of the countless hours he spent in the library. As a Christian, he did not view the life of humankind as merely the passing of the ages but as part of a divine plan. There were also moral lessons to be learnt from the actions of people in the past. In his opening passage he wrote: 'If history records good things of good men, the thoughtful hearer is encouraged to imitate what is good: or if it records evil of wicked men, the devout, religious listener or reader is encouraged to avoid all that is sinful and perverse and to follow what he knows to be good and pleasing to God.'

We have already seen how the history of Britain during this time was dominated by the expansion of Christianity. It was against this background of a patchwork of interconnected pagan and Christian kingdoms that Bede was composing his version of history. He saw Christianity as the guiding force that would bring unity to Britain. He writes that there are five languages and four peoples of Britain. These four – the English, the British, the Picts and the Scotti (Irish people who had settled in Britain and were to become known as the Scots) – all had their own languages. The fifth was Latin, the language of Roman Christianity, which Bede saw as the means by which they would all be united.

He was writing a history of Britain that would not only be the first coherent history of its people (by means of the unifying concept of the AD chronology), but would also outline the manifest destiny of the English as part of the divine plan. Bede's use of the term 'the English people' in this and his other works is very complex and the fine detail need not concern us here. When he describes the history of the arrival of Germanic peoples to Britain, he typically refers to them as Saxons. After their conversion to Christianity he then describes them as English. Sources emanating from Rome before he wrote the *History* described them as English, and it seems Bede was following this lead. For Bede, being English and being Christian were indivisible.

The Reckoning of Time

It was religious motivations such as the calculating of the dates for the celebration of Easter and the use of the AD system of dating that lay behind Bede's scientific and mathematical interests. The Christian religion was the driving force that would lead to scientific progress. Time is one of the underlying themes in both his historical and more technical works. Bede's own stable environment, regulated by the orderly division of time essential to the workings of the monastery, allowed him to concentrate his energies on solving problems concerning time. Although he is now best known as a historian, his *The Reckoning of Time* was hugely influential in the early Middle Ages.

The Synod of Whitby in the year 664 was an attempt to bring the Celtic and Roman churches together in order to reconcile their differences. One of the main points of contention centred on Easter. There was no consensus about when Easter was to be celebrated. Before the Synod, one church could be celebrating Easter while the other was celebrating Lent. This dispute was not just based on theological hair splitting – it was splitting the Christian community apart. The mathematical problems in calculating Easter still remained fundamentally unsolved until the time of Bede. It was such a contentious issue that the normally serene scholar found it impossible not to criticise those he saw as responsible for this state of affairs. When writing about the Irish bishop Aidan (who founded the monastery at Lindisfarne), Bede had many good things to say about him but could not stop himself repeatedly criticising this paragon of the Celtic Church for his 'inadequate knowledge of the proper observance of Easter'.

The unity that Bede strove for in his history could not be achieved without a consensus on the timing of the celebration of Easter. This was why it was such an important issue for him. If Easter was to be related to the Jewish Passover, the Last Supper, then this made the Christian Church dependent on the Jewish calendar, which was lunar. The Christian calendar was based on the Roman calendar, which was solar. Somehow these two points of reference needed to be reconciled. That Easter had to be on a Sunday also had to be taken as part of the equation.

Bede worked out the solution. Earlier scholars had shown that there was a way to reconcile the lunar and solar data, but it was Bede's original contribution to solve this in conjunction with the need for Easter to be on a Sunday. He compiled his exhaustive arguments, which involved a cycle of 528 years – the new basis for working out the date of Easter. For those who could not follow his complex calculations, he appended a series of tables to his book which could be used practically without recourse to the main text. The numerous surviving manuscripts that consist of only the tables show that this possibility was widely taken advantage of by those less learned than himself.

Bede had a need to communicate not only with other learned monks but also with others who did not have the privilege of such an education. He was able to explain complicated things in simple ways. Laura Sole, the curator of Bede's World, a stone's throw from St Paul's church at the Jarrow monastery, gave me an example of his skill as a teacher. He was aware from his reading that the Earth was a sphere and that there were distinct climatic zones, which he divided into five. He explained it to Anglo-Saxons (who would never have seen a globe) by likening it to a huge fire on a cold winter night. If you are too close to the fire, you are too hot to be comfortable. If you are a long way from the fire, you are too far to feel its benefit. If you are in the intermediate zone (Britain being in the temperate zone of the northern part of the world), then the effects of the fire would provide the necessary comfort.

His ability to communicate as a teacher was undoubtedly an important aspect of his influence at the time, but he is nevertheless best remembered as a great scholar and synthesiser of the world of knowledge available to him through books. Yet the raw material that he came across in the monastic library required much moulding for it to be transformed into a vehicle for his own vision. Not only did he have to reconcile diverse chronological systems, he had to find a means to calculate them. The Arabic numerals we use today were not known in the world of Bede and his contemporaries. Roman numerals made complex calculations extraordinarily difficult and so Bede taught a method of calculation using the fingers and other parts of the body. By moving the fingers into different positions it was possible to represent all the numbers up to 9,999. By employing the elbows, shoulders and other body parts you could get up to a million!

It was with the aid of such a system that he constructed his Christian calendar, or computus as it was known, which included his lengthy exposition of how the date of Easter should be calculated. He was not a scientist as the term is understood today, but his work reconciling the lunar and solar calendars and other matters involved complex calculations. The aim of his work was religious but the means to this end necessarily involved the solving of problems by mathematical means. It was to have an effect on the development of learning in the Middle Ages that would result in a more experimental approach to problems. The scholarship of the barbarian had truly come of age.

Bede had travelled little in life, but his mortal remains were to make their own journey after his death. After he died on 26 May 735, he was buried under the south porch of the church at Jarrow. His bones were later reinterred near the altar where they remained until the early part of the eleventh century. It was at this time that they were moved to Durham Cathedral to be placed in the tomb of St Cuthbert. In 1370 they were moved across the cathedral to be housed in a tomb in the Galilee chapel. This was to be his final resting place.

We must now go back in time to the story of St Cuthbert, whose own relics were to one day become the spiritual foundation stone upon which Durham Cathedral was built.

Chapter Eighteen

HOLY ISLAND

It was seen, perhaps, from the back of a dimly lit church as
a mystical object, a visible symbol of St Cuthbert, of God, of
Christ, everything that would act as a power line to God.
I think for all kinds of people it had that electricity about it.

Michelle Brown, curator at the British Library, on the Lindisfarne Gospels

It was St Columba who was the first to establish an Irish
monastery beyond Ireland when he founded that of Iona, an
island of the Inner Hebrides, in either 563 or 565. Iona itself was
later to serve as a springboard for later phases of the missionary
process. The first Irish monk who came to the north-east of
England with the intention of converting the local Anglo-Saxons
left in despair soon after arriving as he found them too rude,
coarse and barbarous. Another would come in his place and have
a good deal more success, effectively beginning the active conversion of the north of England. This was Aidan, an Irish bishop who
came from Iona in 635 at the request of King Oswald, who had
already become a Christian himself earlier while in exile. The king
gave him the island of Lindisfarne to set up his monastery. The

founding of the monastery was to mark the beginning of Christianity in Northumbria.

The tidal island of Lindisfarne is still accessible by a causeway that can be walked across at low tide. Outside the busy tourist season the island is very quiet, preserving something of its ancient tranquillity. According to Bede's account, the original monastery buildings on Lindisfarne were made of timber like the other Anglo-Saxon buildings of the time – unlike the later twin monasteries of stone at Jarrow and Wearmouth. The monastic population of Lindisfarne has been estimated to have been about 600. Although this was an all-male community there were other places, such as Hartlepool, where nuns and monks lived side by side, usually ruled over by an abbess; this system came from Gaul.

Like the twin monasteries, Lindisfarne was a hive of manual and intellectual industry. Its scriptorium produced numerous works, and sometimes the weather conditions meant that the monks could not keep up with the many orders for books. There are little notes written by the monks apologising for not coming up with the goods on account of both their inks and hands freezing due to the cold. Despite these difficulties, Lindisfarne established itself as a centre of artistic excellence and learning that was in many respects way ahead of its counterparts in the supposedly more 'civilised' realms of France and Italy. An obscure island off the coast of northern England peopled by barbarian monks had become one of the leading lights in the Christian world of its day.

St Cuthbert – His Life and Afterlife

The most important saint of this period of British history was Cuthbert. In his lifetime he was an example to those around him. In death the cult that surrounded him was to have a powerful effect on the development of the Church in northern England. He was born in the early 630s. He first entered the monastery of

Melrose on the river Tweed; this was then ruled by Eata, a follower of Aidan. Cuthbert later followed Eata to Lindisfarne, where he was to remain for the rest of his days. Bede describes Cuthbert as an intrepid missionary who would 'visit and preach in the villages that lay far distant among high and inaccessible mountains, which others feared to visit and whose barbarity and squalor daunted other teachers'.

Cuthbert was of a different character to both Biscop and Bede. He was drawn to the life of the hermit and first began to distance himself from the day-to-day life of the monastery by living on the tiny tidal islet called Hobthrush island (colloquially known as St Cuthbert's island) a hundred or so metres off Lindisfarne. This soon proved to be too close for the requirements of a genuine hermitage, as monks from Lindisfarne could not resist the temptation to distract him from his solitary labours of the spirit.

He decided to move to an island some nine miles further out to sea – Inner Farne, or simply Farne Island as it is sometimes known. Here, surrounded only by the seasonal flocks of seabirds, he could pursue his chosen life with more rigour. Although he was living a life of solitude and contemplation, he would find that still others would not let him be. In the year 685, in his absence, the monks of Lindisfarne unanimously elected Cuthbert as their bishop – a post he accepted only after being implored to do so by his followers. He reluctantly returned to Lindisfarne.

Feeling that his end was nigh, Cuthbert returned to Farne Island to die. It was then that another phase of his story began. He asked his brethren to bury him in this isolated spot that he had come to see as his spiritual home. They were reluctant and begged him to allow them to bury him in the church back on Lindisfarne. Once again he finally acceded to their requests. On 20 March 687, by means of a sign that had previously been agreed, a monk stood on high ground on Farne holding aloft a lit candle in each hand.

On Lindisfarne a monk awake and alert in a watchtower saw this signal that meant Cuthbert had passed away. His body was then buried in the church as had been planned.

It was common practice in those days to revere holy men by digging up their bones and putting them in a shrine above ground; it was thought to befit their status. In 698, eleven years after he was first placed in his grave, it was opened by monks who were planning to put his bones into a small reliquary. To their great surprise, his body was said to be incorrupt – that is, it had not decayed. His clothing was also still of pristine appearance. The amazed monks took this as a sign of his great sanctity and placed his mortal remains in a wooden coffin.

This enshrining of Cuthbert's body was to mark the real beginnings of his cult, which was later to spread as far as Germany, Austria and Italy, largely thanks to the writings of Bede. Relics of all kinds were revered. In the eighth century one of the original wooden churches from Lindisfarne was encased in lead and transported to Norham-on-Tweed (where St Cuthbert's relics were also taken some time between 830 and 845). As Richard Bailey, my academic guide on Lindisfarne, explained to me, the timber church, like Cuthbert's body and wooden coffin, had become a sacred relic in its own right.

St Cuthbert's coffin has Roman and runic characters inscribed on it. The runes, the old Germanic script, are usually associated with the pagan period but in Britain they continued to be used occasionally in Christian contexts. There are other examples from Lindisfarne of the use of both scripts, such as a name stone that has the female name Osgyth on it in runes at the top and Roman script at the bottom. Study of the coffin texts has revealed that the runic are dependent on the Roman – that is, the runic writing is simply a transliteration of the Roman. The latter script is dominant and the former secondary. The monks of Lindisfarne placed runes on what was a highly visible and venerated object, the coffin itself. Why?

It was patently an aspect of Anglo-Saxon tradition that did not clash with the Christian message. There are also other indications of the preservation of their ethnic art. A pectoral cross that was placed in the coffin with Cuthbert is adorned with garnets which were, as we know from the Sutton Hoo treasure, a favoured gemstone among the Anglo-Saxons. What was happening was a fusion, and not simply a replacement of one way of doing things by another. Ideas, beliefs and artistic styles were coming to Britain from the Mediterranean world, but they were not just supplanting what was already there. It was not just the runes and the garnets that continued to be used – it was also the spoken language. The liturgy was not just in Latin but also in Old English.

In fact it was not two but three worlds that were coming together, because the Celtic traditions were also part of the lifeblood of Lindisfarne from its founding by Aidan. The greatest expression of this interlacing of separate ethnic traditions is embodied in an illuminated book containing multiple messages: the Lindisfarne Gospels. The book contains not only the four gospels but also a few letters by St Jerome who translated them into Latin. It is generally thought to have been completed in 698 in honour of St Cuthbert, but this date has recently been brought into question as being perhaps a little too early.

Illuminating the Dark Ages

The book is now held in the British Library, as a national treasure. Its custodian, Michelle Brown, told me that one of the many remarkable things about it is that it was the work of a single scribe, the Bishop Eadfrith (with some very minor exceptions). Usually books produced in the scriptorium were the work of many hands. Work of this length and quality would probably have taken him ten years when one considers that he was, as a monk, expected to pray eight times a day and attend to the many other duties of his vocation.

It seemed only appropriate that such singularity of purpose should also have been involved in its binding and external decoration. Eadfrith's successor as bishop was Aethilwald, who bound the book in leather, while Billfrith the Anchorite, a skilled metalworker, adorned its cover with jewels and gold. The work of neither of these men survived, only that of Eadfrith. The book contains a few small areas of unfinished work which may mean one of two things. It has been suggested that he did not wish to show vanity by trying to attain a perfection that might offend God – thus leaving small areas unfinished, tiny blemishes on an otherwise exquisite masterpiece. It is perhaps more likely that Eadfrith died before he was able to complete his great work.

At this time paper was unknown in Europe and books were written on vellum, or dressed calf skin. In theory, at least 130 calf skins were used to make the necessary amount of parchment for the Lindisfarne Gospels. In practice, the number was probably much higher as a book of this truly exceptional quality would require skins of the highest standard – even those with only minor imperfections would have been rejected. It is usually possible to tell with parchment which is the side that had the hair on it and which was the inside of the skin. However, that used for the Lindisfarne Gospels is of such high quality that even the expert eye finds it difficult to ascertain which is which. On the other side of the island from the monastery the site of an old farm was excavated in the 1980s and 1990s and it was identified as a place where they were producing calves for vellum. Such locally available sources would have provided much of necessary vellum, but there was also probably a need to seek skins of sufficient quality from the mainland monasteries as well.

The preparation of the pigments for use as ink was a skill in itself – a subtle alchemy, a combination of artistry and chemistry. About forty-five colours and shades were used in the creation of the Lindisfarne Gospels. Green ink was produced by putting a piece of copper in vinegar or wine, scraping off the resulting green corrosion and mixing it with egg white. Yellow was obtained from arsenic, so great care had to be taken when using this particular colour. Black was derived from soot ground up with some kind of gum or from oak-galls. The source of much of this knowledge was the Mediterranean, but the northern scriptoria did not just blindly imitate – they developed the techniques further. The pen used by Eadfrith was made from either a reed or a quill feather.

The book is not just the envelope for a written text; it is an object in itself. A book such as this, both a supreme work of art and the focus of religious veneration, becomes a cult object. The Bible, the Holy Book, is of course of fundamental significance in the Christian religion so it is not surprising to find books such as the Lindisfarne Gospels being embodiments of the divine message or, as Michelle Brown puts it, 'of the Word made flesh, or rather, the Word made word'. On another level such books, literally and symbolically containing the Christian gospel, were the concrete expression and proof that the mission had reached the far shores of Britain.

The book is also an expression, perhaps even consciously so, of the fusion of cultures that was taking place around the turn of the eighth century. The script shows not only a clear Roman influence but also echoes runic elements in some parts of the book. Much of the ornament adorning the pages has clear precedents in Celtic textile designs, while other aspects derive from Germanic metal-work. Michelle Brown certainly thinks that this work, by drawing together diverse cultural styles, was a means of saying to people who were (through their new-found Christianity) giving up their traditional allegiances that they had a stake in this new order.

Like the coffin of St Cuthbert, the book also provides the historian with a link between the pagan and Christian Anglo-Saxon worlds. The archaeologist Martin Carver eloquently expresses the profound significance of the Sutton Hoo jewels and the Lindisfarne Gospels when viewed together as twin treasures of Anglo-Saxon culture: 'Two great British monuments of native art [stand] clearly at either end of the seventh century, giving the country two stepping stones across the darkest period of its early history.'

It now seems that the traditional date for the completion of the book, 698, needs to be looked at again. Scholarly detective work by Michelle Brown has led her to believe that this date is too early, and that some time between 710 and 720 is much more likely. The date of 698 was suggested because that was the year in which the body of Cuthbert was dug up. The little book that was originally buried with him (known as the Cuthbert Gospel of St John or the Stonyhurst Gospel) had sufficed as one of the cultic objects associated with him so far. But the internal evidence of the text and the techniques used in it suggest to her that the Lindisfarne Gospels seem much better placed at the later date. This dating also helps to explain other aspects of its production. The revised chronology fits well with the fact that Eadfrith died in 721, which would explain why he was unable to finish the last few parts of the text. It also explains why the book was not bound until the time of Eadfrith's successor Aethilwald – it was simply not finished until then.

Returning to the digging up of Cuthbert's remains: as his body was found to be incorrupt, his sanctity grew and his relics were required to reflect this burgeoning status. Michelle Brown suggests that the Lindisfarne Gospels were the literary result of this need for something bigger and more spectacular. She sees this as closely related to the *Life* of Cuthbert that Bede was working on at the same time. Bede's hagiography was actually an expanded version of an earlier life of the saint written by an anonymous monk from Lindisfarne. Bede and Eadfrith may have been in close communication because the book and the *Life* were two parts of a continuing strategy for the further exaltation of the saint. The twin monasteries and Lindisfarne seemed to have been working in unison to forward their mutual aim.

The monastic ideals that had, many centuries before, been born in the harsh and unyielding surroundings of the Egyptian desert were now exerting a powerful influence in what had been outlying regions of Europe. While being the major intellectual force of their time, the monks were also a tough breed. There were some who preferred the isolation of the hermit, like St Cuthbert. Others, most notably Bede, sought to understand and interpret the world from the safety of their own monasteries. Others still, like the greatly neglected Benedict Biscop, were intrepid travellers and risk-takers – but all worked to the same end. They had brought the influence of Rome back to England and, in return, sent their own intellectual and artistic achievements to the continent.

Although decadence and worldliness were already affecting the monastic world by the time of Bede's death in 735, an even greater threat was soon to endanger the intense physical and intellectual labours of the monasteries of north-eastern England. A new wave of northern barbarians was on the way: the Vikings.

Chapter Nineteen

VIKINGS: PIRATES AND POETS

In this year, dire portents appeared... immense whirlwinds
and flashes of lightning, and fiery dragons were seen flying
in the air. A great famine immediately followed those signs,
and... the ravages of heathen men miserably destroyed God's
church on Lindisfarne, with plunder and slaughter.

The Anglo-Saxon Chronicle, ninth century

There is a gravestone from Lindisfarne that has been carved on both sides. One side shows a dramatic scene – the end of the world, a great cross appearing in the sky at the end of time. On the other side there is a war scene showing the Vikings, whose first raid on Lindisfarne was in 793. This event is the point at which the Viking Age is said to have begun. This fact in itself demonstrates how biased and arbitrary the recording of history can be. The barbarians enter history only when they enter the books of the 'civilised'.

From the point of view of the Scandinavian peoples who became known as the Vikings, we can imagine there was no dramatic change in their culture and lifestyle in or even around 793. Most of them would not have been involved in these raids, which were echoes of the earlier Saxon piracy. The initial Viking assaults on Britain are recorded by historians and therefore provide us with a useful inroad to the Viking world. Yet we must not make the mistake of thinking that this specific time marked a drastic change in Scandinavian culture. Later, the Vikings would leave Scandinavia in large numbers, which inevitably changed the make-up of their society more dramatically.

Over the last few decades many historians have felt it necessary to portray the Vikings in a new light. Traditionally they have been perceived as a very destructive force that disrupted the progress of European civilisation. The other, more positive, side of their culture has been brought more into the light of day. In the next few chapters a rounded portrait of these last of the northern barbarians will be given. For the moment, however, we cannot ignore the accounts of their violent pillaging of Britain, which continues to epitomise the image most people have of the Vikings – at least in Britain. The very word 'Viking' has a rather obscure history but seems to derive from the Norse word *vik*, meaning bay, inlet or creek. 'Viking' came to mean a pirate, a robber or a warring seafarer, presumably because such marauders either set sail from inlets or entered them in order to plunder. Although it really referred to only a small minority of the members of the barbarian societies of Norway, Sweden and Denmark, it became a term for them all. Inaccurate it may be, but the term stuck and for this reason we are obliged to use it to this day.

The view from Britain

It was on 8 June 793 that the Vikings sacked the monastery of Lindisfarne. The following summer Jarrow was raided. We have seen how richly furnished the twin monasteries were, thanks to the labours of Biscop and others. The fact that St Cuthbert's pectoral cross and the Lindisfarne Gospels were also both lavishly adorned shows why raiding these monasteries was highly attractive to Viking raiders. There is nothing to suggest that the pagan Vikings had any particular desire to attack the Christian faith or what it stood for; they simply wanted the treasures that were owned by the Church.

One of the leading intellectual successors of Bede was Alcuin of York (*c.* 735–804). A letter he wrote to the monks after the raid on Lindisfarne has survived, and in it he puts forward his opinion that the Viking assault was punishment from God for the sins of Anglo-Saxon society. Bede had said almost the same thing about the sins of the Britons leading to their punishment in the form of attacks by the then pagan Saxons. The monasteries of the Celtic tradition were also not spared the attentions of the Vikings, who plundered Iona in 795 on their way to further forays into Ireland. Further raids on Iona in 802, 806 and 807 led to its community's flight from the island.

These early sporadic and opportunistic assaults were largely the work of Norwegian Vikings. Later more concerted attacks by Danish Vikings would result in more long-term effects on the political landscape of Britain. The attacks inevitably had an effect on the monastic world and repeated assaults led, by 875, to the decision of the monks to abandon Lindisfarne. In the same year St Paul's monastery also closed. The monks of Lindisfarne fled to the mainland, taking Cuthbert and his relics with them. They travelled for a number of years seeking a new home, eventually settling at Chester-le-Street in 883. There is an interesting story behind the decision to found their monastery there.

One of the monks in the community had a vision in which St Cuthbert appeared and instructed him to reach an agreement with the Danes whereby the Church would support a Danish king rather than maintain traditional ties with the Anglo-Saxon monarchy. This was not simply cynicism on the part of the monastic community, for the last Anglo-Saxon kings of Northumbria (before they had to accede their lands to Danish rule) had been plundering the coffers of the Church probably as much as the Vikings. By this time, it was not possible to make a simple equation between pagan, barbarian Viking raiders on the one hand and Christian, 'civilised' Anglo-Saxon victims on the other. It was much more complex than that.

After a century or so of comparative stability, renewed Viking incursions in the reign of Ethelred II led to the relics of St Cuthbert being moved yet again. In 995 Cuthbert's shrine was moved to Durham, where today his tomb is located in the Chapel of the Nine Altars in the cathedral.

Viking Expansion

So far we have only really looked at the Viking presence in these centuries from the point of view of the monasteries and the Church that supported them. There is a bigger picture to consider. We need to explore the Vikings' possible reasons for setting forth from their homelands and discover where else they travelled. Firstly, we must trace them back to their roots. The Gothic historian Jordanes believed that the homeland of the Goths was Scandza (Scandinavia); in Part One of this book, we have seen that archaeology does not back him up on this point.

Jordanes describes Scandza as a 'factory of tribes and surely a vagina of bands'. Although the Germanic Goths do not seem to have been made in this factory, the people commonly called the Vikings can certainly be said to have come off this cultural production line. As we also saw in Part One, the reasons for the Huns' arrival in Europe were not clear-cut and unfortunately the same is the case with the expansion of the Scandinavian barbarians – the north Germanic peoples who were the last of the pagans.

A host of theories have been put forward to explain the seemingly sudden and explosive impact of the Vikings. Overpopulation has been suggested, but not demonstrated conclusively. A climatic change of some kind has also been proposed, but is likewise unsupported by sufficient evidence. An increase in technological sophistication (concentrated in the sphere of ship-building) has been thought to have allowed the Vikings to undertake journeys that would previously have been unfeasible. Yet we know that crossing at least the North Sea was nothing new – the Scandinavian-built Nydam boat of the fourth century being a case in point.

Yet others refer to the fact that the many petty kingdoms in Scandinavia that characterised its political landscape in early times were replaced by fewer but more powerful kingdoms. All these theories are plausible in certain respects and there is probably some truth in them all. All we can say on this point with any real degree of certainty is that an expansion did happen in the eighth century, and the Vikings were to be a force to be reckoned with until the eleventh century, when their story ends. Their early raids centred on the acquisition of portable wealth for practical reasons. This usually took the form of precious metals (coins included) and jewels, or slaves who could be delivered to their masters by boat while working for their passage by one means or another. Kidnapping was also one of their money-making ventures – aristocrats, bishops and other notables could earn them very substantial amounts in the form of ransoms.

The Viking campaigns caused problems not only to the inhabitants of the British Isles but also to those of France (or Francia as it was called at that time). The Vikings were masters not just of the sea; they had vessels that could easily travel far inland up the major rivers of Europe. Danish Vikings were behind a series of dramatic raids in the 840s. In consecutive years, beginning in 843, their ships went up the Loire and raided Nantes, then the river Garonne from which they proceeded overland to plunder Toulouse, and the *pièce de résistance* – a force of 120 ships up the Seine that required paying off to the amount of 7,000 pounds of silver to save Paris from being sacked. To the Vikings, distance was no object: while some of them were engaged in these campaigns in Francia, others were plundering and looting as far south as Seville and Lisbon, both of which were then under Islamic rule.

Their spectacular raids on rich monasteries and cities make for dramatic reading, but they actually tell us very little about the Vikings themselves apart from their love of looting and slave-taking. Lurid and garbled tales of their unsurpassed cruelty have also added to their reputation as one of the most forbidding of all the barbarian peoples of the Dark Ages. The best example of this concerns the supposed actions of a ninth-century Viking leader named Ivarr the Boneless, who was very powerful in the British Isles at the time. He is supposed to have been the fiendish devisor of a particularly imaginative and sadistic way of killing, which became known as the 'blood eagle'. According to one account, it involved the carving of an eagle shape into the back of the still living king of Northumbria, Aella, as a sadistic finale to the conquest of York in 866. The tale got taller in a later version in which Ivarr is reported to have killed not only Aella but also Edmund, his counterpart in East Anglia; this time it involves ripping out the lungs of the victim and draping them over his shoulders in a grisly imitation of the folded wings of an eagle.

Leading modern scholars of the Viking Age such as Else Roesdahl reject the truth of such stories, which seem to derive from nothing more sinister than a misinterpretation of a complex piece of Nordic verse that somehow was transformed into this much repeated anecdote that was said to epitomise Viking barbarity. Such anecdotes highlight the image of the typical Viking as known to most people. We have seen on repeated occasions that the history of 'civilised' and barbarian interactions usually involves the latter being portrayed as outsiders coming from the edge (whether the steppes of Russia, the lands to the north of Hadrian's Wall or from across the seas) to disrupt the centres of civilisation.

Certainly, when we look from the perspective of the monks of Lindisfarne and the Christian kings of the Anglo-Saxon world, the Vikings fit this bill. The British even today have a stereotypical view of the Vikings raping, pillaging and plundering – in short they are still represented as archetypal barbarians. And they did do most, if not all, of the things they were accused of doing in Britain and, indeed, many other places too. But such behaviour was hardly the exclusive prerogative of the Vikings – during these times barbarians and Christians alike were equally ruthless and violent in their political affairs. The Norsemen indisputably came from outside of the Anglo-Saxon and Christian sphere and threw it into disarray.

The sudden appearance of the Vikings right at the end of the eighth century is, as has already been mentioned, really an illusion. We have seen that in the preceding centuries there was much interaction across the North Sea. Yet for whatever reason, trading had turned into raiding and the designation of the Scandinavian barbarians as Vikings begins. As far as we can tell, they were not a disciplined fighting force but were cunning and relied on advance intelligence which would reveal points of weakness that they could exploit. Their swift and sleek ships were highly manoeuvrable, making them masters of the surprise attack. Yet these raiders were not representative of Scandinavian life as a whole. Things must have looked very different from the other side of the North Sea.

The Vikings at Home

The violence that seems to overshadow the Viking raiders does not appear to sit well with their actions at home. The information that we have concerning the old laws of Norway (which have their origin in the time of the Vikings) paints a very different picture. Acts of murder and violence would not go unpunished, and the Vikings had strict codes of conduct. As with many ancient systems of law, homicide was often punished by heavy fines. One source tells us that the murder of a farmer was punishable by a fine of 189 head of cattle. Such hefty fines, coupled with the fact that the murderer's entire extended family were held legally accountable for their kinsman's offence, were considered to act as a deterrent. A murderer could ruin his whole family as a result of his crime.

Laws were made and justice meted out by an assembly of freemen known as a *thing*. Civil disputes and criminal cases were heard at *thing* sites, usually out in the open air. It seems that in early Viking times the most preferred *thing* site would be one of the numerous stone circles that had been erected by their prehistoric ancestors. Many Scandinavian names indicate places that were once used by the assemblies. For all their roaming on the high seas and the rivers, the Vikings were also a people with a distinct sense of place. The foundation of both their economy and family life was the farmstead. This solid infrastructure allowed a thriving trading network to be built up even before the Viking age.

There is firm evidence to indicate that they ran their economy along very precise lines. A pair of scales and ten weights dating from the second century were discovered at an Iron Age burial ground near Hønefoss in Buskerud, western Norway. They are the oldest yet discovered in Norway. The three heaviest weights were 79.4 grams, 53 grams and 26.4 grams respectively. The old Norwegian øre was a basic unit of value that weighed 26 grams. Allowing for very minor inaccuracies, the three weights mentioned above correspond to 1 øre, 2 øre and 3 øre. The fact that the other weights go down to a mere 1 gram shows that accurate measurement was very important. Such scales and weights were used to weigh precious metals. The Viking trading systems that will be explored later in this book patently grew out of the earlier economic interests of the Scandinavian barbarian cultures.

The social world of the Vikings was clearly defined but not absolutely rigid – there was a chance to climb the social ladder or indeed to fall down it. Different variants existed at different times and places in the Viking world, but fundamentally there were three social classes: slaves, freemen and nobles. The slaves were called *traells* and usually had their heads shaved as a mark of their lowly status. They were in some ways similar to the serfs of the later Middle Ages, and worked hard on the farms of their masters and mistresses. They lived modestly and died modestly, being buried in the Viking equivalent of a pauper's grave unless they were 'lucky' enough to be interred with their owner (a dubious honour which usually meant being killed before their time).

There are clear instances where this is verified by archaeology. A tenth-century burial from Stengade on Langeland (one of the Danish islands) revealed the skeletal remains of two men, a master and his slave. The skeleton of the latter is in a strange position which strongly suggests that his feet were bound and that he had been beheaded. There are similar finds, showing that this was not an isolated incident. Although the slaves had no legal rights and could be bought or sold at the whim of the owning classes, their lot does not always seem to have been an unhappy one. They were not typically treated with brutality and often lived fairly secure and comfortable lives. There are even accounts of slaves gaining their freedom. Skilled craftsmen were often in a position to use their talents to buy their way to freedom. On the other hand, a freeman could also become a slave by committing certain crimes.

The class of freemen were farmers who owned the land they worked on. They were sometimes further divided into two groups. The more well-to-do were the *hauld* yeomen who could show that they had lived on their family farms for six generations or more;

the *bonde* free farmers were those who were not able to boast that they came from such stable stock. The structure of society became more complex as the Viking culture expanded, resulting in a more specialised division of labour. Smiths, ship-builders and other craftsmen became highly prized members of society and were to become a new type of freeman. Freemen, as has been noted, were able to attend and contribute to the *thing*.

The Viking aristocracy were the leaders of their society and the kings would be drawn from their ranks. Traditionally, members of this class would be large landowners but with the increasingly profitable opportunities for merchants (or their less scrupulous counterparts – that is, pirates) who were willing to travel far to seek their fortune, a new class emerged – a Viking *nouveau riche* who could buy their way to the top.

Women were not exactly on an equal level with men, but nevertheless had a comparatively high position compared with that which was to be their lot in the later Middle Ages. The most lavish Viking grave that has ever been unearthed is the Oseberg ship burial, and this was the final resting place of a woman (see the next chapter). Female status was largely expressed through the family and home, and there are no records suggesting that women became merchants although, of course, Viking women tended to travel to many of the places that their menfolk visited. Like the Vikings, the Arabs were great travellers and traders. An Arab visitor to the Viking trading centre of Hedeby on the east coast of Jutland (now part of Germany) in the latter part of the tenth century noted that divorce was a woman's right which she could exercise at her own free will. The churchman Adam of Bremen, who visited Denmark a century later, reported that adultery by a man was a capital offence whereas for a guilty woman the punishment was to be sold into slavery.

There was much cultural expression in the sports, games and other pastimes of the Vikings. Horse fighting was more than a sport for them – it was an aspect of their fertility rituals. The winning stallion was traditionally chosen as a sacrifice to the gods. Horse flesh was prized as a meat at pagan feasts, so much so that it was banned in the later Christian era on account of its role in heathen practices. It was not just the dramatic and often bloody sports that were appreciated by the Vikings. Board games were also very popular, as the twelfth-century Isle of Lewis chessmen demonstrates. These pieces, of Scandinavian origin, were carved from walrus ivory. By this time chess had all but replaced an earlier game of subtle strategy named *hnefatafl*. In some respects it is similar to chess in that there is a king and other, minor, pieces. The Vikings would have played it to pass the time on long sea voyages, and the discovery of boards in York and Ireland shows that the game was played in their colonies abroad as well as at home in Scandinavia.

The trading networks built up by the Vikings and their ancestors over the generations brought them in contact with a remarkable range of objects. One of the most dramatic examples of their acquisitions is a small statuette of the Buddha that somehow found its way to Helgö, an island trading centre in Lake Mälaren (to the west of Stockholm) even before the Viking Age. When it was found, it had a leather thong tied round the neck and an arm, which has led scholars to believe that it was worn as a lucky charm or amulet. Exotic and rare items have attracted humanity since the dawn of time and the Vikings were no different, but the amazing distances they travelled to get them demonstrate the extraordinary pioneering spirit of the Norsemen. The native craftsmen of Scandinavia were skilled in their own right but also open to foreign influences. The type of object known as a bracteate, a large golden disc pendant, was based upon imperial Roman medallions. Despite this origin it became a characteristically Scandinavian artefact, starting in the Age of Migration that preceded the Viking era. It was believed to give its wearer protection from harmful forces.

The spirit of the Vikings is embodied in their rich oral tradition of epic tales and poems that were eventually written down in the Christian era. There are the countless sagas that recount the achievements of the Viking leaders and intrepid voyagers. Even more important are the *Eddas*, the sacred poetic repository of the central body of myths of the most northerly of the barbarian peoples. This inner pagan world will be explored in the last chapter of this book; yet even this brief survey of the social world of these people helps to dispel some of the stereotypes that have been built up around them. By looking at the Viking societies in their Scandinavian homeland, we can see their culture in a much more complete way. In addition to a minority of Vikings being infamous pirates, we have shown that some of them were also chess players, antique collectors and poets.

One of the underlying themes of this book has been to seek out the other side of the story – that of the barbarians. The lack of historical records made by the Vikings at this time makes the reconstruction of their own perspectives a difficult task but not a hopeless one. Many of the artefacts and much other archaeological evidence of the Viking Age survives in Scandinavia and beyond. This, in conjunction with the records of those who came in contact with them, can open many doors into their world. I felt that the best way to attempt to see the story from the barbarian point of view was to travel to Scandinavia, to the centre of *their* world.

Chapter Twenty

WARSHIPS AND PLEASURE YACHTS

When you look at a ship like this, you can see that they are not made overnight. It takes thousands of years' experience to make something like this.

Knut Paasche, curator of the Viking Ship Museum

There is surely no city in the world with more ship museums than Oslo. This in itself is a clear testimony to the enduring seafaring traditions of the Norwegians. One of the museums holds the *Fram* ship used by the polar explorer Fridtjof Nansen, and another houses Thor Heyerdahl's papyrus boat *Ra II* and his *Kon-tiki* balsa raft – these are just recent examples of an age-old Scandinavian fascination with the ship-building tradition. I had come to Oslo to see the most famous Viking vessels of them all: the Gokstad ship and the Oseberg ship, both now housed in the Viking Ship Museum. The first had been discovered in 1880 and the other in

1903. Both ships had been buried in mounds with what seem most likely to be their owners inside them.

There must have been literally thousands of Viking ships, but very few remain. There are only three altogether in the Viking Ship Museum – the Tune ship as well as the Oseberg and Gokstad (all were discovered in the environs of the Oslo fjord). The last two are in a wonderful state of preservation; they have been fully restored, as was common practice in the past, and give us an insight into the diversity of vessels that would have existed in the Viking Age. The Tune ship, in contrast, has been left unrestored, even though it was discovered in 1867. However, its time is still to come as the present curator of the museum, Knut Paasche, is now undertaking a full investigation of this neglected poor cousin of the Oseberg and Gokstad ships. The museum also houses the meagre remains of another vessel, the Borre ship (also from the Oslo fjord region), of which only a few rivets and nails survive – as little as that of the Sutton Hoo ship.

The museum was the brainchild of the architect Arnstein Arneberg, who planned it in 1913, but until the museum was completed in 1926 the Oseberg ship was stored at the University of Oslo were it was being restored. This was an extremely difficult job; there were thousands of fragments of the boat that had been damaged and distorted by the pressure of the weight of the mound over a period of more than a thousand years. Yet the jigsaw puzzle was put back together after each piece had been steamed and bent back to its original shape. Frederik Johannessen, its restorer, was later to apply the same techniques to restore the Gokstad ship which, until the end of the 1930s, was displayed in a temporary shed on the grounds of the University of Oslo.

The restored Oseberg ship was moved into the museum in 1926, and the Gokstad and Tune ships joined it in their own respective wings in 1932. In 1957 the fourth and last wing was added to the building and now houses the spectacular collection of artefacts that were found with the Oseberg ship. On 12 June 1975 there was a fire on the external part of the roof, which was made of wood, but thanks to the vision of the original architect the flames were unable to penetrate the inner concrete lining of the vaulted ceiling. The ships that had survived for a millennium were not damaged.

Boat-building has its roots thousands of years back in the Stone Age. By the Bronze Age in Scandinavia (1,800 BC to around 500 BC) both rock carvings and alignments of stones in the shape of boats show their cultural significance to the ancestors of the Vikings. In the early Scandinavian Iron Age, from around 200 BC, the makers of clinker-built boats were already using nails, and the strakes they fashioned were of very similar form to those of the Viking Age ships. The fourth-century Nydam boat and the seventh-century Sutton Hoo ship also provide us with further links to this evolutionary chain that links the prehistoric boats to the Viking ships.

The Vikings also aligned themselves with the age-old tradition of ship-shaped groups of burial stones, for example at Runsa on the shores of Lake Mälaren (not far from where the Buddha statuette was found), which was the site of a Viking fort and cult centre. Upright stones in the shape of boats mark the places of burial both here and elsewhere in Sweden. The discovery of the Oseberg ship and the realisation that it was the centrepiece of a lavish burial site showed the enduring power of the ship as a symbol in the northern psyche.

The Oseberg Ship: A Viking Lady's Pleasure Yacht

Excavation of the Oseberg ship began in summer 1904, under the supervision of Professor Gabriel Gustafson of the University of Oslo. His investigation revealed that, at the time of the burial, the ship was dragged into position and then packed in and covered with a layer of clay. The tight packing of the clay was one of the main reasons for the wonderful state of preservation that greeted the excavators. On top of this layer of clay, heavy stones were placed and the mound built up over the top. The mound would have been at least 5 metres high and 40 metres across (about 16 feet by 130 feet). The purpose of the ship and the mound was very similar to that of Sutton Hoo: to house the body of a dead dignitary of the pagan world.

Oseberg turned out to be a dual burial: two skeletons were found inside and, to the surprise of the excavators, both were female. It is thought that one was a high-born lady and the other her servant or slave, who may have been killed at the time of her mistress's death. (As we have seen, this practice was not uncommon in the Viking world.) One skeleton was that of a woman between twenty and thirty years of age; the other was around fifty, and suffered from arthritis. Archaeologists cannot be sure which was which, but the older one seems the more likely candidate for identifying as the lady.

Unfortunately looters – probably in the Middle Ages – had beaten the archaeologists to the mound and almost certainly removed her jewellery, which is conspicuous by its absence. If there were any weapons buried with her, then they too had been stolen. Nevertheless, a wonderful array of mainly wooden objects accompanied her, among them a finely decorated cart (or wagon as it sometimes referred to), three ornate sleighs and a plain, undecorated, working sled. There were also the skeletons of ten or more horses that were probably from her own stables and slaughtered as a mark of respect at her funeral.

The ship was a large open boat made entirely of oak: 21.58 metres (just over 70 feet) long and 5.1 metres (nearly 17 feet) at its widest part. The depth at midship was 1.58 metres (5 feet) from gunwale to keel, which was itself 19.8 metres (65 feet) long. The oak from which the ship was built has been dated by dendrochronology to the year 820. It has even been possible to say that it was cut in September of that year. The burial has been dated to the year 834, by the age of the timber used to construct the actual burial chamber. The difference in dates shows (again echoing the Sutton Hoo ship) that it was a vessel that had been used for a number of years – something that is corroborated by unmistakable signs of wear and tear.

From a technical point of view, the Oseberg ship has greatly impressed the nautical archaeologists who have studied it; but it is a true work of art as well. It is exquisitely and richly carved in a way that combines its practical features with symbolic designs. There is a snake's head carved on the top of the bow, and its body goes all the way underneath the ship as the keel, terminating at the stern. The Viking ships are noted for their flexibility, and the carving of a serpent seems to be a way of expressing the pliability of the keel.

Although it was extremely well made, it was not designed to endure the rough open seas – this was not a tough working ship used for long-distance trading and raiding by a hardened bunch of Viking seamen. It was a lady's pleasure yacht more suited to sailing up and down the rivers and inlets along the coast. Much skilled craftsmanship had been invested in making sure that it looked the part. The ship is clearly an exceptional vessel and, although its owner is not known, it seems safe to presume it belonged to a female dignitary or her husband. Their status could be that of chiefs, or it may be that she was actually the queen of a regional kingdom, having her grand vessel sailed and rowed on royal business around the fjords. It has been repeatedly suggested that this was the grave of Queen Åsa of the Ynglinge dynasty, the royal house of Vestfold (in the environs of the Oslo fjord), but this cannot be proved.

Amazingly, a whole set of thirty oars – fifteen a side – have been preserved without loss but, although they were clearly buried with the ship, they were not the ones that would have been used to row it in its owner's lifetime. They are simply too short, and might have belonged to another ship of lighter construction. The lack of wear implies that they may rather have been made especially for the burial and in fact be a dummy set, especially as some appear to be unfinished.

The Symbolism of the Oseberg Ship Burial

If we approach the symbolism of ship burials as Martin Carver has done with Sutton Hoo, then the whole Oseberg phenomenon was a grand means of expression, like a poem or a play but using the medium of material culture to get across its message. A play does not need to be realistic in a literal and prosaic sense in order to ring true. Therefore the fact that these oars belonged to another vessel altogether, or may have been a dummy set, is acceptable as poetic licence. The mast and the anchor are likewise too small. Furthermore, the array of objects that were placed in the ship hardly reflect the type of goods that would have been found on board even a pleasure yacht. The Oseberg finds are an expression of the lady's position and place in the world and not merely an inventory of goods.

The land vehicles – the cart, three sleighs and the sled – were all stowed in the funeral boat. The cart is about 5.5 metres (18 feet) long, 1.5 metres (5 feet) wide and 1.2 metres (4 feet) high. The Oseberg cart is the only complete example of its kind to be found in Norway, while elsewhere, as in Denmark and northern Germany, only fragments have been discovered. Interestingly, these fragmentary examples were also found in the graves of women, so clearly it was a kind of transport associated with females in particular. It was previously thought that the cart was just for show, the front axle firmly attached to the chassis thus stopping it from turning. Recent reinspection of the cart has shown that this was not the case. What the cart was used for is unclear. It could certainly have been drawn by horses (there were enough horses in the burial to pull not only the cart but also the sleighs and sled too) but would have made for a very uncomfortable ride as the Viking Age 'roads' were designed more for riders than drawn vehicles.

Its ornate decoration suggests that it might have had a ceremonial role, perhaps loaded with the lady's treasures on important civil or religious occasions – including perhaps her funeral procession. The cart was adorned with four heads, which depict Viking men with neatly combed hair and beards. Such largely realistic portrayals are rather unusual in Viking art. The main body of decoration on the cart is very different from the other items that make up the Oseberg equipment, although it has been suggested that the cart and the ship decoration may be the work of the same craftsman.

All three of the sleighs are made of beech wood and consist of two main parts: an undercarriage and a body. All of them also seem to have got inexplicably mixed up at the time of the burial, as they were found lashed together with ropes but none of the undercarriages were tied to the right bodies! The runners and the bodies are richly decorated and display some of the most bizarre imagery of the whole barbarian period – monstrous animal heads that bear no resemblance to any natural creature.

Another group of extraordinary carvings adorn five animal-headed posts, the function of which is not known. They were made from hard maple wood ideally suited for carving in incredibly fine detail, and are among the most magnificent pieces of Viking Age art to have survived. The difference in the decorative styles has made people think that they were the work of more than one carver – some being described as 'baroque' in style while others are not. While their purpose is unknown, they were certainly not prow figureheads. The Oseberg ship shows that the snake was used as such a figurehead, and written sources tell us that there were other animal heads that were used on the Viking ships. Yet these sources also record the necessity of removing them when the ship lands and taking the head ashore. The reason for this seems to be that the animal head is a means of averting evil influences, and therefore should accompany the crew on land as well as at sea.

It is an on-going policy of the Viking Ship Museum to make faithful copies of all the wooden artefacts in its collection. This work began in 1904, and the staff are now halfway through this monumental task. It is not a question of quantity but quality that makes this such a protracted project. The animal head wood carvings in particular have proved to be nearly impossible to copy. They display a mastery of wood that is seldom seen today – the museum relies on the skill of a Norwegian carver who is probably the only person in the whole of the country able to do work of this standard. A single animal head is a year's work for a craftsman with thirty years' experience.

There were numerous other finds at Oseberg – enough to have cleared out the dead lady's house: five beds carved with animal heads, on one of which her body lay; down-filled bedding; tents (which seem to have been a standard piece of kit when travelling by ship); three oak chests with iron mounts; leather shoes; three large examples of those ubiquitous Germanic personal items – combs; oil-lamps, a frying pan, pot chain, two cauldrons and other kitchen items. A woven tapestry has also survived in part and depicts scenes including a procession of armed warriors (of both sexes) and horse-drawn carts.

Another particularly striking object is the so-called 'Buddha bucket', a yew wood pail with brass bands and rim. The two 'ears' that link the handle to the pail are identical – small bronze human figures. It is because of these that the object is called the 'Buddha bucket', as each figure's legs are crossed in a way very like the lotus posture. Yet it seems that rather than seeking the origin of this image in Buddhist art (which as we have seen was known from at least the actual statuette of the Buddha from Helgö), it has a more likely origin in the traditions of Irish art with which the Vikings were very familiar.

The practice of boat burial was not just for the rich – certainly by Viking times ordinary farmers might be buried in their boats. Presumably this had a religious connotation, but it could also have been because such craft made ready-to-hand coffins. Among both the west Germanic peoples and the Vikings, the ship seems to have played an important symbolic role as the means by which the buried person travels to the land of the dead. In the various cases of boat burial – whether the marshland Saxon chieftain from Fallward, King Raedwald at Sutton Hoo or the present Viking lady – the presence of the dead person's worldly possessions seems to strengthen the idea that they may also have had otherworldly uses.

However, a curious discovery concerning the Oseberg ship may suggest otherwise. A rope that was tied to a stone held the boat fast in its mound. The message seems to be that the mound itself is the final resting place, with its occupant moored here for eternity. The presence of the mooring rope can be interpreted in one of two ways. Firstly, it can be seen to contradict the generally held view that the ship was the symbolic means of travelling over the water to the realm of the dead. If it was moored and therefore secured in the mound, how could it travel anywhere? In this interpretation the worldly goods that surround the deceased are just that – worldly – and have no further role to play in the afterlife. They are buried with the body as a mark of respect and as a message to the living who witness the funeral that the deceased was a man (or in this case woman) of power and prestige.

Yet we can also revive the idea that the ship did play a symbolic role in the drama of an afterlife. In this way of looking at it, the mooring rope and stone announce that the lady has already arrived in the land of the dead. In the process of dying she travelled to the other world, which is now symbolised by the mound in which she, her possessions and her ship reside. The mound was a part of the other world visible in our own.

Gokstad: Ship of a Warrior Chief

The Gokstad ship was buried in a mound that was probably slightly bigger than its Oseberg counterpart. Its dimensions have been estimated at 5 metres (16 feet) high and 43–50 metres (140–65 feet) across. Like the Oseberg ship, this too had been packed with clay which thankfully resulted in much of the wood being preserved. A skeleton was found in the partially preserved timber burial chamber in the ship; it was of a tall man thought to be a chieftain, and about sixty when he died. Robbers had looted any weaponry or other precious metalwork from the chamber, leaving behind what must have been to them less valuable objects.

While there is nothing to really compare with the ornate wood-working of the Oseberg finds, there were nevertheless items of interest. Many of the same items recur in both ships – textile fragments, a sleigh, a number of broken beds, cauldrons and so on – but there are also novel features of the Gokstad burial. The skeleton of a peacock was found in the ship, and a number of skeletons of both dogs and horses were discovered outside the vessel. Substantial fragments of sixty-four shields remained where they had been placed down the sides of the ship (two between each pair of oar-holes). Their preservation was good enough for archaeologists to see that they had all been painted alternately in black and yellow. Three smaller boats also accompanied the main Gokstad vessel. They were equally well made and almost indistinguishable from similar craft still being built in western Norway in modern times. Clearly their construction had been perfected by Viking times and required no further improvements.

The ship dates from the late ninth century and so is some eighty or so years younger than the Oseberg ship. The Gokstad ship is only slightly bigger: 23.24 metres (76 feet) in length, with a maximum width of 5.2 metres (17 feet) and a depth from keel to gunwale midship of 2.02 metres (6 feet 6 inches). It is of really heavy construction – 3 tons of oak designed to endure any conditions and even a transatlantic crossing. An estimated 350 kilos of iron nails were used to strengthen it. It is robust enough to have carried large loads and cargoes, including cattle and other animals that were required to colonise new lands. A crew of thirty-two oarsmen and a few men for sailing could have been accompanied by up to sixty or seventy more people and animals to boot. What the Oseberg ship was for pleasure, the Gokstad ship was for the serious business of long-distance raiding, trading and colonising.

Several replicas of the Gokstad ship have been built and all of them have undertaken long voyages (some with animals on board); more than one of these has crossed the Atlantic without any problem. The first of such voyages was undertaken in 1893 when its captain, Magnus Andersen, was able to proudly display it at the World Exhibition in Chicago. The making of replica ships is still very useful in helping us to understand the craft skills and technology that were used in Viking times.

A number of replicas are being made at the Ship Museum at Roskilde to the west of Copenhagen in Denmark, including a full-scale Viking ship. This major project of experimental archaeology has shown the boat-builders there that the most important person in the making of a Viking ship was the man who designed the stern post and the keel. If this was right, everything else followed smoothly – provided the level of workmanship was maintained. He was as important to the outcome as an architect is for a house.

The Borre find is the most modest of all the exhibits in the Viking Ship Museum in Oslo. It is a ghostly ship, its presence marked only by rivets and nails. Yet this is not its only similarity to Sutton Hoo. As with the other three ship burials from the Oslo fjord, this vessel too was buried in a mound. It was not a solitary mound but one of a number that may have housed other members of its occupants' lineage. It is thought probable that this group of mounds belongs to the northern branch of the Ynglinge dynasty (which included Queen Åsa), but the assigning of particular mounds to particular members of this pagan lineage has proved as difficult as in the case of Sutton Hoo.

In this shadow ship of Borre, however, there was a small but important find: a single rock crystal. Rock crystal is one of the prized items of the Viking Age. There were a few areas in Norway and on mainland Sweden producing it, but the industry was centred on the island of Gotland in the Baltic Sea. This was, in Viking times, a centre of commerce and a thriving crossroads of trade. It was to be my next port of call.

Chapter Twenty One

GOTLAND: A BARBARIAN BANK

Gotland has aptly been called the world's largest treasury. From the Viking Age alone, over 700 hoards have been discovered. In proportion to its area, the island has the greatest abundance of treasure hoards in the world.

Maria Domeij, *Treasures of Gotland*

There were a number of trading towns in Scandinavia that grew up as the Viking merchants expanded their horizons. Hedeby in Jutland (Schleswig, northern Germany) and Birka on an island in Lake Mälaren, Sweden, are among the most well known. There were no towns in Scandinavia until around the beginning of the eighth century, and even after that the settlements that arose were not towns as we might understand them. Few had any stone buildings, and their wooden houses were very much like those built in villages – there were simply more of them.

At Hedeby (which has been studied by archaeologists for a century) there are clear indications that a local trading network had been set up to allow the townspeople more time to concentrate on trade and production. Rural villages would supply the town with food from their farms in exchange for items such as combs and jewellery made in workshops in the town. At its height in the tenth century, it probably had a population of about 1,500. Freedom from the daily toil of farming allowed some of the townspeople the chance to develop their longer-distance trading opportunities.

Goods and merchants came to Hedeby and Birka from both eastern and western sources, some from remarkable distances. In the middle of the tenth century an Arab traveller named Al-Tartushi wrote about his visit to Hedeby, which he describes as 'a large town at the very far end of the world ocean. It has freshwater wells within the city. Its people worship Sirius except for a few who are Christians and have a church there.' Some of the numerous Viking Age graves that have been excavated at Birka contain Chinese silk, probably obtained by Viking traders via middlemen based around the Caspian Sea. The Baltic Sea was a crossroads for the seaborne trade routes that linked the western and eastern markets during the Viking Age (from the eighth to the eleventh centuries) – and Gotland was literally right in the middle of this sea of commercial opportunities. A large island about 106 miles long and 31 miles wide, it is some 50 miles from the Swedish mainland.

The Silver Age of Gotland

Gotland's hoards have become widely known to international treasure hunters in modern times. Dan Carlsson, an archaeologist based at Gotland University, told me that recent attempts by foreigners and Swedish nationals to dig up hoards had led to prosecutions, and resulted in the use (but not ownership) of metal detectors being made illegal in Gotland without special permission, a ban that was more recently extended throughout Sweden. The Viking Age hoards are mostly silver and the total weight of those found so far is about 2 tons. This is far more than has been found in the whole of the rest of Sweden. There are undoubtedly many more hoards still buried in the soils of Gotland, so the ban on the use of metal detectors was imposed for good reason. A single hoard that was found recently comprised 70 kilos of silver. There are probably one or two hoards on every farm on Gotland.

The silver that makes up these hoards is usually found either in the form of coins or so-called silver bracelets. Despite the latter's name, Dan Carlsson told me that he had never found any of them on the wrists of either the male or female skeletons that he had excavated. These silver bands actually seem to have been the nearest thing to 'currency' known at the time. They are standardised in weight and obviously were used in transactions in which their value would have been well understood. We have seen in an earlier chapter that scales and weights were used in Scandinavia long before the Viking Age.

Numerous portable scales and associated weights have also been found in Viking Gotland, but for the larger amounts of silver being exchanged bigger scales must have existed, although such artefacts have yet to be found. Of those weights that have been found the great majority have turned up at sites that were used for the Viking assemblies of freemen – the *things*. Perhaps the *thing* was the forum where merchants could make public oaths concerning their business. It is also a possibility that the weighing of weights themselves might have been conducted in full view of the other men attending the *thing*.

Before rivers of silver started to flow into the Viking world, gold (mostly in the form of Roman coins) was the main precious metal – so much so that the period from about AD 400 to 550 has been dubbed the Golden Age of the North. It was out of this that the Scandinavians developed their gold bracteates, in the traditions of the Roman medallions. As this Golden Age marked the links with the Roman world, so the Silver Age that began later, in the ninth century, showed the links that were being forged with a new super-power on the world stage: the Islamic empire of the Arabs. Most of the coins that found their way to Gotland in the earlier period of its economic heyday were Arabic coins from the east, while others came from as far afield as Sassanian Iran and Moorish Spain. Later, from around 975, the majority of coins came from the west, from Anglo-Saxon England and Germany, indicating that the eastern trade routes had fallen into decline.

Coins from various sources were part of the trading system that flourished in Gotland, but they were not used like modern currency. Their source or their value in terms of the coinage system to which they belonged were of no interest to the Vikings – it was simply their weight that mattered. There are many coins in the hoards that have been cut in half or into quarters in order to balance the scales. The use of coins as currency did not start in Gotland until the middle of the twelfth century.

How did the Gotlanders become so rich? It was certainly not because they had any raw materials of value to outsiders; nor was their own craftsmanship or manufacturing industry (for which see below) sufficient on its own to explain all of their wealth. The answer seems to lie largely with their role as middlemen. These days Gotland is far from the trade arteries that dominate the western world, but in Viking times the Baltic was the hub of a vibrant economy – the island's inhabitants were able to trade exotic items both ways, accumulating huge hoards of silver in the process. They were shrewd businessmen who took their cut as middlemen, but they were also daring entrepreneurs willing to risk life and limb to bring back goods from the ends of the known world.

Rock crystal was one of the main kinds of specialist goods controlled by Gotlandic middlemen. It was imported probably from the Black Sea region or from Basra in Persia (an important eastern centre of the crystal industry), and was used, among other things, for making beads and pendants. Rock crystal is an extremely hard substance and difficult to work; how the island craftsmen managed to drill holes in it is something of a mystery, but drill it they did. The fact that the archaeologists have found raw material, half-finished beads and fully crafted beads shows that not only did the islanders import rock crystal, but they also crafted it locally rather than buying it in finished form.

An even greater mystery are the bigger rock crystals found on Gotland; these are some 4 or 5 cm (up to 2 inches) in diameter. Rather than being simply ornamental like their smaller counterparts, they had a practical function – as magnifying lenses that would have been used by craftsmen who, after years of close work, would find their sight failing. The lens are made to a standard that modern experts in optics have found to be amazingly high. There is not sufficient evidence to ascertain whether these were also manufactured on the island or imported in their finished form. Such rock crystals must have been highly sought after and therefore, no doubt, extremely expensive.

They also had another use as so-called sun stones. Sun stones can be used for navigational purposes when the sky is overcast and the sun not directly visible. With the magnifying glass of rock crystal, the sunbeams would be concentrated in one spot and allow the navigator to work out the position of the sun. They worked, in a way, as a kind of compass. The confusing of these dual functions of the larger rock crystals – as magnifying lens and sun stone – has led to them being interpreted as the lens for a Viking telescope, which seems extremely unlikely to have been the case.

There is evidence that trading in iron and specifically in swords was also high among their business priorities. Arms dealing was no doubt as highly lucrative in the past as it still is today. This trade continued into the Christian era; one Pope wrote to the local bishop, instructing him to tell the Gotlanders to cease selling swords to heathens. Among the exotica that found its way to the island are four or five so-called 'resurrection eggs', made of clay. They came from Kiev in the Ukraine and indicate that some of the Swedish Vikings at least had their initial contacts with Christianity from the Eastern Orthodox church before the faith arrived from western Europe.

Even when we realise that the hoards were the result of the Gotlanders' joint roles as middlemen and bold travellers, we still need an explanation of why they buried their wealth in the ground. It of course shows a great surplus in wealth; that so much silver could be taken out of circulation without damaging their economy is a staggering fact. It was literally disposable wealth. They seem to have typically put their nest-eggs under their houses, perhaps depositing a little each year so their 'savings' grew over time. Were they just saving for a rainy day, or to have something to pass on to their children?

It has been suggested that they may have been placed in the ground as an offering to the pagan gods. To us today this sacrifice may seem a plain absurdity – but it is not so different to what happened to their money next. The very earth on which they lived and farmed was a bank to the barbarians, yet with the rise of the new religion of Christianity among them they were to pull their money out of nature's bank and reinvest it in the afterlife promised as a return by the Church. In the first centuries of the Christian era in Gotland, the islanders paid for the building of the numerous stone churches that mark the parishes of the island. The silver that had lain in the ground was turned to stone.

The Picture Stones: Doorways to Another World?

While rune stones are comparatively widespread in mainland Scandinavia, Gotland has very few. Instead, the Vikings of this island raised memorials to those who died far away from home, and whose bodies had either been lost at sea or could not be brought back to be buried for some other reason. Travellers who never came back from their adventures on the Russian rivers or in the Arab trading areas are remembered by their families who put up these stones for them. These memorials are known as picture stones and are a distinctively Gotlandic contribution to Viking culture. At the base of some of these standing stones animal bones have been unearthed, suggesting that feasts or memorial meals took place at the site of the memorial. Most of the stones that were carved and once painted in bright colours (little of this pigment remains today) on their surfaces show no runes like the famous stones of mainland Scandinavia, but vivid pictures that tell us something about the lives of the Gotland Vikings as well as something about their beliefs concerning the afterlife.

Over 400 picture stones have been found to date. New finds are not that uncommon. While I was there, a picture stone was brought in to the museum storehouse – it had been uncovered by men digging in the ground by the side of a road in order to lay fibre optic cables. Although these stones once stood proud and erect in the landscape, few now remain in their original setting. Many reside in the national collections in Stockholm, while many are also kept in the Historical Museum of Gotland in the island's capital, Visby. The earliest examples date from the fifth century (that is, before the Viking period), and the latest from the twelfth century when the pagan Viking Age gave way to the Christian era. As memorials, they were placed in prominent spots in the landscape – at the side of tracks and roads, near bridges and close to the sites used for the *thing* assemblies.

Many of the picture stones were shaped like doorways, and this has led to suggestions that they can be seen as portals to the world of the dead, as markers of the transition between life and death. Others have seen some stones as symbolically shaped as axes or phalluses. Whichever interpretation is correct, they remain a source of symbolic and practical information about the world of their creators.

Early symbols include the motif of horses confronting each other, which reflects not only the Vikings' love of stallion fighting for sport but also probably stands as a symbol for the battle between positive and negative forces, between good and evil. This motif has also been linked to fertility rites. Dragons, snakes and other monstrous images on some of the picture stones appear to be linked to Norse mythology as it is known through the early-thirteenth-century *Prose Edda* and other literary sources. Some of the pagan gods are also present, Odin the most prominent among them. There is a scene on one picture stone (the Hammars stone from the Lärbro parish of Gotland, dated to the period 700–800) that depicts human sacrifice. It shows an armed warrior with a noose around his neck waiting to be hanged while another man, his head face down on an altar, seems about to be speared to death.

Many picture stones have a number of panels on them in which different scenes are shown. Typically, those at the top of the stone reflect the world beyond – many depict the deceased being greeted in Valhalla, the Viking heaven, by a Valkyrie (a female spirit who attends to dead warriors) with a drinking horn full of mead. Other stones, such as one found under a church floor in the Ardre parish, shows Sleipnir, the eight-legged horse of Odin, being ridden by a dead man to Valhalla. We have already met Sleipnir in relation to the riddles of the Anglo-Saxons, and once again there is a riddle to solve.

It has long perplexed scholars of Norse mythology that Sleipnir is not simply reserved for his owner Odin, king of the gods, to ride. Why are dead warriors allowed to ride the god's mount? The German scholar Detlev Ellmers has convincingly solved this problem. Using continental sources that record the customs of this time, he notes that when honoured guests of a king arrived by sea they were greeted at the shore with horses to ride to the regal hall. Often, if the guest was distinguished enough, the king would send his own horse out for his guest to ride back to the hall. In this explanation, Odin as king of the gods sends his own horse Sleipnir for the deceased to ride to the heavenly hall of Valhalla.

The Vikings of Gotland, being of course surrounded by sea, also used the ship as a potent symbol of the journey to the other world. Yet the boat depicted on this picture stone clearly represents a worldly vessel too. Nautical archaeologists, lacking material proof of the kinds of rigging used in Viking ships, have found such images very useful in their making of replica vessels. In addition to fleshing out the picture of the rigging and other practical features of the ships, we can also see that the boats portrayed on the picture stones are quite small. Typically they show crews of fifteen to twenty or even less. These kinds of boats are very different from the Gokstad and Oseberg ships – less grand but more useful for trading down the Russian rivers. The larger vessels were simply too big to be hauled overland, which was something the Norse traders with the east had to do routinely. Often there were considerable overland distances to get from one river to the next, and the ship had to be small enough for its crew to pull it.

While I was in Gotland I was fortunate enough to have a close look at a replica of such a ship (the rigging mirrors that on the picture stone, as shown in the illustrations). This ship, named *Krampmacken* ('The Prawn'), was housed in a boat shed on the coast. Dan Carlsson introduced me to a colleague of his named Jonas Ström, who was one of the crew who had rowed, sailed and pulled it from Gotland to Istanbul via the rivers and roads of eastern Europe on an expedition that took place in the 1980s. With the help of wheels – which the Vikings may or may not have used to help them – and modern road surfaces, Ström and the others were able to move the boat an average of 25 kilometres (just over 15 miles) per day overland and obviously much more rapidly down the rivers.

Although this faithful replica of a Viking trading vessel could, with some concerted effort, be brought out of its boat shed by means of manpower alone, Carlsson and Ström decided that this time it would do no harm to tow it out with the help of a Volvo. As the ship was hauled out of the shed, I remarked to Ström that it was rather fitting that this modern Swedish vehicle was pulling an ancient kind of Swedish vehicle. He turned towards me with a wry smile, and corrected me by pointing out that this Viking-style vessel was not Swedish but Gotlandic. The islanders have a very distinct identity and their dialect is difficult for many mainlanders to follow. Many of the older people have never visited mainland Sweden. This independent spirit of the Gotlanders runs very deep and certainly has its roots in the Viking Age, if not before.

The social world of Viking Age Gotland was very different to that of mainland Sweden. There were no kings, no lords and no upper class whatsoever. It was a society of farmers who doubled up as traders. From the evidence of the distribution of the hoards (which are as common in the middle of the island as they are in the coastal areas), it seems that all the islanders had a stake in the trading network that linked them with the outside world. Treaties were made with other societies in the Baltic region and tribute was paid to the Swedish kings – the price of independence. Such a society was suited to the particular circumstances of living on an island and, in the absence of a permanent centralised power such as a king, the whole administration was run by the *things*. Each part of the island (which has been, since the introduction of Christianity, divided into parishes) had its own local *thing*, then there were a small number of regional *things* and the *althing* which representatives of all parts of the island would attend. The *althing* would meet once a year in midsummer in the middle of the island to discuss matters of importance to the whole island community.

The democratic leanings of this island community stood in contrast to the centralised kingdoms that were emerging in mainland Scandinavia, but they were echoed elsewhere – in the brave new world of the Nordic colonies in Iceland and beyond.

Chapter Twenty Two

NORTH ATLANTIC COLONIES

*Thule... the very last of named places: a place at the limits of
the cosmos. The lure of such an island fired the imagination,
and as knowledge of the northern lands expanded, so Thule
retreated, staying always just beyond the familiar.*

Christina Horst Roseman, *Pytheas of Massalia*

We have seen how the Vikings' small ships made it possible for
them to raid down the French rivers and trade down the Russian
rivers. The larger vessels, epitomised by the Gokstad ship, were
able to spread the Viking influence further across the seas. The
Vikings' travels by ship brought them into contact and conflict
with numerous peoples who had their own established cultural and
trading networks. While the Norsemen were bringing their own
influences to bear on the existing cultural mosaic of the Old World,
they were also being greatly transformed in the process. Yet there
is another part of their epic story that took place far from the
centres of either Islamic or Christian civilisation. Their pioneering

spirit took them beyond the confines of that world into the uncharted seas of the North Atlantic.

Ultima Thule: the Quest for the Far North

In the fourth century BC, Pytheas of Massalia (the name once given to the ancient port of Marseilles) wrote in his book *On the Ocean* about a northern island that he named Thule. Exactly which place he meant to designate by this name remains a mystery. Western Norway, the Faeroe Islands and Iceland have all been put forward as candidates. The writers who followed Pytheas in mentioning this fabled northern land are equally vague concerning its whereabouts, even down to the time of Bede. A ninth-century Irish monk named Dicuil who was based in France hints that Thule may be identified with Iceland, and by the eleventh century Adam of Bremen says just this in explicit terms. A recent review of this ancient mystery by Christina Horst Roseman suggests that Pytheus' Thule may be the Faeroe Islands.

In a book written in 825, Dicuil states that from the beginning of the eighth century it was the practice of hardy monks to set forth in small boats (probably *currachs*, leather or skin boats of a type in which legend would have St Brendan reaching America) and to settle on whatever desolate or windswept island they reached first, by God's will. These voyaging monks beat the Vikings to both the Faeroe Islands and Iceland. They were known to the Vikings as *papar* ('fathers'). The arrival of the Vikings usually led to the swift departure of the monks, who would either leave in search of a new uninhabited place to live or be forcibly removed by the Norse immigrants. The Vikings reached the Faeroes some time between 860 and 870.

The founding father of the Viking colonisation is given in the account of the *Saga of the Faeroe Islanders* as Grim Kamban. Scholars see the name Kamban to be a Celtic one, and have therefore suggested that he may have been a Norwegian who set out from either Ireland or the Hebrides, both of which had already been settled by the Vikings. Archaeological evidence from the islands reveals traces of the Viking presence – farmsteads, pagan burials, coin hoards and, dating from the later period, the remains of a number of wooden churches. The Faroes lie about half-way between the Shetlands and Iceland and it was to the latter that a major migration was to take place.

The Founding Fathers of Iceland

The volcanic landscape of Iceland presented a new world to the Vikings in a number of ways. Its distance from other lands – over 250 miles from the Faeroes, 500 miles from the northern tip of Scotland and 620 miles from the Norwegian homeland – made it isolated and largely independent of the outside world. A twelfth-century source tells us that the voyage to Norway took a week, and to Britain five days. Iceland's climate and ecology differed from the other lands the Vikings knew, and farming land was limited by glaciers and mountain ranges. The fact that there were no indigenous people there (and only a handful of *papar* leading the lonely life of the hermit) meant that they did not have to fight to establish themselves, and there was no native culture to assimilate – they had the freedom to settle anywhere they wanted. The Vikings brought their own cultural baggage with them but, when they arrived to settle this new world, they were to create a different way of living – built on the past but adapted to a novel present.

Twelfth-century sources credit a Norwegian named Floki with the Norse discovery of Iceland. He is said to have set out from the Faeroes some time early in the ninth century, travelling north. During the course of his voyage he released two ravens to see in which direction they would fly. By following them, he was led to Iceland. He is also supposed to have been the first to call it Iceland after enduring a particularly severe first winter on this new-found land. Apocryphal stories aside, the period between 870 and 930 was the time of the 'land-taking' (*landnám*) during which between 10,000 and 20,000 Vikings emigrated to Iceland. Men, women and children, along with their animals and supplies, poured into Iceland. The majority came from Norway directly but others came from the Norse settlements in Celtic lands – Ireland, the Scottish mainland and the Hebrides.

After this original period of colonisation, the people of Iceland were brought together by the founding of the *Althing*, a general assembly along the lines of that which also existed in other Norse communities such as Gotland. It would be a mistake to think of Iceland as a unified state, for despite the existence of the *Althing* the emphasis was more on a loose-knit and decentralised society than an authoritarian and autocratic kingdom. The existence of local and regional *things* allowed each part of the island's community to continue to assert itself. There were no kings in Iceland and the leadership of the people fell to *godar* (chieftains; singular *godi*), whose role was more political and priestly than military. The *godar* had to persuade their followers, or *thingmenn*, drawn from the ranks of farmers who owned their land freehold, to support them on the basis of mutual interest. They were also repositories of the pagan religion and responsible for public ceremonies and rituals.

Other familiar Norse beliefs have also been proved by archaeological discoveries to have travelled with the Vikings to Iceland. Excavations at the site of a farm on the coast of Patreksfjord in north-western Iceland led by Thórr Magnússon revealed the presence of a tenth-century boat burial. Many of its features reflect patterns that are similar to Viking ship burials elsewhere, and also to Saxon and Anglo-Saxon practices. It is one of the richest burials discovered in Iceland, despite the fact that it was robbed in former times and probably much of its contents have been lost.

The boat was buried under a mound, and when it was excavated the archaeologists found little trace of the vessel except the iron nails that once held it together. The layout of the nails was sufficiently preserved for the dimensions of the boat to be calculated: about 6 metres (20 feet) long and 1 metre (just over 3 feet) wide. Fragments of wood led the excavators to propose that it was made of spruce or larch. Two whalebone pieces were also found; these were originally attached to the inside of the gunwale and used to limit the friction caused by anchor or tow lines.

Bones of seven young people – four female, three male – were found in the area where the boat would have been, but Magnússon believes that six of these were thrown in some time after the burial, possibly by the looters. The original and intended occupant of the grave was probably one of the young women. The body was accompanied by an array of objects which, like King Raedwald's much richer grave goods, seem to show a mixture of pagan and Christian elements. Alongside some small bronze items including a pin and two bracelets, two bone combs, thirty glass and amber beads, part of an Arabic coin and some lead balance weights, was a little Thor's hammer made of silver and a tiny broken bronze bell.

These last two items show the transition was under way from paganism to Christianity. The Thor's hammer is just over 3.5 cm (11/2 inches) long and was a common kind of pagan amulet believed to protect its owner from baleful influences. The bell is similar to a few others found in Viking Iceland, and has been identified as Celtic or Anglo-Saxon but certainly from the British Isles; such bells are known to have been used in Christian ceremonies. Interestingly enough, as Magnússon points out, there are early written records stating that the people who came to colonise the Patreksfjord area were Vikings from earlier settlements in the British Isles. The boat burial shows how the Christian communities among which the Vikings had previously lived before coming to Iceland had started to influence their religious beliefs.

This gradual transition was soon to be formalised by the *Althing*, which ratified the peaceful and painless conversion of Iceland to Christianity in the year 999 or 1000. Many of the pagan *godar* moved fairly effortlessly into the role of Christian priest. The free state of Iceland was increasingly coming under the expansionist eyes of the Norwegian kings, and by the 1260s was paying tax to the sovereign – formal acceptance of the end of its independence, which it was not to regain until 1944.

Icelandic society was something of an anomaly in early medieval Europe. Jesse L. Byock, a leading specialist on early Icelandic society, notes just how precocious their social order was: 'To succeed, a *godi* had to have charisma as well as skill in managing relationships with *thingmenn*, in supervising disputes and feuds, especially in the final court and arbitration stages, and in winning legal cases. Despite the deference accorded to successful *godar*, the society's egalitarian ethos was so strong that the *godar* participated in governmental processes that were often proto-democratic.' Icelandic society was probably more democratic than any other society in the Europe of its time. It was not racked by the wars and displacements of population that almost routinely disrupted the peace of mainland Europe. Yet it was not free of disputes and troublesome individuals.

One of these, a violent and disreputable man named Eirik the Red, was tried for murder by one of the regional *things* (the Thorsnes *thing* in the west of the country). He was found guilty and temporarily banished from Iceland, probably in the year 982. He had heard about a land further to the west discovered by a seafarer named Gunnbjörn after he was blown way off course by a storm on his way from Norway to Iceland. Eirik set out on an expedition to discover this new land for himself, and thus took the first step towards the Norse colonisation of Greenland. According to a short but informative historical text written in the early twelfth century and entitled *The Book of the Icelanders*, Eirik discovered that unlike Iceland, Greenland was not an uninhabited land but it was sparsely populated by *Skraelings*, that is, the Inuit (Eskimo) people. He returned to Iceland, having served his time in exile, in 985 or thereabouts and set about persuading others to follow him back to the new land.

A Green and Treeless Land

Eirik knew the importance of a name in trying to 'sell' the new land to would-be settlers; he chose to name it Greenland to make it sound as inviting as possible. Although he has been berated for what many believe was little better than a confidence trick, parts of Greenland were actually very suitable for farming. Certainly his description of the new country was far more accurate than that of Adam of Bremen, who expressed the opinion that Greenland was so named on account of the colour of its salt water – which made its inhabitants greenish in colour too!

Twenty-five ships are reported to have left Iceland on course for Greenland, but only fourteen arrived at their destination; the others either turned back to Iceland or were lost. In some respects, Greenland was more attractive than Iceland – the pasture was good, having never been used by farming people before (the Inuit were hunter-gatherers). On the other hand, there were no trees to greet the settlers and their houses were thus usually made from turf and stones and driftwood when available. Nevertheless, the wildlife offered numerous opportunities for trading. Luxury items and crucial imports such as iron and timber could be bartered for marine ivory (in the form of narwhal and walrus tusks), exotic furs, falcons and even the occasional live polar bear.

The most well-known Viking site in Greenland is Brattahild on a plain close to Eiriksfjord, the inlet that Eirik claimed on his arrival in the new colony. Archaeology has so far revealed only one pagan image among the artefacts from Greenland – a broken loom weight with a hammer of Thor etched on it, found at the site of a barn at Brattahild. There is also a small church with thick turf walls at the site, and this is thought to be the earliest place of Christian worship in Greenland. It is usually identified as the church built by Eirik's wife Thjodhild shortly after she was converted to Christianity by her son Leif the Lucky. Legend has it that Eirik remained an unrepentant pagan and his newly converted wife refused to live with him.

Sagas, Maps and Artefacts

Eirik's son Leif had tired of Greenland and was restless to explore even further to the west. In 985 a ship en route from Iceland to Greenland was blown off course and a previously unseen wooded land was sighted. Bjarni Herjolfsson, who was on board, named it Markland (meaning 'Woodland' or 'Forestland'). His vessel then proceeded north past a barren rocky land he called Helluland ('Flatstoneland') and eastwards back toward Greenland. Leif is said to have heard about this accidental voyage and tried to retrace the route taken by Bjarni. To do this he had, of course, to start in Greenland and proceed from there to Helluland (now thought to be Baffin Island) and on to Markland (the Labrador coast). From there Leif pressed on further south for two days until he reached a place he called Vinland ('Vineland' or 'Wineland', now thought to be Newfoundland) on account of the wild grapes he is said to have found growing there. Leif and his crew landed and wintered over in this new world before returning to Greenland in the spring. The following year Leif's brother Thorwald voyaged to Vinland, and was killed by an arrow fired by a *Skraeling* (in this case the term refers to an Indian native of the region rather than an Inuit, as was the case in Greenland).

Despite these references in the sagas and other early sources, there was no concrete proof to demonstrate the Norse presence in North America. Then in 1957 a map was launched into the scholarly world that seemed to provide a dramatic vindication of the Viking voyages. The Vinland map, as it is known, is drawn on vellum and was described by the curator of the map collection at Yale University Library as 'of late medieval type... [it] contains the earliest known and indisputable cartographic representation of any part of the Americas, and includes a delineation of Greenland so strikingly accurate that it may well have derived from experience'. The curator went on to note that it may be the only surviving medieval example of Norse mapmaking. Despite having certain reservations about its authenticity (it seemed too good a find to be true), Yale University Press decided to go ahead and publish it in 1965 with a detailed analysis of its contents and its implications. Since its publication, analysis of pigment in the ink used to draw the map indicates that it was of a type that would not have been available until the late nineteenth century. Such analysis has led most experts to reject the Vinland map as a forgery.

The sagas and early records of the Viking period had not, after all, been proved by the discovery of this map. Yet during the 1960s another more tangible means of proving the Vikings were the first Europeans to reach the Americas was under way. A Norwegian explorer named Helge Ingstad was convinced that Vinland was northern Newfoundland, and decided to try to find archaeological proof of the Norse presence there. Ingstad describes how a fortunate meeting with a local man named George Decker led to his momentous discovery. Ingstad had been surveying a number of possible sites along the north coast of Newfoundland and had reached a small fishing village named L'Anse aux Meadows, the last place on his list. It was there that Decker directed him to a cluster of overgrown bumps in the landscape, which Ingstad could see must be the site of long abandoned houses. This was where he decided to dig for the evidence he was looking for.

The site of L'Anse aux Meadows turned out to provide the firm evidence that the Vikings were in America, yet the site also showed signs of being temporary. The remains of eight structures were found by Ingstad and subsequent archaeologists. They were made of turf and were very similar in style to Norse buildings found in Iceland and Greenland, but they lacked the stone foundations that characterised the permanent houses of these Viking colonies. There was no question that Vikings had stayed here for a time – a bronze pin, a spindle whorl and the signs of a smithy were all identified as their artefacts. Is this site just a vindication of their fleeting presence in the New World or was it, as some have suggested, a transit camp used sporadically by Vikings probing further to the south, making other journeys of which we know nothing?

Whichever role L'Anse aux Meadows played, it is ironic that just as the Vikings were in the process of discovering a new world, their old pagan world was coming to an end.

Chapter Twenty Three

RAGNAROK: END OF THE VIKING WORLD

In this conflict all the great gods must be destroyed,
and the monsters with them.

Hilda Ellis Davidson, *Gods and Myths of Northern Europe*

Ragnarok is the name given in Norse mythology to the end of the world. At this time, after a number of cataclysmic events – an interminable winter, earthquakes and the darkening of the sun – all the gods are killed in conflict with giants and monstrous beings. Such is the mythic view of the final apocalypse. From the perspective of history, the pagan gods (the Aesir and the Vanir) were destroyed by the coming of a new set of beliefs in the form of Christianity. The changes wrought by this missionary faith went far beyond the realm of worship: society itself was changed, literacy and books began to exert more and more influence over the destiny of the European continent, and the roots of modern science began to emerge out of the strivings of religiously motivated individuals.

Christianity was not the only religious force that the Vikings came in contact with during their countless voyages through numerous parts of Europe and beyond. The influence of Islam and the Arabs during the Dark Ages is often overlooked. The Arabs, like the Vikings, were great merchants and travellers and the two did business together. Probably the most important Arabic source concerning the Vikings is Ibn Fadhlan, who encountered them on the banks of the river Volga and left a record of the experience in 922.

To a Muslim like Ibn Fadhlan, cleanliness was an important religious duty and one that he noticed was very much neglected by the Vikings. He recounts his horror on observing that they did not wash after eating, urinating, defecating or having sexual intercourse. He says more positive things about their appearance, which he admires: they are 'perfect physical specimens, tall as date palms, blond and ruddy'. He tells us too that they had simple prayers, in which they asked their god to send them a rich Arab merchant who would be willing to buy all their goods and not haggle too much!

An Eyewitness Account of a Viking Ship Burial

Although these snapshots of cultural exchange are interesting in their own right, Ibn Fadhlan also recounts more detailed information about the funerary rites that surrounded the death of a Viking chieftain. His account is an extremely valuable one because it adds many eyewitness details that archaeological discoveries can never provide. There on the Volga the familiar practice of boat burial was performed, but with many unfamiliar details.

Ibn Fadhlan first describes how the dead chieftain was placed in a grave for ten days accompanied by fruit, beer and a lute. During this time special grave clothes were made for him. If a man was poor, then a modest boat would be made for his funeral; his corpse would be placed in it and the both of them burned on a pyre. A wealthy man's worldly possessions would be split three ways: a third was left for his family, a third for the cost of his grave clothes, and the other third for making beer for the funeral. On his death, his family would demand a volunteer from among their slaves to die with their master. Normally – and as on the occasion witnessed by Ibn Fadhlan – it was a female slave who would agree to this ultimate self-sacrifice. Once the slave had consented, there was no turning back. While the (presumably lavish) clothes were made for the dead chieftain, the condemned slave would be constantly attended by two other slaves whose tasks even included washing her feet. She would drink and sing as though she was happy to be going to the other world. As the female spirit or Valkyrie that was believed to greet the dead warrior in Valhalla with a drinking horn, so the female slave was to accompany her master across the divide between the two worlds, that of the living and the dead.

On the day of the funeral the dead chieftain's boat that had been moored on the river was hauled up on to dry land. A wooden scaffold was then set up around it. Vikings began to walk around the structure, speaking words that Ibn Fadhlan could not understand. A bier was then carried to the site and put on the boat. There was a mistress of ceremonies, an old woman called by the Vikings the 'Angel Of Death'. Fadhlan describes her as 'a strapping woman, massively built and austere of countenance'. Byzantine carpets and silk cushions were brought in, and she arranged the cushions on top of the bier. The scene was now set for the corpse to be carried to the funeral site. The body was dug up and the wooden coffin removed. The corpse, which had turned black due to the freezing conditions, was then stripped of the clothes in which the chieftain had died. Both these clothes and the items that had been placed in this temporary resting place were discarded.

The corpse was then dressed in the newly made clothes – a sable fur cap, a tunic and cloak with gold buttons and other fancy trappings. Once he was fully dressed, he was carried over to where the boat lay and placed inside a tent on top of it. Fresh fruit and beer were placed around the body along with aromatic herbs, bread, meat and onions. The next stage in the proceedings consisted of a series of animal sacrifices. The first to be dispatched was a dog, which was cut in two and then cast into the boat. Two horses were slaughtered with swords after they had been ridden into a sweat, and then also cut up and placed in the ship. Two cows and a cock and a hen were similarly sacrificed and their carcasses thrown in.

While these sacrificial preparations were taking place, the female slave who was soon to die went into the tent of each and every Viking freeman to have sexual intercourse with them. Each of them would say to her: 'Tell your master that I do this thing for the love of him.' The girl was then taken to a wooden structure rather like a door frame, and was lifted up by the Viking men who were present so that her eye level was above the top of the frame. She said something that Ibn Fadhlan could not understand, then she was lifted up again twice more, each time speaking different words. She then cut the head off a hen and cast it into the boat. Ibn Fadhlan asked his interpreter what had been said, and was told that the first time she had cried out: 'Look. I see my father and mother.' The second time: 'Behold, I see my dead relatives seated around.' And finally: 'Behold! I see my master in Paradise, and Paradise is green and fair, and with him are men and young boys. He is calling me. Let me go to him!'

She was now prepared to die. She took off the two bracelets she was wearing and gave them to the Angel of Death whose task it was to kill her. She also removed her two finger rings and gave them to the daughters of her executioner. The girl was taken into the ship but was not yet allowed to enter the tent. She drank two cups of beer and sang her goodbyes. She tarried too long over her swan song and the Angel of Death had to hurry her along, firmly putting her in the tent and following her in. Then the gathered Viking men began to make a fearful noise by beating their shields with sticks. Ibn Fadhlan tells us that this was done to drown out the cries of the victim, in case her screams put off other girls from volunteering themselves as sacrifices in the future. Six men then entered the tent and had sexual intercourse with her. After this she was laid down by the side of her dead master. Two of the men held her hands, while another two held her feet and the others held the two ends of a rope that the Angel of Death had put round her neck. As the rope was tightened to strangulation point, the old woman stabbed the girl repeatedly in the chest.

After this human sacrifice had been made, the dead man's closest relative set fire to the pile of wood that had been placed under the ship. Others were then permitted to follow suit by casting their own firebrands on to the wood pile. The ship and all its contents, the sacrificial bodies of the animals and the girl along with the tent and the dead chieftain's richly garbed body, were all soon engulfed in flames and, according to Viking belief, the man and his slave were transported to the pagan paradise of Valhalla.

The kind of pagan Viking funerals that Ibn Fadhlan witnessed on the banks of the Volga were soon to be a thing of the past. Valhalla itself, the spiritual home of the Viking warrior, was soon to be demolished and the Christian heaven built there in its place. As the Vikings had themselves predicted, all the gods – including Odin, lord of the great hall of Valhalla – were to die at Ragnarok: the end of the world.

Vikings, Visigoths and Moors
Most of the Viking interactions with the Islamic world took place

in the east. The Swedish Vikings travelled much further east than is generally realised. The Volga river down which they sailed their ships ran through the ancient market town of Bulgar (near to the modern city of Kazan). It was a trading centre controlled by Bulgar tribes, who have been described as the Huns under a new name. It was through Bulgar that much of the vast amount of Arabic silver eventually found its way to Gotland and other places.

Tribes lower down the Volga seem to have made trading agreements with the Abbasid caliphate shortly after it deposed the existing Umayyad dynasty (based in Damascus) in the middle of the eighth century. This change of power at the very heart of the Islamic world resulted in the exploitation of silver-rich mines in Central Asia, which had a knock-on effect for the Viking economy. In the east the Vikings generally travelled in small boats (like the *Krampmacken* replica from Gotland), and unlike their western counterparts they were not really in a position to launch massive assaults and raids.

The Umayyad dynasty that had lost its eastern power base to the Abbasids was able to establish itself in southern Spain (or al-Andalus as the Muslims called it) from the eighth century. By this time the inhabitants of Spain had ceased to be viewed as a mixture of Romans and Goths. The distinctive identity of the Romans had all but dissolved into the Visigoth kingdom that ruled Spain. But the vibrant and strident culture of a still young Islamic world was to prove a more powerful force than the desultory kingdom of the Visigoths.

The Arabs had completed their invasion of Roman North Africa in 698 and had set their sights on crossing the straits of Gibraltar. Their army was largely composed of Berbers – the name given by the early Arab geographers to the indigenous population of North Africa. The Arabic word *barbara* means 'to talk noisily or confusedly', and some believe it to derive from the Greek word for barbarian. The city of Toledo fell in 711 or 712 and within a decade the force of Arabs and Berbers (Moors as they came to be collectively known) had extended their rule beyond the Pyrenees as far as the city of Narbonne. The Visigoth kingdom was consigned to history.

The Moors' hold on the northern regions of Spain and parts of southern France was never very firm, and the centre of their thriving culture was to be in the south. There was an initial period of Arab rule in which governors subordinate to external authorities in both North Africa and Damascus administered al-Andalus. After the overthrow of their power base in Syria, the members of the Umayyad dynasty fled to Spain where they ruled first as *amirs* (kings) from 756 to 929 and then as caliphs from 929 until their demise in 1031.

Three Viking forces are on record for their attempts to raid this stronghold of Islam. The first took place in 844, when a number of towns were sacked and the city of Seville was temporarily overtaken by the northern barbarians. The second raid was part of probably the most audacious and epic voyage of piracy undertaken by any Viking force. It began in 859 on the Loire river, where two Viking leaders named Bjorn Ironside and Hastein decided to loot their way to Rome, taking in Spain, North Africa and the Balearic Islands along the way. This time Moorish Spain suffered more dramatically, many of its cities being sacked by the Scandinavian buccaneers. The Vikings reached Italy but not Rome itself; nevertheless they were so successful that, having made a round trip back from the Mediterranean to their stronghold on the Loire, they were now very rich men. In 866 a third raid on some of the northern towns of Moorish Spain was ineffectual and the Vikings were easily expelled. From this time on, the Vikings seem to have given up raiding Spain and left the Moors in peace.

Al-Andalus: a Centre of Civilisation at Europe's Edge

Al-Andalus became a flourishing centre of civilisation and was in many ways far more advanced technologically and scientifically than the contemporary Christian world. A great mosque, the Mezquita, was built on the site of a church in Cordoba in the eighth century and expanded during the course of the next two centuries. After the end of Arab rule it was turned back into a Christian place of worship, although its patently Islamic architecture makes it difficult to perceive it as such. Today in Cordoba one can still hear the faint echoes of the golden era of Islamic dominance in the voice of the single *muezzin* calling the faithful to prayer from the sole surviving working mosque in the city. This small and modest building stands merely a stone's throw from the vast mosque of ancient Cordoba now transformed into the city's cathedral. When I visited the modern mosque at the time of the midday prayers, the congregation was made up of only four people, a poignant reminder of days long past.

Not only did al-Andalus have trading links with the Islamic world to the east; its scholars also carried out a great number of translations into Arabic of Greek writings which, in turn, did much to keep the learning of the classical world alive. Its Golden Age was under the reign of the caliph Abd al-Rahman III (912–61) and his son al-Hakem (961–76). The first of these two caliphs was responsible for building the huge palace complex of Madinat al-Zahra west of Cordoba. The site covers an area of 112 hectares and, despite having received the attention of archaeologists since 1911, only a tenth of it has been excavated so far. It is an extraordinary site and was once adorned with beautiful gardens and flowing fountains. Against such an idyllic backdrop the arts and sciences flourished, and paper – still unknown in the Christian world – was readily available. Medicine, mathematics and astronomy were among the subjects that were greatly advanced in the heyday of al-Andalus.

Cordoba was home to the man who has been described as the father of modern medicine: Abul Qasim al-Zahrawi (936–1013), or Albucasis as he was known in the Latin world. Julio Samso, a specialist on the history of science in al-Andalus, described him to me as probably the best surgeon of the Middle Ages. His massive treatise on surgery was to have an enormous impact on the subsequent development of western medicine. He illustrated his book with drawings of the medical instruments he used, along with details of their particular functions.

I was able to borrow some accurate replicas of some of the instruments Albucasis describes, and I took them to a surgeon at a local hospital to get his professional opinion on their practical value. He was greatly surprised at the similarity between these replicas and their modern-day counterparts – even my untrained eye could see clear correspondences in the size and shape of numerous different instruments: scalpels and other more specialist tools of the trade to remove blood clots, to operate on the nasal bone, for dentistry and for eye operations.

It was also in the allied fields of mathematics and astronomy that Islamic science in al-Andalus excelled. We have already seen in the Christian world, with the calculations of Bede concerning Easter and other matters, that religion was often the driving force for scientific investigations. Similarly, Islamic science was stimulated by the needs and requirements of religion. Muslims are required to pray in the direction of Mecca and this was simple enough when they were still in their Arabian homeland. But in places far away such as Spain it was not straightforward at all – complex calculations were involved.

A device known as an astrolabe was used; this allowed the position of both the sun and stars to be calculated, and also meant that the hours for the five daily prayers could be worked out. The astrolabe was not an Arabic invention but a Greek one that was later modified by Muslim scientists who adapted it for their religious requirements. The Christians had lost all contact with the astronomical science of the Greeks and only rediscovered it through Islamic middlemen in Spain.

Christianity and Islam were the superpowers of a rapidly changing world, but Spanish Christianity slowly and inexorably pushed the wave of Islamic expansionism back into North Africa. Europe became the uncontested spiritual empire of Christianity, and the Vikings were among the last barbarians on the continent to be brought under its sway. The pagan Ragnarok had come to pass.

Perhaps the most enduring legacy of the Vikings is not their material goods that have been unearthed by archaeology, but their stories and their wisdom that are embodied in the words of the *Voluspa*, a poem written around the year 1000 when the old gods – the Aesir and the Vanir – were giving way to Christianity. It is a fitting epitaph for a pagan Norse world that ended but always believed its time would come again:

In later times
a wondrous treasure,
chessmen of gold,
will be found in the grass
where the Aesir had left them
ages ago…

Barren fields
will bear again,
woes will be cured…
There shall deserving
people dwell
to the end of time
and enjoy their happiness.

Afterword

The aim of this book has been to give, as far as possible, the barbarian side of the Dark Ages story. I have drawn on three main sources of information concerning the history and culture of these people: contemporary accounts by Roman or Christian writers; later accounts by the barbarians themselves once they have developed their own literary traditions (usually after they adopted Christianity); and archaeological data in the form of sites, artefacts and human remains. Each of these sources has its inherent shortcomings: Roman and Christian accounts are often biased and selective in what they tell us; the barbarians' own accounts are often infused with legend and propaganda; and the material evidence from the ground cannot always be taken at face value. Nevertheless, they are all essential and rich sources of information.

Moral issues play a big part in many early accounts of the barbarians. In some cases the barbarians are used as a moral example for the writer's own people to take to heart. Tacitus portrays the Germanic peoples as noble savages who still lived a life of honesty and integrity, unlike his own Roman readers who have sunk into moral decadence. Christian authors also used barbarians as moral exemplars. The fifth-century priest Silvian compares the Goths and Vandals favourably to the Romans – barbarians honour their own people while the Romans think only of their own personal gain. And the Goths are praised for migrating far in search of freedom, rather than enduring the state of 'slavery' imposed on the Roman Christian in a rapidly decaying empire.

On the other hand, Silvian expects the Hun to cheat, the Alan to be greedy and the Saxon to be cruel, because they are all either pagans or heretics (by which he means Arians). They are like this because they do not know any better, whereas the Christian has no excuse for harbouring such sinful intentions. There were many influential

Christian writers who had very clear views about the role of the barbarians whose attacks they had to endure – numerous churchmen interpreted these attacks as divine punishment. It was not just Attila who was believed to be the Scourge of God. The Celtic Gildas and later the Anglo-Saxon Bede both see God's work behind the raids of Germanic tribes. Later still, Alcuin sees the Viking sack of Lindisfarne as just a punishment meted out to a sinful Anglo-Saxon people.

These kinds of record tell us next to nothing about tribal customs and beliefs in the Dark Ages, but much more about the imperial or Christian perspectives of their authors. For most of these ancient writers, barbarians could be a number of things – evil, ignorant or, less often, noble savages and moral exemplars – but they were never allowed to be themselves. In short, their value was deemed to lie merely in their role as the shadow of the Roman or Christian way of living, or as a mirror in which the civilised could contemplate themselves.

Our best contemporary sources are those authors who do not have an axe to grind but simply report what they see, hear and read in a reasonably unbiased way. Unlike many other ancient authors, Tacitus does much more than moralise. In his *Germania* he provides a fascinating and informative account of the Germanic tribes of his time, details of which have been backed up by archaeological finds (such as the distinctive hairstyle known as the Suevian knot). He is not the only literary source to show a genuine interest in the habits and customs of barbarian society. Priscus provides a unique insight into life among the Huns in the time of Attila, and the Arab traveller Ibn Fadhlan's descriptive account of the Norsemen he encountered on the Volga sheds light on many otherwise unknown aspects of life and death among the Vikings. It is contemporary accounts such as these that are invaluable in trying to reconstruct something of the barbarian cultures of the Dark Ages.

The barbarian world was always one of shifting alliances, ethnic diversity and cultural complexity. We have seen that apparently simple questions like who were the Huns or who were the Goths are not as straightforward as they might first appear. This is not merely because the Roman and early Christian writers were too engrossed in their own societies to provide enough accurate ethnographic or historical information. It was also because the Huns and the Goths were not single, unified societies living in isolation – they were composite entities. For example, the Gothic migration from north-eastern Europe down to the Balkans was not the movement of a monolithic nation travelling from one place and arriving at another intact and unchanged. It was a society that was run by an elite who saw themselves as a Gothic dynasty, but many of the people who joined them along the way had other ethnic origins.

The barbarian and pagan chieftains and kings retained power not only through their ability to meet the economic needs of their followers. It was also a widespread practice among such leaders to provide themselves with a noble pedigree. This typically meant that they would not only demonstrate an ancient lineage that linked them back to the world of the ancestors (as in the case of Raedwald's Wuffinga dynasty in the Anglo-Saxon sphere), but also claim descent from mythical figures (such as Mannus among the ancient Germanic people that Tacitus encountered, or the Gothic cultural hero Filimer). Fact, legend and myth became inexorably intertwined in the fluid oral traditions of the barbarians.

Such traditions were transformed when the barbarians began to write down their own history. What had once been mercurial was now fixed in the form of the written word. When Jordanes wrote his book *Getica* he not only recorded the origin and history of his own Gothic people as he saw it; he also partly created it. He moulded his own people's vision of themselves and their past – he was literally making history. This is even more explicit in the Christianised vision of Bede and his history of the English people.

These were not attempts to give largely impartial accounts of the past; they were part of the act of creating a past for a barbarian people and thereby, to an extent, creating that very people by trying to make solid the fluid material they were working with – the earlier orally transmitted lineages and legends.

Archaeology, our third source of information concerning the Dark Ages, provides us with another form of solid evidence. The presence of objects does not always indicate the presence of their makers. There are artefacts that can be identified broadly as originating with a particular ethnic group – Saxon pottery and brooches, for example – but we cannot be sure that the discovery of such objects at British sites necessarily demonstrates a Saxon presence (though it certainly proves a Saxon influence). In other words, while there is no simple correlation between people and objects, the characteristic artefacts of the different barbarian cultures have allowed us to trace migrations and other movements across the continent of Europe and, in the case of the Huns, beyond. They provide frameworks not only across space but also across time: artefacts can provide a chronological sequence in the absence of sufficient historical documents.

The work of archaeologists also provides a different kind of evidence concerning the values and customs of barbarian peoples from that given by written accounts. Objects speak to us: the jewellery made by barbarians on the Danube startles with its beauty and sophistication, the Anglo-Saxon sword tells the story of the remarkable technological achievements wrought in the forges of the Dark Ages, and the vestiges of a golden bow testify to the military prowess of the horse archers of the Huns. When such important objects are found together with many others in an assemblage (as is often the case with burials), a multi-faceted view of a barbarian world emerges; we have seen this in, for example, the Sutton Hoo burial. This in turn links in with other assemblages far away from it in both space and time. We can see a great

Germanic cultural tradition expressed in the form of ship burial throughout the northern European world: in the marshland home of the Saxon chieftain of Fallward in Germany, in the lavish burial of Sutton Hoo, in the Oseberg and Gokstad finds, and among the immigrant population of the Icelandic fjords.

The interplay between the Roman (and subsequently Christian) 'civilised' world and the barbarians (who later became more often known as pagans) was the essence of the Dark Ages. There are underlying patterns in the way in which these two worlds interacted. Typically, we first hear of the barbarians as violent raiders who suddenly appear – hordes of Huns or Vandals, Saxon pirates, Viking looters. After this initial phase more permanent relations are forged out of necessity, and often reluctantly. Dangerous barbarian tribes are paid off with gold or with the promise of land. The Romans employ them in the army and follow a divide-and-rule policy by pitting one barbarian force against another. Barbarians make their permanent settlements inside the 'civilised' world – Goths enter the Roman Empire, Vikings stay in Anglo-Saxon England. The barbarians were transformed from being outsiders and were assimilated first into the Roman Empire and second into the Christian faith.

Barbarian cultures were dramatically transformed by their encounters with 'civilisation', but so too was the Roman empire radically altered by their presence. The pressure of the barbarians within its boundaries caused the empire to implode, and the provinces to take the first steps towards becoming the countries that we see today on the map of Europe. In the regions beyond the reach of empire, the emergence of national kings would occur later and largely under the auspices of the Church. The barbarian societies of the Dark Ages were to provide the fertile soil from which the nation states of today were eventually to grow. And this very soil continues to yield up artefacts that testify to the great cultural achievements of the barbarians.

Further Reading

Among the most important works to provide an overview of the early Middle Ages or Dark Ages are Roger Collins's masterly *Early Medieval Europe 300–1000* (2nd edn, Palgrave, Basingstoke, 1999); J. M. Wallace-Hadrill, *The Barbarian West 400–1000* (Blackwell, Oxford, 1996); and H. Wolfram, *The Roman Empire and Its Germanic Peoples*, trans. Thomas Dunlop (University of California Press, Berkeley, 1997).

On the treasures of barbarian peoples and my source for the tale of the Pietroasa treasure, see H. Wolfram, *Treasures on the Danube: Barbarian Invaders and their Roman Inheritance*, ed. G. Langthaler (Böhlau, Vienna, 1985).

On the Huns, see Patrick Howarth, *Attila, King of the Huns* (Constable, London, 1994), and E. A. Thompson, *The Huns*, afterword by Peter Heather (rev. edn, Blackwell, Oxford, 1996).

For a highly informative overview of the Goths, see P. Heather, *The Goths* (Blackwell, Oxford, 1996); on more specific topics, see S. Salti and R. Venturini, *The Life of Theodoric*, trans. S. Copper (Edizioni Stear, Ravenna, 1999); and the chapter by Roger Collins on Visigothic Spain in *Spain: A History*, ed. R. Carr (Oxford University Press, 2000).

On the west Germanic peoples, the Anglo-Saxons and related matters, there are a number of easily obtained translations of Tacitus, *Beowulf* and Bede's *Ecclesiastical History of the English People*. The standard introduction, highly informative on all periods from the end of Roman rule to 1066, is J. Campbell (ed.), *The Anglo-Saxons* (Penguin, Harmondsworth, 1991). P. B. Ellis, *Celt and Saxon: The Struggle for Britain AD 410–937* (Constable, London, 1993), gives a view of the period with a strong Celtic bias. M. Welch, *Anglo-Saxon England* (jointly published by Batsford and English Heritage, London, 1995), gives an overview of the archaeology.

On particular Anglo-Saxon sites: M. Carver, *Sutton Hoo: Burial Ground of Kings?* (British Museum Press, 1998), is a highly readable account of the various excavations and excellent on the meaning of the finds; A. C. Evans, *The Sutton Hoo Ship Burial* (British Museum Press, 1994), is by the curator of the Sutton Hoo treasure and provides a detailed and lively description of all the objects, most of which are also illustrated. Archaeological monographs of a more technical nature are C. Haughton and D. Powlesland, *West Heslerton: The Anglian Cemetery*, 2 vols (Landscape Research Centre, 1999), and S. West, *West Stow Revisited* (St Edmundsbury Borough Council, 2001).

A detailed description of the making of the replica of the Sutton Hoo ship can be found in Edwin and Joyce Gifford, *Anglo-Saxon Sailing Ships* (Creekside Publishing, 1997, reprinted from the *Mariner's Mirror*).

Those interested in taxing themselves with Anglo-Saxon riddles are directed to J. Porter, *Anglo-Saxon Riddles* (Anglo-Saxon Books, Hockwold-cum-Wilton, 1995). Anglo-Saxon Books have also published a host of books on other aspects of Anglo-Saxon life, including language, food and drink, martial arts, runes and magic.

Note: The West Stow Country Park and Anglo-Saxon village is open to the public. It is 6 miles north-west of Bury St Edmunds. For those who wish to know more about the Angelcynn, see their website: www.angelcynn.org.uk/

On the Vikings: Else Roesdahl, *The Vikings* (rev. edn, Penguin, Harmondsworth, 1998), is a very readable and wide-ranging book. The lavishly illustrated *Cultural Atlas of the Viking World*, ed. J. Graham-Campbell (Facts On File, New York, 1994), is also recommended, as are J. Byock, *Viking Age Iceland* (Penguin, Harmondsworth, 2001), and H. R. Ellis Davidson, *Gods and Myths of Northern Europe* (Penguin, Harmondsworth, 1990), and E. Nylén, *Stones, Ships and Symbols: The Picture Stones of Gotland from the Viking Age and Before* (Gidlunds, Stockholm, 1988).

Index